GLORIOUS HOPE

Women and Evangelical Religion in
Kent and Northamptonshire, 1800-1850

GLORIOUS HOPE

Women and Evangelical Religion in
Kent and Northamptonshire, 1800-1850

by

Sibyl Phillips

Compton
Towers
Publishing

ISBN 0-9545478-0-2

Printed and bound by The Gemini Press, Towcester, Northamptonshire
First published in 2004 by Compton Towers Publishing
102 Northampton Road, Roade, Northampton, NN7 2PF

To Bill

and the Cockram family

CONTENTS

LIST OF ILLUSTRATIONS

Between pages 202 and 203

PREFACE AND ACKNOWLEDGEMENTS

An interest in the local history of women and religion has been with me for many years. It stemmed from an early awareness that my maternal grandmother, christened Mary Jane, daughter of Daniel Arthur Rowlands (1812-80) of Cardigan, was descended from the Rowlands of Nantcwnlle, a small parish in the former Welsh county of Cardiganshire. The family's noted ancestor, Daniel Rowland(s) (1711-90), was curate of Nantcwnlle and neighbouring Llangeitho from 1734 until 1767. His grandfather, father and brother had all been incumbents of the two parishes at some time during the seventeenth or eighteenth centuries. Daniel Rowland, along with Howell Harris, was at the forefront of the Great Evangelical Awakening in Wales when John Wesley was establishing his Methodist Revival in England. Wesley's *Journal* confirms that he and Rowland knew each other and preached together at Machen, near Newport, on 16 October 1741. On that occasion Rowland, who was bilingual, delivered his sermon in Welsh and Wesley his in English. However, Rowland's Evangelical ministry was firmly opposed by Bishop Samuel Squires, of St. David's, and his curacies were terminated in 1767. Nevertheless, as Eifion Evans's full-scale biography of Daniel Rowland recounts, the powerful Welsh preacher continued his ministry until he died at the age of seventy-nine.

My great-grandfather, Daniel Rowlands, finished his working years as superintendent excise officer for Cardiganshire, but his two brothers were clergymen. In each successive generation, members of our side of the Rowlands family have been ordained and several of them christened Daniel. I still have a family tree written out by my grandmother which shows our descent from John Rowland, vicar of Nantcwnlle in the seventeenth century. Amongst those of us whose names have been added in the twentieth century is Daniel John Rowlands, former Dean of Gibraltar, now retired and living near Cardigan.

Why and how popular Evangelicalism had such profound effects on the domestic, parochial and social lives of nineteenth-century women were questions that led me to research the topic as a Ph.D. student at the Centre for English Local History, University of Leicester. This book has developed from my investigations. It aims to illustrate, examine and explain a diversity of female responses to Evangelical religion in Kent and Northamptonshire between 1800 and 1850. Fellow researchers will understand my excitement on discovering that another well-known Evangelical clergyman, Thomas Jones of Creaton (Northamptonshire), who had such great influence on the lives of women featuring in my Chapters three and four, knew the revivalist Daniel Rowland intimately. Jones had been brought up in Cardiganshire and had wished to marry Rowland's daughter, but his proposition failed. During the course of my investigations other coincidences have inspired me to contact people I would otherwise never have met, and to look for that extra piece of evidence to confirm associations I suspected to have existed between people and parishes.

I am indebted to all who kindly assisted me in any way during the period of this research. My sincere appreciation goes to the archivists and staff of Northamptonshire County Record Office for always attending to my requests promptly and with patience, but I am particularly grateful to Crispin Powell for sharing his professional knowledge on several occasions in answer to my queries. The Canterbury Cathedral Archivists, too, showed much courtesy in meeting my demands. I thank Leicester University librarians for their help, the authorities at Cambridge University Library for allowing me access, especially to their rare books room, and The Open University Library for permitting external membership. Deserving of special mention is the late David Cozens, head of the Local Studies Room in Canterbury City Library, who brought to my attention many documents that proved vital to my earliest investigations of Kentish people and places. I owe my greatest debt of gratitude to Professor Keith Snell, my supervisor at Leicester, whose constructive criticisms and encouragement sustained my enthusiasm throughout what proved to be a most enjoyable research experience.

ABBREVIATIONS

N.C.R.O. = Document in Northamptonshire County Record
            Office (followed by call number)

Bos.Coll. = The Bosworth Family collection (uncatalogued)

HBC   = Hackleton Baptist Church records

S(T)   = The Strong Family collection

Chapter 1

INTRODUCTION

The first half of the nineteenth century saw a preponderance of women in English Protestant church and chapel congregations and their associated local activities.[1] William Wilberforce, leader of the Evangelicals in Parliament, had declared in 1799 that women's very nature made them 'more favourably disposed' than men 'to the feelings and offices of Religion'.[2] Although women and religion in localized settings are the primary concern here, this study can also contribute something to other popular fields of research, such as family and community history, the history of women and women's issues. I anticipated that family history, socio-economic circumstances, local environment and childhood exposure to particular denominational influences were of greatest significance in shaping the spiritual beliefs and activities of the women and girls identified here. Therefore, these elements of their lives are investigated thoroughly in the following chapters. It will be evident that social class and family influences were the most dominant factors in deciding the spiritual allegiance of these women and the parts they played in their Anglican or Dissenting communities. Local religious traditions also were extremely important and, where relevant, the historical development of Evangelicalism in certain parishes is traced.

However, female responses to Evangelical religion were often determined by wider influences than the parochial and these can usually be contextualized as theological, political, intellectual, geographical and social. Such aspects will be covered to a lesser or greater degree here when they can be related to the spiritual attitudes and activities of specific women. Consequently, this investigation is interdisciplinary and wide-ranging, pointing to avenues of research that can bring something new to the local history of women and Evangelical religion. Early on in my enquiry I realized that men, through their inevitable domestic, parish and other relationships with women, also needed to come under a good

---

1   See L. Davidoff & C. Hall, *Family Fortunes: Men and Women of the English Middle Class, 1780-1850* (1987), pp.107-8, 131.

2   W. Wilberforce, *A Practical View of the Prevailing Religious Systems of Professed Christians in the Higher and Middle Classes in this country contrasted with Real Christianity* (1799), p.259.

deal of scrutiny. The approach throughout the book is fundamentally historical and there is no intentional bias towards any particular religious viewpoint. The focus here is mainly on individuals but chapter four concerns, for the most part, female groups involved with Evangelical mission at parish level. Each chapter is a separate study. However, the third and fourth are related insofar as they are centred on the same geographical area of Northamptonshire. Furthermore, the methodology is not that of comparing one micro-study with another, nor of contrasting Evangelical activities in the built-up areas mentioned with what was happening in the named rural parishes.

Late twentieth-century studies of Evangelical religion have, as Frances Knight observed, 'become considerably more sophisticated' and one of the 'new and much needed' scrutinies is David Bebbington's *Evangelicalism in Modern Britain: A History from the 1730s to the 1980s* (1989)[3]. Bebbington's book is a valuable historical source explaining the development of Evangelical ideas and practices within different denominations. His work has enabled some influential personalities, investigated in my research as local figures, to be placed in their national religious contexts. Like other historians of nineteenth-century religion and society, I have accepted David Bebbington's identification of the four main characteristics of Evangelicalism as '*conversionism*, the belief that lives need to be changed; *activism*, the expression of the gospel in effort; *biblicism*, a particular regard for the Bible; and what may be called *crucicentrism*, a stress on the sacrifice of Christ on the cross.'[4]

For Evangelicals, spiritual conversion was central to becoming a Christian. They believed that the innate sinfulness of all human beings alienated them from God. The individual must recognize his or her own iniquity, wholeheartedly repent and acknowledge Christ's redeeming grace and promise of salvation. 'Preachers urged their congregations to turn away from sin in repentance and to Christ in faith.'[5] Only through faith might the sinner be assured of justification. Conversion was to be a life-changing event or process.

3   F. Knight, *The Nineteenth-Century Church and English Society* (Cambridge, 1995), p.10.

4   D. W. Bebbington, *Evangelicalism in Modern Britain; A History from the 1730s to the 1980s* (1989, 1993 edn), p.3. Like Bebbington, I shall use a capital 'E' when referring to 'members of any denomination dedicated to spreading the gospel' (Evangelicals) or 'any aspect' of the popular Protestant Evangelical movement that began in the 1730s (Evangelicalism), *ibid.*, p.1.

5   *Ibid.*, p.5.

Many Evangelical women and men reported that it had been a sudden and dramatic spiritual transformation. For others their change of heart came gradually, sometimes after much painful soul-searching and lack of assurance that their sins were forgiven. Examples of the process can be found in this present investigation. Occasionally historians have judged the individualism of 'vital' religion excessive, but there was also a strong corporate sense of purpose in local Evangelical communities, to which many women responded.

The converted were dutifully bound to express their faith through activism. They should do all in their power to convert others, to live a pious and exemplary moral life themselves and to practise their belief in showing concern for fellow human beings. Although good works alone could not win salvation, Evangelicals allowed they could rightly be considered 'evidence of a justified state', and confirmation of the individual's living faith.[6] Evangelical activism took many and varied forms. As evidence from Kent and Northamptonshire will indicate, its nature depended largely on denominational ideas, priorities in specific religious communities and the socio-economic status and inclinations of dedicated lay-people in particular localities.

The third main feature of the Evangelicals was 'their devotion to the Bible' (biblicism).[7] Evangelicals believed the Holy Scriptures to be inspired by God and therefore the source of all spiritual truth. Although, as will be explained in the Conclusion, there were progressive disagreements concerning this during the nineteenth century, it will be apparent that the theological arguments on the matter did not affect the views of women at the centre of this study. Among Evangelicals, reverence for the Bible was unrestrained. Their preachers based sermons predominantly on biblical passages. Local evidence from Kent and Northamptonshire confirms that the pious frequently quoted directly from the Bible or adapted its verses when writing personal letters, obituaries, published works, including hymns and epitaphs to loved ones.

The doctrine of Christ's death on the cross as the atonement for human sins had been central to Christianity since apostolic times, but Evangelicals 'tended to take crucicentrism beyond the

6   B. M. G. Reardon, *From Coleridge to Gore: A Century of Religious Thought in Britain* (1971), p.27.
7   Bebbington, *Evangelicalism*, p.12.

Catholic position'[8]. They believed that Christ had died as a voluntary substitute for human beings who 'were so rebellious against God that a just penalty would have been [their own] death'.[9] Man's reconciliation with the Almighty was won through Christ's atonement. The Gospel records of events on Calvary were of supreme significance for Evangelicals and parts of this present study illustrate that the image of the cross could inspire many of their writings. Evidence will reveal how important was the atonement to the Evangelicals featured in Chapters three, four and five, who were moderate Calvinists, though some were Anglicans and others Dissenters. Strict Calvinists believed that Christ had died only for God's elect band of sinners, whom he had predestined for salvation. The Almighty alone could effect their conversion and they contributed nothing in the process.[10] The moderates held that all mankind could be saved. Conversion was an individual turning to Christ in faith. Thus, each man or woman was responsible for his or her own destiny.[11]

However, Chapter two concerns a woman member of the Church of England who opposed Calvinism of any degree. She was anti-Evangelical and can be judged Arminian in persuasion. 'The Order of the Administration of Holy Communion' in *The Book of Common Prayer* contains 'The Prayer of Consecration', which tells that Christ's atonement was 'for the sins of the whole world'. This was Arminian belief, but it was through the operation of God-given free will to do good or evil that humans could work out their own salvation. For Arminians, God's grace was believed to operate through Church ordinances, and by 'strict observance of these and living, as far as possible, a holy life', some people might persevere and finally be saved.[12]

The three separate collections of documents on which this present investigation is based are deposited in Northamptonshire County Record Office. They have provided a wealth of primary sources for my case studies. Handwritten correspondence constitutes much of this material. In the early nineteenth-century,

8   G. M. Ditchfield, *The Evangelical Revival* (1998), p.27.

9   Bebbington, *Evangelicalism*, p.15.

10 See D. W. Bebbington, *Holiness in Nineteenth-Century England: The 1998 Didsbury Lectures* (Carlisle, 2000), pp.32-3.

11 *Ibid.*

12 Ditchfield, *The Evangelical Revival*, p.71. Wesleyan Methodists and the Evangelical New Connexion of General Baptists also upheld Arminian doctrine.

most families and friends separated by considerable distances could sustain an intimate relationship only by occasional meetings and written communication. Letters often satisfied the human need to relate life's events to affectionate and sympathetic 'ears'. Correspondence quoted here tells much about the experiences and emotions of their writers and shows, along with further miscellaneous items, that Evangelicals were more likely than some of the less pious to express their faith in writing. Many widely assorted, contemporary documents investigated throughout the following chapters tell much about both the spiritual and secular lives of the women studied. Original spelling, capitalization and punctuation have been retained in all quotations.

The significance of Evangelicalism in the day-to-day existence of English women during the first half of the nineteenth century has remained an under-researched topic. Detailed evidence left by ordinary families and individuals is scarce and not often available to the researcher. Therefore, historians find it difficult to establish the specific religious beliefs and practices of inconspicuous families, and to ascertain how their members fitted into the local interaction of religion and society. However, personal accounts of life within some well-known Evangelical households are available in contemporary biographies.[13] Christopher Tolley's *Domestic Biography: The Legacy of Evangelicalism in Four Nineteenth-century Families* has relied mostly on family letters and other personal writings by descendants of the prominent Clapham Sect. Tolley has acknowledged that finding documentary evidence from which to recapture 'the precise texture of any domestic religious environment' is not easy, and 'with the nineteenth century the task becomes especially hard'.[14] Frances Knight, in *The Nineteenth-Century Church and English Society*, has considered at length what Anglicanism meant for ordinary people in England during the period, yet has confirmed that 'glimpses of lay life in the nineteenth-century Church tend to be fleeting, and often mediated through clerical eyes'.[15] The documentation which has survived is more likely to be concerned with 'the externals of religion' than

---

13 See D. M. Rosman, Chapter 11, 'Faith and family life', *Evangelicals and Culture* (1984), pp.97-118.

14 C. Tolley, *Domestic Biography: The Legacy of Evangelicalism in Four Nineteenth-Century Families* (Oxford, 1997), p.7. The families were descendants of the Clapham Sect Evangelicals, Zachary Macaulay, Henry Thornton, James Stephen, William Wilberforce.

15 Knight, *The Nineteenth-Century Church*, p.23.

with 'the interior world of the believer. Any sort of systematic understanding of the latter is unattainable; all that can be done is to strike a few matches in an otherwise dark landscape, and to peer briefly at what is illuminated.'[16] Statements such as these serve to enhance the value of the primary sources on which the case studies in this present investigation are founded. Personal documentation from the first half of the nineteenth century is particularly scarce. Furthermore, my work relates to identifiable women living in different localities whose responses to Evangelicalism, whether favourable or unfavourable, were influenced by their own special circumstances. Some had close domestic relationships with clergymen. For all the women at the centre of this study, it can be claimed that their full histories have never before been investigated and some rich sources for research into the meaning of Evangelical religion in women's lives have so far remained untapped.

Chapters two, three and four here mainly concern female members of the Church of England and illuminate a few domestic and wider local scenes in parts of Kent and Northamptonshire at a time when Evangelical religion was expanding within the Established Church. They illustrate that Evangelicalism could arouse strong antipathy in some Anglican women, while for others it was a positive rule of life. However, it must be stressed that the Evangelical revival of the first half of the nineteenth century was not limited to a single denomination and to centre this investigation on Anglican women would tend to underplay its impact on female Dissenters. Therefore, my fifth chapter concerns a young woman belonging to an expanding Particular Baptist community in rural Northamptonshire, who was converted in 1826.

Much literature of various kinds has been read in the course of this research. Some was written during the lifetimes of the women featuring in the investigation, but a good deal of it has been produced in recent years. Essential reading has been extensive, mainly because my case studies concern women from two separate factions within the Anglican Church as well as an Evangelical Dissenter, and they have been considered independently in their own local and religious contexts. The problem has been that of containment. The range of material explored is indicated in the list of primary and secondary sources at end of this book. There is

16 *Ibid.*

room here in the Introduction to mention only a limited number of relevant publications.

The Bible, often just the New Testament, was probably the only book to be found in many Christian homes during the first half of the nineteenth century, but a mass of supplementary religious literature was also available. Published biographies, tracts, periodicals, hymns, and fiction for all age-groups found a wide readership. Doreen Rosman's *Evangelicals and Culture* has addressed the relationship between Evangelicals and their cultural activities. She has considered a good deal of the literature produced for and by Evangelicals and looked at the forms of recreation, other than reading, that were permitted within the boundaries of Evangelical 'seriousness'. Whereas Rosman has covered a range of nineteenth-century popular reading matter, Elisabeth Jay has concentrated on contemporary fiction. In *The Religion of the Heart: Anglican Evangelicalism and the Nineteenth-Century Novel*, Jay has seen how major novelists of the time characterized Anglican Evangelicals, illustrating that some drew on personal acquaintance with 'the religion of the heart' for their fictional representations.[17] Some of the published material and authors mentioned in these two books receive appropriate attention in my chapters.

Many strands of Establishment law and policy were interwoven with the fabric of religion and society during the first half of the nineteenth century. Frances Knight's *The Nineteenth-century Church and English Society* has brought several of the strands together. Yet, the religious life of every English parish, though a microcosm of the national structure, was shaped considerably by its own landscape, demography and socio-economic forces. All this is confirmed in my investigation of local communities in Kent and Northamptonshire. To set the whole study in contemporary religious, political and social contexts, some detailed historiographies of relationships between the early nineteenth-century Church, State and society in England have been consulted. E. R. Norman's three opening chapters of his intensive survey, *Church and Society in England, 1770-1970* have proved particularly informative.[18] Dealing with the end of the eighteenth and the first half of the nineteenth centuries, they have spelt out the

17 E. Jay, *The Religion of the Heart: Anglican Evangelicalism and the Nineteenth-Century Novel* (Oxford, 1979).

18 E. R. Norman, *Church and Society in England, 1770-1970: A Historical Study* (Oxford, 1976), pp.15-122.

interdependence of Church and State, their attitudes towards society and the constitutional adjustments deemed necessary to retain support for the Establishment and restore national stability.

After the French Revolution, political uncertainties in England alarmed parliamentarians and churchmen. Some Bishops claimed that 'it was the rejection of religion that had brought disaster and tyranny to France.'[19] It was clear that large sections of the population in Britain were spiritually destitute. The Anglican Church was suffering acute problems of plurality of livings, non-resident, poor quality clergymen, increasing dissent and growing indifference among the people. Then suddenly the Church appeared in the 1790's 'a weak barrier to revolution, and many of its leaders knew it'.[20] At the beginning of the nineteenth century radicalism and civil unrest were on the increase in England, and public morality among rich and poor alike was considered by many to be at a low ebb. Church and State needed to work together. Clerics turned to the State for assistance in bringing the masses within the fold of Christianity.[21] However, as Frances Knight has claimed, 'it was often admitted quite candidly that the Church's main function was social control; though this was not to imply that it did not also have the function of saving souls'.[22] Bishops were conspicuous in the House of Lords but, as Gilbert has shown, it was the parochial system that provided the basic structures of local government, social control, education and poor relief in England well into the period covered by my research.[23] Supportive evidence of this can be found in some of the documents mentioned below concerning Kent and Northamptonshire. Anglican Church problems were further compounded by the agrarian and industrial revolutions, the closer social relationships between clergy and the land-owning class after parish enclosures, the patronage system (one of the most difficult matters to resolve), the dilapidated state of parsonages and churches, increasing population and the inability to provide places of worship with sufficient numbers of free seats for the poor. Most of these factors have been recognized by

---

19   *Ibid.*, p.20.

20   R. A. Solloway, *Prelates and People: Ecclesiastical Social Thought in England, 1783-1852* (1969), p.47.

21   Norman, *Church and Society*, p.46.

22   Knight, *The Nineteenth-century Church*, p.11.

23   A. D. Gilbert, *Religion and Society in Industrial England: Church, Chapel and Social Change, 1740-1914* (1976), p.75.

historiographers of early nineteenth-century religion and society in England as being largely responsible for the multitudes who did not attend Anglican Churches but were ready to respond to the conversionist and less formal methods of Evangelical Dissent. Several parliamentarians and ecclesiasts recognized that Church reform was essential and urgent.

A. D. Gilbert's *Religion and Society in Industrial England: Church, Chapel and Social Change, 1740-1914* has explored the links indicated in the title. His explicit analysis of the social constituency of Evangelical Nonconformist denominations and reasons for their expansion has been applied in the local contexts of my investigation. Some documentary evidences of expanding Dissent during the first half of the nineteenth century are examined to see if trends in the localities concerned agree with Gilbert's statistical tables.[24] Contemporary Government records of population figures and employment patterns for relevant parishes are analyzed to show if these elements affected local growth of Evangelical religion. Although historiographers have written much on the appeal of Evangelicalism to people living in developing industrial areas of England, there is insufficient room here to feature women from a rapidly expanding urban district.[25] However, my second chapter relates to a woman living in Canterbury, which did experience a population increase from 10,200 in 1811 to 13,649 in 1831, with 542 more families employed in trade, manufacture and handicraft at the end of that twenty-year period.[26] Nevertheless, the city did not become highly industrialized.

The home was the most important centre of Evangelical influence. It was the parents', though often the widowed mother's, responsibility to bring the family to early conversion, as death struck down many infants and adolescents. The young must be spiritually prepared for a sudden meeting with their Maker.

---

24 Gilbert, *Religion and Society*, Tables 2.1 & 2.3, pp.34,38.

25 One such community was Carr's Lane Independent Chapel in the centre of Birmingham. Its minister, John Angell James, was well-known for his acceptance of women's subordination: see Davidoff & Hall, *Family Fortunes*, pp.126-130. James's congregation was mainly lower middle-class.

26 *Abstract of the Answers and Returns, pursuant to an Act, passed in the Fifty-first Year of His Majesty King George III intituled "An Act for taking Account of the Population of Great Britain, and of the Increase or Diminution thereof", 1821* (1822), p.147; and *Abstract of the Answers and eturns, pursuant to an Act, passed in the Eleventh Year of the Reign of His Majesty King George V intituled "An Act for taking Account of the Population of Great Britain, and of the Increase or Diminution thereof, 1831*, Vol. I, (1833), p.278.

Christians shared a core of beliefs in the central importance of the family, and among the middle classes there developed a common culture based on 'the distinct and separate spheres of male and female'.[27] The man's world was work, the woman's domesticity.[28] Of course, this was not always entirely practicable for the poor, or for widows who needed to provide an income if they were left with a family to support. Examples of Evangelical mothers who found themselves in the latter situation feature here in local settings. 'Women's profession was', as Hannah More the celebrated Evangelical put it, 'to be wives and mothers', but once this work had been completed conscientiously they could think of doing some religious and philanthropic work outside.[29] Along with their practical help, middle-class women could usefully bring their social attitudes and religious beliefs to bear upon the poor. However, women's active participation in both church and chapel life was restricted by contemporary attitudes towards women's place in society. The spiritual equality of both sexes was confirmed in Galatians 3:28 – 'there is neither male nor female; for ye are all one in Christ Jesus' – yet most Evangelicals upheld the message contained in Genesis 2:18, that God had created woman as 'help meet' to man. Generally, men occupied leading positions in most local and national religious institutions, but women were necessary to act in supportive roles. Documents from Northamptonshire substantiate this. Yet some women held considerable power as ecclesiastical patrons and a few who appointed Evangelical clergy are identified in parishes featured here.

The notion of women's subordination had been challenged. In 1795 Mary Wollstonecraft (1759-97), feminist and acquaintance of an intellectual group of political writers and reformers known as the English Jacobins, had published her *Vindication of the Rights of Woman*. Directed towards an upper and middle-class readership, this work advocated equality of the sexes and equal opportunities

---

27 Davidoff & Hall, *Family Fortunes*, p.74.

28 K. D. M. Snell has argued that Victorian ideas of the proper role for women were
     established after a trend towards female confinement to the home in agricultural areas
     had already been set; technical advances in farming methods had resulted in
     employment of men rather than women: see K. D. M. Snell, *Annals of the Labouring
     Poor: Social Change and Agrarian England, 1660-1900* (Cambridge, 1985, 1995 edn),
     pp.51-2,56.

29 Davidoff & Hall, *Family Fortunes*, p.116, quoting H. More, *Coelebs in Search of a Wife:
     Comprehending Domestic Habits and Manners, Religion and Morals* (2 vols, 1808, 1809 edn).

in education. Wollstonecraft firmly refuted the arguments supporting woman's subordination and also spoke out against bringing up daughters to be dutiful without questioning. She declared:

> Girls are more kept down by their parents, in every sense of the word, than boys. The duty expected from them is like all the duties arbitrarily imposed on women, more from a sense of propriety, more out of respect for decorum, than reason; and thus taught slavishly to submit to their parents, they are prepared for the slavery of marriage.[30]

Whilst it is acknowledged that aspects of this parental control affected individual women mentioned in my study, in some Kentish elite families, wives and daughters recently converted to Evangelicalism were responding by challenging these traditional attitudes. It can be argued that the Bible supported their new ideas of freedom to oppose family members when it came to the matter of religious allegiance and carrying out God's work. Matthew 10:34-37 permitted defiance of close relatives:

> Think not that I am come to send peace on earth:
> I came not to send peace, but a sword.
> For I am come to set a man at variance against his father
> and the daughter against her mother, and the daughter
> in law against her mother in law.
> And a man's foes shall be they of his own household.
> He that loveth father or mother more than me, is not
> worthy of me: and he that loveth son or daughter
> more than me, is not worthy of me.

Wollstonecraft continued with this comment on the upbringing of children. 'A slavish bondage to parents cramps every faculty of the mind' and, 'if the mind be curbed and humbled too much in children; if their spirits be abased and broken much by too strict an hand over them; they lose all their vigour and industry'.[31] Some Evangelicals were the strictest of parents. In their eyes, children were born wicked and moral training must start in infancy.

---

30 M. Wollstonecraft, *A Vindication of the Rights of Woman* (1795), in R. Todd & M. Butler (eds), *The Works of Mary Wollstonecraft*, V (1989), p.226.

31 *Ibid.*

Excessive anxiety led some Evangelical parents to look for signs of an infant's spiritual response and their joy at recognizing it.[32] Equally, they could be horrified at the 'slightest signs of declension' indicated by minor acts of disobedience.[33]   Children's behaviour was often judged in terms of adult moral values.[34]   Many Evangelicals believed childish misdemeanours to be 'inherently hateful as offences against God, incurring divine punishment.'[35]   In simplistic terms, devils in hell awaited the naughty child, but a good child would go to heaven.   E. P. Thompson has seen how these attitudes were brought into Methodist Sunday Schools.   His views have been summarized thus by Thomas Laqueur:

> These schools acted upon Wesley's doctrines of the aboriginal sinfulness of the child; they practised a kind of religious terrorism on the young, convincing them of their spiritual unworthiness and offering hard work, adherence to duty and submission to the wishes of their betters as a kind of exculpatory act.   Far worse than being merely agencies of moral rescue, Sunday schools weakened the wills and corrupted the souls of their inmates, making them the victims of an objectively hostile ideology.[36]

This statement can also apply to Evangelical Sunday schools within other denominations, which is confirmed by evidence on the strict teaching methods and catechizing suffered by young attenders in some Northamptonshire villages.

The central sources for chapter two of this present study are eighty-six extant letters written by Mrs Anna Maria Lukyn,[37] the spinster daughter of an Orthodox Anglican clergyman with an ancestry of ecclesiastical service and civic duty in Canterbury.   As her family history indicates, she had inherited associations with

---

32 Rosman, *Evangelicals and Culture*, p.98.

33 *Ibid.*

34 *Ibid.*, p.99.

35 *Ibid.*

36 T. W. Laqueur, *Religion and Respectability: Sunday Schools and Working Class Culture, 1780-1850* (1976), p.188, citing E. P. Thompson, *The Making of the English Working Class* (1963), pp.50, 361, 375-83, 401.

37 Styled 'Mrs' according to the conventions of the day for unmarried women of mature years.   In the only surviving letter written by Mrs. Margaret Strong (to her daughter-in-law Mrs Strong, Manor House, Standground, Peterborough), Anna Maria is referred to as 'Mrs Lukyn', N.C.R.O., S(T)113 (undated).

High Churchmanship. Mrs Lukyn's letters were written between 1809 and 1835 to a friend, the wife of Dr. William Strong, Archdeacon of Northampton. The Archdeacon's immediate ecclesiastical superior was Bishop Marsh of Peterborough, a High Church Arminian, renowned for his opposition to Evangelical religion.[38] Peter Nockles has warned of the need for care when attempting to clarify labels, such as 'High ' and 'Low', which were given to different Anglican Church parties before 1833, that is prior to the Tractarian era. He has given this definition that could also be applied to Anglican High Church party adherents of the early nineteenth century. They 'tended to uphold in some form the doctrine of apostolic succession' and on this was founded a 'strong attachment to the catholicity and apostolicity of the Church of England as a branch of the universal catholic church', which could not include 'those reformed bodies which had wilfully abandoned episcopacy, so that a distinction was made between Nonconformist congregations and continental Protestant churches.'[39] Other important elements of High Church belief were the supremacy of the Scriptures and their interpretation according to the Prayer Book, the Catechism and the Creeds.[40] Stress was also laid on the doctrine of sacramental grace in the Eucharist and baptism. For many High Church adherents, the basis of their practical Christianity lay in acts of self-denial, rather than any subjective conversion experience or unruly manifestations of the Holy Spirit.[41] Furthermore, High Church party members firmly upheld the union of Church and State, the latter being considered divinely appointed as guardian and promoter of the former.[42] In some modern histories of Anglican Church debates, the terms 'Orthodox' and 'High Church' have been used interchangeably.[43] This will be done here. As Knockles has pointed out, some of the Orthodox were more High Church than others on particular points of doctrine and practice, lying somewhere within a broad spectrum of theological emphasis, but all were 'basically allies

---

38 See P. B. Nockles, 'Church parties in the pre-Tractarian Church of England 1750-1833: the "Orthodox" - some problems of definition and identity', in J. Walsh, C. Haydon, S. Taylor (eds), *The Church of England, c.1689-c.1833: From Toleration to Tractarianism* (Cambridge, 1993), p.342.

39 Nockles, *Ibid.*, pp.335-6.

40 *Ibid.*, p.336.

41 *Ibid.*

42 *Ibid.*

43 *Ibid.*, p.338.

united in defence of the cause of orthodoxy against the Church of England's Dissenting and Unitarian opponents'.[44]   Abundant evidence will show that Mrs Lukyn can be classed within this spectrum of orthodoxy for these reasons. She strongly supported the ecclesiastical authority of the Established Church and its traditional ministerial functions. She partook of the sacrament at least four times a year, was anti-Roman Catholic, firmly opposed Evangelicalism within the Church of England, and its expansion within Dissent. Thus she conformed to what Bebbington, too, has seen were elements of the High Church tradition of the late eighteenth and early nineteenth centuries.[45]   For a close study of one woman's negative responses to Evangelicalism, Mrs Lukyn's letters are of special value and might even be recognized as something of a rarity.   Many additional sources, such as parish records in Canterbury Cathedral Archives, newspapers, published and unpublished material in the Local Studies Room of the City Library and details of monuments recorded by Canterbury Archaeological Trust have been studied. Therefore, Mrs Lukyn can be placed accurately in contexts of her family history, religious affiliations and Kentish society.   She is taken as representing a certain set of Orthodox Anglicans whose attitudes and views I am endeavouring to define with greater precision.

The chapter begins by tracing some of Mrs Lukyn's forebears back to the early eighteenth century and identifying her contemporary network of friends and family. Evidence confirms that she belonged to a distinct social and cultural community united by class status and Orthodox Anglican allegiance. This included not only Mrs Strong and the Archdeacon, but also her relatives and friends in Canterbury and other areas of Kent. As late as the 1850s, according to Alan Everitt, the small parishes of the downlands and chartlands of the County 'were still dominated by numerous little parks and manor houses, just as they had been in the sixteenth and seventeenth centuries...Honywoods and Derings, Oxindens and Knatchbulls...Austens...these and similar Kentish dynasties still exerted in the first half of the nineteenth century the same autocratic influence as in the days of Charles I. In a single great county cousinage, they were yet more powerful.'[46]   Mrs Lukyn counted some members of the Kentish landed gentry amongst her

44   *Ibid.*, pp.339-40.

45   Bebbington, *Holiness in Nineteenth-Century England,* pp.7-9.

46   A. Everitt, *The Pattern of Rural Dissent: the Nineteenth Century.* (Leicester, 1972), p.60.

closest friends and she has given insight into their shared social life and religious bonds.

The next section of this chapter is on 'Literature' and will confirm that Mrs Lukyn read widely. She criticized some contemporary authors and their works, and an endeavour is made here to explain how and why she occasionally did this in terms of Evangelical religion. Evangelicalism was the subject of much literature of her time. I have included a few of the authors who interested Mrs Lukyn and Mrs Strong, two High Church women friends familiar with cathedral life in Canterbury and Peterborough. Mrs Lukyn's criticisms of recently published works afforded another medium for expressing her antipathy towards Evangelicalism, a movement growing ever stronger in both cities.

This chapter's last section, on 'Religion', is the longest. It opens with reference to the Evangelical call for improvement in the nation's public and private morals. Then follow extracts from Mrs Lukyn's letters which contained her most candid remarks about parish clergy and their ecclesiastical superiors, especially those connected with Canterbury Cathedral. Her belief that Anglican inadequacies were contributing to growth of Evangelical religion in Canterbury and other parts of east Kent is made all too clear. Mrs Lukyn's responses to the impingement of Evangelicalism on local society end the chapter. Today the intimacy of her correspondence gives unusual access to the changing worlds of religion and society in Kentish settings during the early nineteenth century. That the letters were written by a resident of Canterbury, but are deposited in Northamptonshire County Record Office, may explain why they have until now remained untapped sources for research into the history of their county of origin. All efforts to trace Mrs. Strong's replies to Mrs Lukyn have proved fruitless.

The third chapter of this book is based on a newly-deposited, significant collection of documents concerning the Bosworth family of Spratton, near Creaton, Northamptonshire. It is written around four sisters, 'cradle-Christians' born into an Evangelical familial home. Domiciled in a coaching inn situated in a rural area of the county, the extended household included the well-known, unmarried Evangelical clergyman, Thomas Jones (of Creaton). An exceptional opportunity has been presented to gain insight into the significance of Evangelicalism in the lives of four generations of women belonging to a Northamptonshire family community where Evangelical religion was part of their everyday existence.

How Thomas Jones came to take up the curacy at Creaton and live in the Bosworth's hostelry at nearby Spratton is explained in the first part of the chapter. A short history of the family's long-standing association with Evangelical religion at Creaton is included. Analysis of personal letters from Thomas Jones to the Bosworth daughters, and others between family members and friends reveals how relationships within this Evangelical network were formed and maintained. Furthermore, the correspondence and many additional sources illustrate the diversity of responses to Evangelicalism from the Bosworths and other local women. Local landscape, land ownership and demography are assessed for their influence in shaping the Evangelical communities at Creaton and Spratton.

Chapter four is linked with the previous chapter, although it exhibits local women's more public activism. Focussing on the corporate Evangelical mission of women living in Thomas Jones's own and nearby parishes, it deals mainly with Creaton Branches of The Church Missionary Society and The British and Foreign Bible Society. A run of annual reports from a rural branch of one of the early nineteenth-century charitable institutions is an unusual find.[47] Fortunately, several consecutive Annual Reports from the Creaton Branch of the C.M.S. have survived, and the kind of evidence they give of female support in a country area is probably not often available. There is also an extant copy of the first Annual Report from the Creaton Branch of the B.F.B.S. This has been particularly useful as it describes the inauguration of the Branch and gives insight into its first year's work. Some of the local women who responded to the Evangelical call for mission are identified, and it will be shown how a few rural auxiliaries of these two national societies really functioned. The Bible Ladies, who made regular house-to-house calls in their parishes to collect contributions, were expected to carry out philanthropic work among their poorer neighbours. Within the middle classes it was agreed that woman's natural instincts for caring for the family and her practicality fitted her for charitable work outside the home.[48] Creaton records illustrate that Evangelical organizations for mission enlarged the opportunities for lay women to play an active part in parochial life, but their roles were subordinate to those of the men who

47 F. K. Prochaska, *Women and Philanthropy in Nineteenth-Century England* (Oxford, 1980), p.28.
48 *Ibid.*, pp.7–8.

dominated national missionary societies. Elizabeth Elbourne wrote in 1993: 'There is reason to believe that research into the neglected area of local "cultures of mission" would yield a rich harvest'.[49] This was a correct estimation. Chapter four ends with investigation of other ways in which local women responded to the Evangelical requirement for activism.

Chapter five, as already indicated, relates to a community of Particular Baptists in rural Northamptonshire. Primary and secondary sources are investigated and confirm that this was established at Hackleton by noted Evangelicals of historical importance, both locally and nationally. Details of landscape, enclosure, demography and employment patterns are included to show that these favoured the local expansion of Dissent. Original records from Hackleton's Particular Baptist Church reveal the place of women in its activities. Explanation will be given of how one of them, a young lace-maker named Eliza Westbury, established her own identity by writing a dramatic, versified account of her gradual spiritual conversion and many hymns of publishable quality. Central to this chapter is an extant copy of a small printed book containing a few details about her life, the long record of her conversion and several of her hymns. I have analyzed some of her works to indicate their reflection of Evangelicalism, and present my argument that the style and content of Eliza's verses were influenced by William Cowper and John Newton, the famous Evangelical writers of the *Olney Hymns* (1779). Olney is about eight miles from Hackleton, lying about four miles over the Buckinghamshire border.

49   E. Elbourne, 'The foundation of the Church Missionary Society: the Anglican missionary impulse' in Walsh, Haydon, Taylor, *The Church of England*, p.264.

Chapter 2

MRS LUKYN'S LETTERS FROM
CANTERBURY 1809-1835

Canterbury Sep. 24 1809

My dearest Madam,

You must have possessed the power of reading the human heart, and have learned how deeply esteem and affection had impressed the remembrance of yourself, and our excellent Dr. S[trong] to have formed any idea the pleasure your billet gave me. as I had not dared to hope it I feel still more grateful for the remembrance.[1]

There is an unmistakable image of gentility reflected in these few words. They begin the first of the eighty-six private letters written by Mrs Anna Maria Lukyn, a resident of St George's Place in the ecclesiastical metropolis of England during the early decades of the nineteenth century. The somewhat educated literary style is typical of Mrs Lukyn's correspondence to Mrs Margaret Strong, who lived at Thorpe Hall, Peterborough, Northamptonshire, with her husband, Archdeacon William Strong. He was a man held in high regard, as an Orthodox Anglican, in his Peterborough Diocese and beyond. The cathedral city of Peterborough stands at the western edge of Fen country and is about 150 miles distant from Canterbury. Between one and six of Mrs Lukyn's dated letters covered each year from 1809 to 1835.[2] The six last-numbered in the collection are only parts of letters and have at least the first page missing hence the dates are not indicated.[3] In 1809, when Mrs Lukyn was fifty-seven, the close friendship between herself and the Strongs appears to have been in its early stages. It was to endure for almost twenty-six years.

The reading of only a small, random selection of her letters is sufficient to confirm that Mrs Lukyn was part of an elite Kentish society. Reading them all will show that she had a keen, knowledgeable interest in the ecclesiastical world of Canterbury and was a woman confined by the conventions of Anglican

1 Northamptonshire County Record Office, S(T)230.
2 N.C.R.O., S(T)230-309.
3 N.C.R.O., S(T)310-315.

institutional religion. It may well have been for more than sentimental reasons that her correspondence was not discarded by Mrs Strong. Perhaps Mrs Lukyn's historic family background was the extra element added to her detailed, often gossipy reports on contemporary matters, that made the letters thought worthy of preservation.

2.1 FAMILY, FRIENDS AND SOCIAL NETWORK

Genealogical details can make tedious reading, but it is necessary to give them a good deal of space here to set Mrs Lukyn in context of her family's place in local religious and social history. Furthermore, examination of her own domestic background and that of her various friends will indicate why it was unlikely her responses to Evangelical religion would have displayed anything other than firm loyalty to the Established Church and to the State. Undoubtedly, this loyalty was the overriding influence on her views of Evangelicalism and had been shaped during the formative years of her life, in the mid–eighteenth century.

As A. D. Gilbert has pointed out, in England up to the third decade of the nineteenth century the 'unreformed Establishment' still exercised 'communal functions' of 'non–recurrent rites...annual rituals and festivals' which brought communities together.

Thus religious conformity at once symbolised and reinforced the cohesion of an established social order. Symbolically it was a person's affirmation of the basic moral values, social conventions, and cultural mores of his community: and it symbolised, too, his own acceptance by that community and his integration within it. In this way the Establishment performed important identity functions for individuals and social groups...The parson, like his lay counterpart, the gentleman landowner, in theory was an exemplar to the lower orders of morality, propriety, and patriotism; and even when theory and practice coincided only imperfectly, the alliance of squire and parson, operating through the informal 'influence' of rank and status, through a variety of parish officers and institutions, or through the immense authority of the local magistracy, was able to exercise a clear leadership role in local societies. The preservation of the existing order, the maintenance of social harmony and social tranquility: this was the *raison d'etre* of the Church of England as a religious Establishment.[4]

My first chapter has already indicated that, by the early nineteenth century, the 'existing order' was under threat and later evidence will show that Mrs Lukyn was well aware of the contemporary challenges to the Established Church. Like many others of her time, she saw Evangelicalism, within and without the Church of England, as posing one of the threats to the old order. Undoubtedly, expansion of the Evangelical element within local Anglicanism was of personal concern to her. Moreover, her letters will show how much she was disturbed by the growth in Nonconformity being achieved by the proselytizing methods of Evangelicals in Canterbury and other parts of Kent. Throughout England, Dissent and Methodism were expanding so rapidly that by the first decades of the nineteenth century 'many clergy felt that they were in danger of being swamped'.[5] Mrs Lukyn's reactions were to be expected when several of her family, friends and acquaintances or their relatives, were exercising, or had exercised clear leadership roles in Church and society, particularly in Kent and Northamptonshire.

2.1.i Family background

During the seventeenth and eighteenth centuries, Mrs Lukyn's forebears had been men of no mean authority and influence within the Establishment in Canterbury. Memorials in the city's St Margaret's Church testify to those erstwhile members of her family who fulfilled diverse ecclesiastical and civic functions. She could have been justifiably proud of her great-grandfather, Paul Lukin,[6] for he was a notary, appointed procurator in the Ecclesiastical Courts of the Archbishop and the Archdeacon of Canterbury. He served as procurator for fifty years, during which time sessions of the Prerogative Court were held in St Margaret's Church. In his additional office as auditor of the Metropolitan Ecclesiastical accounts for twenty years, he would have had close contact with the Dean and Chapter of the Cathedral. Paul Lukin died on 11

4   Gilbert, *Religion and Society*, pp.75–6.
5   J.Walsh & S.Taylor, 'Introduction: The Church and Anglicanism in the "long" eighteenth century', in Walsh, Haydon & Taylor (eds), *The Church of England*, p.19.
6   The name was changed from Lukin to Lukyn by the next generation.

June 1716 at the age of seventy-two, and his wife, Grace, on 20 November of the same year aged fifty-eight. They were buried in St Margaret's Church where a fine memorial to them both bears a long Latin inscription.[7] Grace Lukin was the daughter of Martin Hirst, registrar of the Archbishop's Court, and Lucie his wife, both of whom were interred in the Cathedral. Paul and Grace Lukin's son, John, a Canterbury barber-surgeon, was Anna Maria's grandfather. He died in 1754 and his Will was proved 'at London...before the Commissary of the Prerogative Court of Canterbury' on 30th October of that year.[8] It contained this request:

> ...as my body must return to the Dust from whence it was taken I desire it may be deposited in the most private manner possible in St Margaret's Church by the Monument of my family at the discretion of my Executrixes[9].

His 'desire' for a private funeral may well indicate that John Lukyn was one member of the family who shunned publicity and there is nothing of note written about him in the local histories. His wife Anne, whom he had married in 1720 at Thanington Church near Canterbury, was the daughter of another outstanding Canterbury city worthy, Anthony Oughton and his wife Anne, whose father was Sir James Bunce of Kemsing. Anthony Oughton served as Common Councillor, Sheriff, Chamberlain and twice as Mayor of Canterbury (in 1702 and 1730).[10]

---

7   Z. Cozens, *Ecclesiastical Topographical History of Kent, I* (1975), p.178. Memorial placed by their son, John: see photograph of stone number 221, St. Margaret's Church, Canterbury, north wall, Canterbury Archaeological Trust Ltd. 'In 1942 the church and surrounding area was extensively bomb-damaged and after the war the parochial use of the church ceased. In 1958 it was opened as the Church Institute for the Deaf and Dumb in Canterbury and East Kent. The Institute moved in 1983 and the building closed': see T. Tatton-Brown, St. Margaret's Church, Canterbury (Canterbury Archaeological Trust, 1986). The Church now accommodates The Canterbury Tales Visitor Attraction which opened in 1988. St. George's Street, not far from St. Margaret's, also was probably damaged in air raids. It now contains post-war houses and Mrs Lukyn's home cannot be located.

8   Public Record Office, PROB11/811 F191RH+F192LH.

9   *Ibid.*

10 Gardiner, *Story of St Margaret's Church*, p.9. A memorial to Anthony and Anne Oughton was placed in this Church.

It might have been difficult for Anna Maria's father, Anthony Lukyn, son of John and Anne, to follow after his male ancestors of such local high office. However, it appears he was the first of this direct line of Lukyns to acquire a university education and to be admitted to Holy Orders. In 1744 (aged 17) he became a student at Christ Church, Oxford, and was awarded a B.A. degree in 1748.[11] He was ordained at Peterborough in 1753. Unfortunately, his father died the following year. In August 1755, Anthony Lukyn was appointed chaplain to the Countess of Aberdeen,[12] and, in September of the same year, domestic chaplain to the Countess dowager of Aberdeen.[13] He died on 12th November 1778 at the age of fifty-one and his death was announced in the *Kentish Gazette* of 14th November, thus:

On Thursday died in this city, the Rev. Anthony Lukyn, M.A., Rector of St. Mildred, with St. Mary Castle, and All Saints [Canterbury], in the gift of the Lord Chancellor; and Vicar of Reculver[14] and Hoath, in the gift of the Archbishop.

Anna Maria's father had been appointed to these livings only six years earlier.[15] His demise was also recorded in the November issue of the *Gentleman's Magazine*.[16] Like his forebears, Anthony Lukyn was buried at St. Margaret's Church, Canterbury, where he and his one brother and two sisters had been baptized.[17] Surprisingly, there seems to be no record of a memorial to him being placed there. Yet he was the subject of a portrait by the court

11 See J & J. A. Venn, *Alumni Cantabrigienses: A Biographical List of All Known Students, Graduates and Holders of Offices at the University of Cambridge, from the Earliest Times to 1900, Part II, from 1752-1900*, IV, (Cambridge, 1951), p. 233.

12 *The Gentleman's Magazine*, XXV (1755), p. 382.

13 *Ibid.*, (Sept. 1755), p. 429.

14 Reculver Church, an early Saxon Abbey, stood just above the shoreline. Only its famous twin towers remain. Nineteenth-century watercolours of the Church are on loan from Canterbury City Library to Herne Bay Visitors' Centre.

15 It was not until 1773 that he gained an M.A. degree from King's College, Cambridge, his B.A. having been incorporated from Oxford: Venn, *Alumni Cantabrigienses*, pt. II, IV (1951), p. 233. This was probably a strategic move to gain preferment: see R. Price, *Diary (1769-1773)*, p. 140, unpublished shorthand manuscript, transcribed by F. Higenbottom (1959), Canterbury City Library Local Studies Room.

16 *Gentleman's Magazine*, XLVIII (Nov. 1778), p. 550.

17 *St Margaret's Church Registers of Baptisms and Burials*, Canterbury Cathedral and City Archives (microfilm, U3/6/1/1).

painter, John Wollaston. It is not known who commissioned the work, but 'on the back of the stretcher of the painting there [was] an old tag inscribed: "Anthony Lukyn, A Celebrity of Canterbury, The Painter John Wollaston, Painter to George II".[18]

Anthony Lukyn was survived not only by his daughter, Anna Maria, but also by his wife, Elizabeth, his sister, Anna Maria, and his three other children, Paul, Anthony and Grace. They were all mentioned in his Will, dated 9th February, 1778, written only a few months before he died.[19] After the death of his 'very kind and much esteemed Sister' and the death or re-marriage of his wife, Anthony Lukyn's children were to inherit

> equally between them share and share alike as Tenants in Common and not as Joint tenants…All that Messuage or Tenement with the Catherines Yard Garden and Appurtenances there unto belonging situate and being in the parish of Saint Margaret in the said City of Canterbury [and the] Rest and Residue of [his] Personal Estate.

Anna Maria was aged about twenty-six when her father died and, no doubt, she felt an ensuing responsibility for her mother and the other younger members of the family. She was sufficiently well provided for in her later life to receive an adequate income from rents and monetary interest to enable her to lead an independent existence, even if prudence was necessary at times. Her sister, Grace, married a Reverend Applebee, with a living in Essex.[20] Anna Maria was on such good terms with the couple, often spending holidays with them and their daughters, that it is unlikely there was any serious difference of opinion between them on matters religious. The family clerical tradition continued, for the Applebee's daughter, Grace, married a 'Mr Williams', whom Mrs Lukyn mentioned to Mrs Strong as 'a gentleman your son probably knew by name. he was a Fellow of I believe St John's,

18 Canterbury City Library, *Letter* from National Portrait Gallery, London (5 June 1959), to Canterbury City Librarian, quoting letter from Vose Galleries, Boston, Mass., U.S.A. The portrait was said to be dated 1742 but the mature appearance of Anthony Lukyn makes this unlikely to be accurate. Photographs of portrait in possession of Canterbury City Library and S. M. Phillips, kindly donated by Vose Galleries.

19 Centre for Kentish Studies, Maidstone, PRC17/100/f114, proved 23 November 1778.

20 N.C.R.O., S(T)238.

Cambridge...2 or 3 years since, he had a living at Forton, near Bury. I believe a good one.'[21] Only one of Anna Maria's brothers was alive during the period covered by her letters. He lived in Epsom but, it seems, was never ordained.

What appears to have been Mrs Lukyn's last letter was dated 'February 1835'.[22] She was able to continue her correspondence until about two months before she died on 17th April 1835. Her funeral took place almost a fortnight later, on the 30th, at St Margaret's Church, and it is likely that she was buried in the churchyard.[23] It was probably at the instigation of her nieces that a combined memorial to Anna Maria and her Aunt was placed on the west wall inside the Church.[24] These two unmarried female members of the Lukyn family, though they shared the same names and stone, were given individual epitaphs. Clearly, each was thought of as a woman in her own right. The honour of a memorial placed inside the Church indicated that they still upheld the family status. This illustration shows the overall design of the stone,

whilst the inscription reads:

21 N.C.R.O., S(T)314.
22 N.C.R.O., S(T)309.
23 *St Margaret's Church Parish Registers of Baptisms and Burials*, Canterbury Cathedral Archives, (microfilm U3/6/1/1).
24 St Margaret's Church, Canterbury, west wall, stone no. 218; Canterbury Archaeological Trust, Ltd, photocopy (1997).

SACRED
TO THE MEMORY OF
ANNA MARIA LUKYN
ELDEST DAUGHTER OF
JOHN LUKYN, Esqr
BY ANNE DAUGHTER OF
ANTHONY OUGHTON Esqr
DIED
JULY THE 21st 1803
AGED 83

"HOW GOOD SHE WAS AND WHAT HER VIRTUES WERE,
HER GUARDIAN ANGEL SHALL ALONE DECLARE."

ALSO

IN AFFECTIONATE REMEMBRANCE OF
ANNA MARIA LUKYN
THE ELDEST DAUGHTER AND LAST SURVIVING CHILD OF
THE REVEREND ANTHONY LUKYN
AND ELIZABETH HIS WIFE
WHO DIED
APRIL THE 17th 1835
AGED 83

"MORE WOULD YOU KNOW. GO LEARN FROM
EVERY YEAR.
THE GOOD HOW HONOURED, AND THE KING
SO DEAR."

The last two lines quoted in the epitaph are, of course, to 'our' Anna Maria but their source is unknown. They may well be thought more secular than sacred, and knowing their original context might be helpful in interpretation. However, it can be considered an astute choice of quotation reflecting her intellect and love of literature. The learning connotation could, of course, be to both academic and religious knowledge. It might be asked if the reference in the second line is to celestial or terrestrial honours, and does 'the King' mean 'the King' of England, or 'the King' of Heaven? They are legitimate questions in view of Mrs Lukyn's unashamed support of both Church and State. Epitaphs to contemporary Evangelicals were usually more obviously spiritual, often giving signs of biblicism, conversionism or crucicentrism, characteristic elements of Evangelicalism identified by Bebbington. Good examples of this will introduce Chapter 3. The simple floral decoration heading the memorial stone was probably chosen specially, for it symbolized the younger Anna Maria's love of cultivating her garden. This leisure pursuit, considered by Evangelicals to be permissible as 'that most innocent of pleasures, supposedly sanctioned by Milton's Eve',[25] was one she shared with Archdeacon and Mrs Strong. In October 1831, she told them: 'I saved only one plant of your beautiful Hock seed, winter kill'd the rest, but that one was a Giant, and single, cover'd with bloom, and nearly as tall as myself.'[26]

Efforts to trace the distaff side of Anna Maria's family have proved unrewarding. Any additional information to justify her acceptance within a privileged society would be interesting but is not really necessary. However, there may have been maternal influences that helped to shape her negative responses to Evangelical religion.

2.1.ii Communication

Force of circumstances allowed Mrs Lukyn and Mrs Strong to meet seldom more than once a year. Clearly, they maintained their close friendship predominantly through their long letters sent every few months, but this was not unusual for women of their class and time. Travel was often slow and uncomfortable. Therefore, where personal circumstances allowed, and accommodation could be provided, visits to relatives and friends tended to run into weeks, rather than days. Mrs Lukyn wrote to Mrs Strong on 14th February 1815: 'my dear, my beloved Sister, the friend, and darling companion, of my whole life has spent the last month with me, and stays one fortnight more.'[27] For the upper classes, the employment of servants - and Mrs Lukyn did employ two maids and a cook - made the extra domestic work of entertaining negligible for the host and hostess. For the less well-off, circumstances could be very different. Intervals between meetings were usually regulated by home circumstances, working commitments, or money. In the early nineteenth-century atmosphere of mass population movement, wide physical separation from relatives and friends was

25 Rosman, *Evangelicals and Culture*, p.121.
26 N.C.R.O., S(T)295.
27 N.C.R.O., S(T)246.

common. An acute sense of loss of identity and companionship was felt by many women. This was particularly so for those who were disadvantaged by illiteracy or found the cost of travel prohibitive. Increasing numbers realized that the informal, welcoming style of Evangelical places of worship assuaged feelings of isolation to a much greater extent than the traditional formality of most Anglican churches, and could become a prime focus for social and cultural life.

Mrs Lukyn only occasionally made spiritual reference in her letters, which is particularly surprising when it is remembered that they were addressed to the wife of an Archdeacon. Letter writing had become a cultivated art within the upper classes, especially amongst the women, who usually had plenty of leisure time to fill. The more intimate the relationship between correspondents, the more gossipy and unguarded their letters tended to be. This applied to Mrs Lukyn as much as to others, even to the extent that prudence appears to have guided someone, probably Mrs Strong herself, to incise a few of the letters judiciously to remove certain passages. It can be deduced from their contexts that these passages almost certainly included lines which recounted the scandalous behaviour or misfortunes of specific persons, some of whom were ecclesiastics. Mrs Lukyn's propensity to gossip may be seen as incompatible with Christian charity, but Doreen Rosman's discussion of the gossiping which took place between some Evangelicals has revealed that such double standards were by no means infrequent among those appearing to be the most pious.[28] Obviously, Mrs Lukyn felt she could express herself as freely in writing as she would have done in intimate conversation with the friend she saw so infrequently. However, on one occasion she made this apology for what she thought were her literary deficiencies:

> ...I am conscious my unconnected epistles demand all the partiality of friends to tolerate them. I never in my life could plan a letter, except on business, and then found it quite different when indeed, from what I had perhaps intended, tho' answering the same purpose. nor can I always conjecture when I begin a letter, what the third line, or any that follows will be were I not too old to amend, after all the fine things my dear Madam you have

28 Rosman, *Evangelicals and Culture*, pp.90-1.

said, I should study a little, for something shrewed or
sensible, or at least for a well turn'd period. But I cannot;
so must e'en go on my old way, relying on your
indulgence, *and discretion* also, for the freedom with which
I give my opinions, on subjects of which I am very
incompetent to judge, only unfortunately, my hasty
form'd opinions go for nothing tho' I knowingly never
borrow without marking the quotation.[29]

Nevertheless, there is a confident subjectivity in most of Mrs
Lukyn's letters. This, of course, must be borne in mind when
interpreting her ideology, her accounts of personal experiences and
her comments on people and events, particularly when relevant to
this present discussion of Evangelical religion. Undoubtedly, most
of her opinions on religious matters in general, and Evangelicalism
in particular, ran in parallel with those of Archdeacon and Mrs
Strong. Otherwise, her relationships with such a prestigious
ecclesiastic and his wife could neither easily nor pleasurably have
been sustained during some of the most contentious and changing
times in the modern history of the Church of England.

2.1.iii Social network

Mrs Margaret Strong was born in 1755. She was three years
younger than Mrs Lukyn, which made her fifty-four when she
received the first of the letters. The friends shared a similar
immediate family background. This must have proved a good
foundation for their mutual understanding of church life and
contemporary Anglican difficulties. Margaret Strong's father, the
Rev. John Wakelyn, was awarded a B.A. from Magdalene College,
Cambridge, in 1720-1 (M.A. in 1725); he, too, was ordained priest
at Peterborough, but thirty years earlier than Anthony Lukyn.[30] For
the last years of his life Wakelyn was rector of Fletton in
Huntingdonshire (1730-60). He was also chaplain to the Earl of
Westmoreland. Margaret was an infant, aged about five, when he
died. William Strong (born on 13th February 1756) was the 'only
son of Isaac of Peterborough, gent', and his university education
was at Queen's College, Cambridge (B.A. 1779, M.A. 1782, D.D.
1802).[31] On 23rd October 1781, he was ordained priest at

29 N.C.R.O., S(T)268.
30 Venn, *Alumni Cantabrigienses*, pt. I, IV (1927), p.312.
31 Venn, *Alumni Cantabrigienses*, pt. II, VI, (1954), p.69.

Peterborough and became Archdeacon of Northampton from 1st December 1797, also Chaplain to the King and to the Bishop of Lincoln.[32] Archdeacon and Mrs Strong's son, William, followed his father into the Anglican Church ministry, but not until a few years after leaving Cambridge University. In her letter of November 1819, Mrs Lukyn declared: 'How happy, my dear Madam, must you and ye Dr. be at your son's having chose a profession to which he is so bright an ornament. never surely did Church and State stand in greater need of such!'[33] He was to become a Justice of the Peace and Chaplain in Ordinary to Queen Victoria.[34]

It was in writing to Mrs Strong on 21 June 1827, after hearing of the death of her grandson, aged seven, that Mrs Lukyn gave the longest reference there is to her faith:

> tho' I sympathize with you, in losing such an angel, can scarce condole; because of his acceptance (without sin and so early pious) we cannot entertain a doubt. Of the best, when arrived at in years of maturity, we can only alas express an humble hope.[35]

This dismisses the subject very briefly and unemotionally compared to Evangelical female responses to bereavement news, with the writers' certainties of human salvation through faith. Several examples of such belief can be found in my next chapter. Evidence will also show that probably, by the age of seven, most Evangelical children had been instilled with ideas of their innate sinfulness and that God's forgiveness could be gained only through repentance. It can be understood that Mrs Lukyn's expressed belief tied up with the sentence ending the 'Publick Baptism of Infants' in *The Book of Common Prayer*: 'It is certain by God's word, that Children which are baptized, dying before they commit actual sin, are undoubtedly saved'. Archdeacon Strong died on 8th September 1842 and his body was interred in Peterborough Cathedral. Mrs Strong lived to age ninety-three and was buried in the Cathedral precincts on 30th November 1848.[36]

32 *Ibid.*
33 N.C.R.O., S(T)261.
34 J. Grant (ed.), *Northamptonshire: Historical, Biographical and Pictorial* (published for subscribers, no date, but c.1915).
35 S(T)283, N.C.R.O.
36 Rev. H. Longden, *Northants and Rutland Clergy from 1500-1900*, XIII (Northampton, 1942), p.101.

There is much other substantial evidence to confirm that Mrs
Lukyn belonged to a distinct social and cultural community united
by class status and Orthodox Anglican allegiance. This included not
only Archdeacon and Mrs Strong, but also Mrs Lukyn's friends in
Canterbury and other areas of Kent within a radius of about ten
miles. Some were landowning families living in what Alan Everitt
termed 'little parks and manor houses' in the County's downland
and chartland areas. He has claimed that undoubtedly 'the weakness
of rural Nonconformity in much of Kent was largely due to the
remarkable strength of the old squirearchy' in these parts.[37]

In the *Kentish Herald* dated Thursday, April 21, 1836, the
following announcement appeared in the 'Deaths' column:

> On the 19th instant, at her house, in St. George's Place,
> Canterbury, aged 80 years, Mrs Dealtry, who was the eldest
> sister of the late Sir Edward Dering, bart., of Surrenden
> Dering, in this county, and great aunt to the present Sir
> Edward Cholmeley Dering, bart.

The most oft-repeated name in Mrs Lukyn's letters was that of
Mrs Dealtry, and the Dering dynasty was one of the most powerful
in this area of Kent. In the very first of her letters, Mrs Lukyn
wrote: 'The rain has prevented my going to Mrs Dealtry which I
shall do as soon as possible, as you refer me to that for more
particulars; and as I hope a frank, she will probably be glad to write
in it.'[38] It seems likely that it was through the Strongs that Mrs
Lukyn and Mrs Dealtry became acquainted. Conveniently, the two
ladies lived near to each other in St George's Place. Although
married, Selina Dealtry did not live with her husband. She had
married Skinner R. B. Dealtry at Lambeth Palace, London, in
September 1796. His father was George Dealtry, Master of the
Skinners Company (1755). After ordination, Skinner Dealtry
served in the Anglican Church in Ireland for the whole of his
ministerial life, and at the time of his death in 1830 he was Prebend
of Wicklow and Chaplain to the Archbishop of Dublin.[39]
According to Mrs Lukyn, his widow 'behaved with great propriety

37 Everitt, *The Pattern of Rural Dissent*, p.60.

38 N.C.R.O., S(T)230.

39 Venn, *Alumni Cantabrigienses*, pt. II, II (1944), p.263: Skinner R. B. Dealtry, Trinity
    College, Cambridge, B.A., 1777; M.A. 1780; M.A. incorp. at Dublin 1783; LL.D. (Hon.
    causa, Dublin) 1783.

on his death, but [was] obliged to go to Law for the small part of her property settled on her'.[40]

No doubt, Mrs Dealtry had been brought up on her family's estate at Surrenden-Dering which stood in the Parish of Pluckley. Pluckley Rectory, in 1839, was 'the seat of the Rev. Cholmeley Edward John Dering, M.A., Prebendary of St. Paul's Cathedral, London, Rector of Pluckley, Chaplain to the Queen, and a Magistrate for the County'.[41] Cholmeley Dering was Mrs Dealtry's half-brother, and Pluckley Rectory was 'a handsome modern mansion, in a very beautiful situation, commanding a most extensive prospect over the weald of Kent'.[42] For a period, from January 1813, she had moved from St George's Place and was 'comfortably situated in a Prebendal house' furnished for her by her 'good brother' but, according to Mrs Lukyn, she seemed 'not a degree happier than before'.[43] In March 1821, Mrs Dealtry returned to St George's Place, 'about 6 or 7 doors beyond' Mrs Lukyn, who had been asked to assist in finding a suitable property for her.[44]

Another resident of Canterbury, a Mrs LeGeyt, also shared Mrs Lukyn's network of Anglican kinship. Like that of Mrs Dealtry, Mrs LeGeyt's name appeared with regularity in the letters, but she may well have been of more modest descent. Yet, among the memorials on the walls of the Cathedral cloisters, there is one to Mrs Anna Maria LeGeyt, her husband and four of their children. Almost certainly this relates to Mrs Lukyn's friend and her family, who were 'of the Archbishop's Palace'. Ledgers below the memorial mark the places where those named on it were buried. Why they lived at the Archbishop's Palace is not apparent, but families unconnected with the Cathedral occupied houses on Palace land and their prerogative was to be buried in the precincts. How Mrs Lukyn and Mrs LeGeyt had first become friends is also not clear, but probably the connection was ecclesiastical for the Strongs usually visited Mrs LeGeyt during their stays with Mrs Lukyn.

Certainly Philip, one of the LeGeyt sons, had been ordained. He held preferments in Canterbury Diocese from 1803 and

40   N.C.R.O., S(T)293.
41   C. Greenwood, *An Epitome of County History: County of Kent*, I (1839), p.283.
42   *Ibid.*, p.283.
43   N.C.R.O., S(T)241.
44   N.C.R.O., S(T)266.

became Chaplain to the Duke of Kent.[45]   Clearly, he was not
Evangelical. Despite his earlier disappointment 'at not having the
Living at Margate',[46] Mrs Lukyn was able to write on 30 January
1813: 'Mrs LeGeyt's son is distinguishing himself as a strenuous and
I am told able defender of our established Church against the strong
attacks of a Methodist Clergyman in this neighbourhood, and a
party of Dissenters.'[47]

During the autumn, Mrs Lukyn usually visited friends who
lived within a limited area located about twelve miles from
Canterbury. On 12 November 1810, she explained to Mrs Strong:

> You would have heard from me long since, had not my
> intended visit of a week been prolonged to different
> friends to seven. From Bridge Hill I went to Mrs
> Beckingham of Oswalds... from Oswalds I went to Mr
> Hammonds at St Albans Court, from thence to Deane
> Park, then at the earnest request of a party of old-maids
> like myself back to Bridge Hill.[48]

This was a round of some of the 'numerous little parks and
manor houses' in the area. The Hammond family were landed
gentry and among Mrs Lukyn's closest friends. She had known
them from her childhood and it seems there had been family
connections for at least two generations. At the time of her visits
the owner and resident of St Alban's Court, in the parish of
Nonington, was William Hammond. He followed a long line of
worthy ancestors who had lived there from the sixteenth century.[49]
His wife was the 'eldest daughter of Osmund Beauvoir, D.D.', and
his brother, Anthony, was 'rector of Ivychurch and vicar of Limne'.[50]
Greenwood described the Hammond's mansion thus:

> St Alban's Court is pleasantly situated, being sheltered on
> the east and west by gently rising grounds, and by groves

45 J. M. Cowper, *Memorial Inscriptions of the Cathedral Church of Canterbury* (Canterbury,
    1897).
46 N.C.R.O., S(T)235.
47 N.C.R.O., S(T)241.
48 N.C.R.O., S(T)235.
49 Sir B. Burke, *History of the Landed Gentry of Great Britain and Ireland*, I, A. P Burke and
    brothers (ed.), (1894 edn), p.882.
50 E. Hasted, *A History and Topographical Survey of Kent*, IX, (Canterbury, 1800, 1972 edn),
    pp. 255-56.

of lofty trees on the south, which give the spacious north front of the mansion a picturesque effect, as seen in the approach from Knowlton Court, from which it is distant only one mile. About the same distance southward is Fredville, and very near it, on the northwest, is Goodnestone Park. St Alban's Court is about nine miles north-west from Canterbury.

The scene is idyllic. The area has retained its rural, open landscape, but part only of the St. Alban's Court of Mrs Lukyn's time remains. It has been reduced to 'a fragment of what was quite a large house, part half-timbered, mostly of red brick'; the 'original date-stone' shows the year of construction as 1556.[51] In my later, more detailed discussion of early nineteenth-century Evangelicalism within this region of Kent, the proximity of St Alban's Court to Fredville and Goodnestone Park will be shown to have had significance. The memorials in Nonington Parish Church testify to the virtues of Hammonds of former generations. William Hammond died on 20th November 1821, aged seventy, leaving his wife and seven children. Two days afterwards Mrs Lukyn wrote to Mrs Strong:

> While finishing this, one of the best of men, has been summon'd to the reward of his numerous virtues. You have heard me mention Mr. Hammond of St Albans Court who as well as his charming wife were my *uniformly* intimate friends, from early youth at whose hospitable and splendid Mansion, I annually spent part of every Nov.[52]

In connecting Mr Hammond's heavenly 'reward' specifically with his 'virtues', Mrs Lukyn was expressing Arminianism. Significantly, she made no mention of his having been saved through spiritual conversion, one of the fundamental characteristics of Evangelicalism.   Mr Hammond's elder son, William Osmund Hammond, married Mary, the daughter of Sir Henry Oxenden,

51 N. Pevsner and J. Newman, *North East and East Kent* (1969, 1998 edn), p.405, in B. Cherry & J. Nairn (eds), *The Buildings of England* series. The present St Alban's Court, dated 1878, was built in Elizabethan style for William Hammond's grandson, Walter Oxenden Hammond, *Ibid.*, pp.404-5. Now occupied by the Evangelical Bruderhof Community.

52 N.C.R.O., S(T)268.

Bart, and became a Magistrate and Deputy Lieutenant for the County of Kent. He continued the family's residence at St Alban's Court.[53]

The village of Bridge lies adjacent to Bourne Park, Bishopsbourne. 'Bridge Hill' can be recognized as the present Bridge Hill House now developed into flats. Undoubtedly, it is what Newman called 'Bridge Place' and described as 'a fragment of the major mid-c17 brick house'.[54] Writing in November 1816, Mrs Lukyn commented on one of her annual visits there:

> I received yours of Oct. 4 at Bridge Hill, where I passed an agreeable, tranquil month. I could not withhold from the Baroness the gratification of the favourable impression she had made on you. More especially as I know it was mutual. The King wishes him [the Baron] to be near him but the Baroness will not go, and the Baron ever gratefully and affectionately yields to her every wish. This account I have repeatedly learnt from both in the ease of friendly conversation.[55]

Current investigation has not revealed who exactly the Baron and Baroness were but, clearly, Mrs Lukyn was on very familiar terms with them. Apparently through her they had been introduced to Archdeacon and Mrs Strong.

In 1800, Bourne Park was owned by Mr Stephen Beckingham. Oswalds was a dower house attached to the Park and at that time was inhabited by his brother, the Reverend Beckingham. No doubt Mrs Beckingham was the clergyman's wife but perhaps in 1816 she was a widow. By 1974 half of Oswalds had been demolished. However, its later owners 'were trying to restore it to its original glory', but they would 'never be able to replace the three beautiful gardens which opened from one to the other and stretched right into Bourne Park'.[56] The reduced house still stands about one and a quarter miles from Bridge Hill. The whereabouts of Deane Park has not yet been ascertained.[57]

53 Greenwood, *Epitome of County History*, p.349.
54 Pevsner and Newman, *North East and East Kent*, pp.160-1.
55 N.C.R.O., S(T)253.
56 B. Conrad, *Coach Tour of Joseph Conrad's Homes* (1974), p.9. In 1919, Oswalds was bought by Joseph Conrad, the author, and it became his last residence.
57 There is a house, Denne Hill (1871) at nearby Womenswold: see Pevsner and Newman, *North East and East Kent*, p.116.

The elite members of society living in this area of Kent constituted a formidable power block within a radius of only a few miles. Yet it will be illustrated later that an Evangelical challenge to the traditions of local religious and social life was to be led by female members of some of the very families to which they belonged.

2.2 LITERATURE

In an article printed in *The Edinburgh Review (or Critical Journal)* of November 1812 its editor, Francis Jeffery, estimated that in 'this country' at that time, there were probably 'not less than two hundred thousand persons who read for amusement or instruction among the middling classes of society. In the higher classes, there [were] not as many as twenty thousand'.[58]   Mrs Lukyn and members of her social circle might properly be included in the latter figure.   Increasingly, literature was being recognized as a powerful medium for dissemination of religious views.   Elisabeth Jay has quoted that 22.2 per cent of all the books published between 1801 and 1835 were religious in content.[59] Undoubtedly, Mrs Lukyn herself was a voracious reader. It is clear that she shared her literary pleasures with the Strongs, for she regularly expounded about what she had been reading. In her letter of 15 May 1824, she wrote: 'I wish much to see you both here again when I come down to breakfast, our dear Archdeacon making his memorandums, and looking over the shelves, and noticing how many books I have bought, since he was here'.[60]

It is important to remember that this section on 'Literature' is a study of how some contemporary authors were received by Mrs Lukyn at her level of perception. A good deal of her reading matter, including articles in periodicals, was related to contemporary religious issues. It was not unusual for new works in poetry or prose, written by some authors of distinction, to be discussed within her network of spiritual kinship. Mrs Lukyn's own approach was often critical and her comments on certain publications have been a useful supplement for revealing her responses to Evangelicalism. Though a non-professional reviewer, she has confirmed her ability to argue in a limited way. Often, in comparatively few words, she said enough for us to understand

---

58 'Crabbe's Tales', *The Edinburgh Review*, XX (Edinburgh, 1812), p.280.
59 Jay, *The Religion of the Heart*, p.7.
60 N.C.R.O., S(T)274.

what point she was trying to make. Investigation has usually shown that her comments were related to topics discussed within influential literary, religious and political circles of the time. Only a very small number of the many authors and their publications written about by Mrs Lukyn can be mentioned here. These few will be dealt with at some length because the writers and their newly published works were subject to much criticism by contemporary religious commentators. Though the demands of writing about 'Literature' have necessitated some particularly long quotations, a little space will be allotted to writers and printed works not referred to by Mrs Lukyn where they have contributed to my argument.

2.2.i Early nineteenth-century periodicals

The growing interest in serious reading matter was accompanied by the innovation of several religious periodicals for Orthodox Anglicans, and for Evangelicals. Their reviews of new publications, both sacred and secular, could be long, searching and, of course, biased. But, undoubtedly, the *critiques* were often relied upon as important guides before spending money on a newly-published work. That a review could persuade Mrs Lukyn to a likely purchase, can be seen from this comment in her letter of March 1824: 'saw in the Gentleman's Magazine...a work by the Member [Bishop] for Gloucester so highly praised, and the extracts so excellent shall endeavour to procure it'.[61] The rise of the periodical press was 'a notable feature in the history of the [Established] Church' during the first decade of the nineteenth century.[62] Reference will be limited here to the following publications. The *British Critic* was produced for High Churchmen, but was mentioned only very seldom by Mrs Lukyn. The *Christian Observer*, launched at about the same time (1802), was the organ of the Evangelical party within the Anglican Church and, as one might expect, was never referred to in her letters. Neither was the *Eclectic Review*, first printed in 1804 for the Eclectic Society, an organization for Churchmen and Dissenters which after 1814 represented Dissenters only. Non-religious literature was favourably reviewed in both the *Christian Observer* and the *Eclectic Review*, but their judgements were always guided by

---

61   N.C.R.O., S(T)274. This was Bishop Monk, a staunch Tory and former Dean of Peterborough, see Norman, *Church and Society*, pp.74, 85, 92.

62   J. Overton, *The English Church in the Nineteenth Century, 1800-1833* (1894), p.200.

Christian principles.[63]

The *Gentleman's Magazine: and Historical Chronicle* seems to have been Mrs Lukyn's favourite periodical. Probably she had been familiar with it from childhood, for it was first published in 1731 and was very popular with the clergy. Its Establishment biases were reflected in the choice of 'Essays, Dissertations, and Historical Passages' that appeared within its pages, together with the long lists of clerical preferments and obituaries. Letters to the editor often expressed anti-Evangelical sentiments. This extract is taken from one printed in 1812, headed 'Evening Lectures not suited to Country Parishes'. It could scarcely have been more partisan:

> The church being generally but indifferently lighted up, the most unseemly noises proceed from the more gloomy parts of it, not immediately under the observance of the preacher. Besides, *deeds of darkness* not unfrequently are committed by the younger part of the audience, on their return home to their distant hamlets, which more than counterbalance any possible good that may be supposed to accrue from the establishment of evening lectures *in villages*. Extemporary evening lectures have lately been introduced into the neighbourhood of my residence; and it will not be a monstrous breach of Christian charity in suspecting the reverence of the Clergy who introduce them. The country parish priest who conscientiously discharges the important duties of the pastoral office confers more real benefit on the hearts and souls of those committed to his charge, than wild extemporary harangues possibly can effect, which generally have no other result but enslaving the mind to a species of religious phraseology, and of producing either the most daring presumption, or the most gloomy and deplorable despair. [Signed] A Christian of the Old School.[64]

Such descriptions might well have strengthened Mrs Lukyn's antipathetical responses to 'the religion of the heart'. However, by August 1823 she had become somewhat tired of argument, for she explained: '[I] avoid everything controversial; more particularly

63 Rosman, *Evangelicals and Culture*, p.166.
64 *Gentleman's Magazine*, LXXXII (1812), pp.224–5.

religious. at one time there was too much in the Gents Mag. and I found the possibility of doubts being so much easier raised, than solved. I carefully shun them.'[65]

The *Edinburgh Review*, first published in 1802, received only occasional mention by Mrs Lukyn. Not strictly a religious periodical, this was a quarterly devoted completely to reviews mainly of books on politics, science, and religion. It was more liberal in its approach than the *Gentleman's Magazine*, and in its early days was usually fair to both sides in discussing matters of dispute between sectaries and Orthodox Anglicans. But, as it became more and more Whig dominated, one can detect that the *Edinburgh Review* would not tolerate any extreme views expressed by any religious faction.[66] Evangelicals outside the Anglican Church produced plenty of their own periodicals during the early nineteenth century. Titles of the *Evangelical Magazine*, the *Wesleyan Methodist Magazine*, and the *Baptist Magazine* indicated their separate allegiances. As might be expected, Mrs Lukyn never referred to any of these.

2.2.ii Romantic and Evangelical literature
The Romantic movement was part of the early nineteenth-century changing intellectual climate which was tending to move away from the rationalistic and mechanistic philosophy of the previous century. In David Bebbington's view,

> Romanticism was well fitted to be a vehicle for religious thought. This was the movement of taste that stressed, against the mechanism and classicism of the Enlightenment, the place of feeling and intuition in human perception, the importance of nature and history for human experience. Wordsworth, Coleridge, Keats, Shelley and Byron represented its various expressions in English verse.[67]

Bebbington has not insisted on there being 'an intrinsic bond between the Romantic and Evangelical' but has seen that

---

65 N.C.R.O., S(T)272.
66 See for example 'Publications on the education of the poor', and 'Papers on toleration', *Edinburgh Review*, XIX (1811-12), pp.1-41 and 149-164.
67 Bebbington, *Evangelicalism*, pp.80-1.

frequently in the minds of commentators 'such a connection did in fact subsist'.[68] It is not surprising that contemporary Romantic authors, as well as their works, were open to critical comment in terms of religion. B. M. G. Reardon has claimed that 'a fresh interpretation of the very nature of religion was to become a main feature of romanticist thought' at the opening of the nineteenth century.[69] The move was away from 'Natural theology' - belief in a God revealed in his created natural world - to "revelation" read in the light of human experience, in which feeling and volition are elements more potent than the critical intellect.'[70] In their re-assessment, Romantics accentuated the stimulus of imagination and subjectivity in human response. Reardon has expressed the negative side of Romantic introversion thus:

> The sense of self is obsessive and inescapable. Its shadow falls across every experience. The result can be morbid, a persistent inward suffering...wordly sorrow...from which there seems no relief except in death...The Romantic soul was painfully aware of the burden of human existence.[71]

These distressing reactions can be acknowledged as having much in common with the extreme melancholy some Evangelicals experienced through the deep soul-searching demanded by conversion. Mrs Lukyn read some of the Romantics - Byron, Southey and Scott - and her criticism of Byron's *Childe Harold's Pilgrimage* has illustrated that she understood there to be a connection between the Romantic and Evangelical.

George Gordon, sixth Baron Byron of Rochdale (1788-1824), was 'in many eyes, the very embodiment of the Romantic spirit'.[72] Byron, a writer of religious and political revolt, was 'by far the most controversial of the romantic poets.'[73] Despite his dissolute private life, his works found a ready market. His sexual immorality, including a likely incestuous relationship with his half-sister, was incompatible with the Christian idea of exemplary behaviour.

---

68   *Ibid.*, p.81.
69   B. M. G. Reardon, *Religion in the Age of Romanticism: Studies in Early Nineteenth Century Thought* (Cambridge, 1985), p.29.
70   *Ibid.*
71   *Ibid.*, pp.14-15.
72   Reardon, *Coleridge to Gore*, p.9.
73   Rosman, *Evangelicals and Culture*, p.181.

Nevertheless, many religious members of society found Byron's literary attractions irresistable. It is worth allocating a good deal of space to him here.

Mrs Lukyn wasted little time in procuring one of Byron's most disputable narrative poems - *Childe Harold's Pilgrimage* - very soon after it was published in 1812. In August of that year, she wrote to Mrs Strong:

> I have just begun Ld Byrons popular poem of Childe Harold. hitherto it has not quite answered my high expectations tho' I find many beautiful passages, and two kinds of Ballads he introduces in the 1st Canto are pathetic in the extreme, more especially as he is supposed to designate himself under the Childe H.[74]

The general opinion was that Harold was a representation of the poet himself and it was on this premise that much strong criticism was founded. Thus, the pious could attack the author along with his poem, but in his 'Original Preface' to it, Byron insisted that Harold was 'the child of imagination'.[75] It would have been surprising if a connection between Byron, himself, and Childe Harold had not been assumed, for the history of their lives appeared so similar. The *Edinburgh Review* gave over eleven pages to discussion of the poem. It described Byron's hero as 'a sated epicure - sickened with the very fulness of prosperity - oppressed with *ennui*, stung with occasional remorse; - his heart hardened by a long course of sensual indulgence, and his opinion of mankind degraded with his acquaintance with the baser part of them.' This was written of Lord Byron himself:

> It is impossible not to observe, that the...sentiments and reflections which he delivers in his own name, have all received a shade of the same gloomy and misanthropic colouring which invests those of his imaginary hero. The general strain of those sentiments, too...run directly counter to very many of our national passions, and most

74 N.C.R.O., S(T)240. The beginning of this letter is missing but, as usual, Mrs Strong noted the date of her reply at the end: 'August 1812'.

75 G. Byron, *Childe Harold's Pilgrimage and other Romantic Poems* (1807-23), J. D. Dump (ed.)(1975), pp.3,5.

favoured propensities...Neither are his religious opinions
more orthodox, we apprehend, than his politics; for he not
only speaks without any respect of priests, and creeds, and
dogmas of all descriptions, but doubts very freely of the
immortality of the soul, and other points as fundamental.[76]

But Mrs Lukyn's mention of Byron in an Evangelical context does
not appear until March 1814 and was this:

> ...as that Sect [Evangelicals] love desperate cases I earnestly
> wish they would undertake Ld Byron. more wretched than
> he describes himself, they could not make him and this
> acknowledged misery carries with it the antidote to his
> infidelity, which might be dangerous if it made him
> happy.[77]

Seemingly, still convinced that Childe Harold was a
personification of Byron himself, Mrs Lukyn expressed her view in
somewhat sarcastic terms. It was true that Evangelicals 'did love
desperate cases' for they gained many proselytes from among those
suffering physical hardship and mental distress. The wretched were
often ready to accept the message that, through conversion, they
could attain a better life in the next world. Mrs Lukyn's somewhat
sarcastic suggestion that Byron might find happiness through
Evangelicalism is based on its tenets of repentance and justification:
the process of 'the crushing sense of sin and defilement, the
discovery of salvation through the blood of Christ, and finally the
assurance of pardon and the joy that comes with it'.[78] But
Mrs Lukyn considered, perhaps not seriously, that such a
readily-available 'antidote' for misery caused by an uneasy
conscience might make Byron 'dangerous' in a continuing lack of
restraint. He would know that a spiritual panacea for the pains of
guilt was always at hand and therefore he might sin repeatedly.
    Mrs Lukyn probably enjoyed contributing in her own way to
the wider debates about a possible change in Byron's attitude
towards religion. Some contemporary Evangelicals refused to
accept 'that a man would willingly choose misery' and 'assumed

76 'Lord Byron's *Childe Harold*', *Edinburgh Review*, XIX, pp.466-7.
77 N.C.R.O., S(T)243.
78 J. R. H. Moorman, *A History of the Church in England* (1953, 1973 edn), p.319.

that he was ripe for conversion'.[79] However, the following extract is from a letter written by Sir Walter Scott,[80] in which he reported a conversation that had taken place between himself and Byron, his close friend:

> I [Scott] remember saying to him that I really thought that, if he lived a few years, he would alter his sentiments. He answered rather sharply, 'I suppose you are one of those who prophesy I shall turn Methodist?' I replied, 'No; I don't expect your conversion to be of such an ordinary kind. I would look to see you retreat upon the Catholic faith, and distinguish yourself by the austerity of your penances.'[81]

That Byron made immorality attractive, was a widely-held opinion, but according to the *Christian Observer* he 'never attempted to suggest that vice brought happiness'.[82] True to its cause, the *Evangelical Magazine* 'condemned him for prostituting his gifts, for spreading profanity and corruption, and for perpetrating false and morbid views of human nature.'[83]

Debates about the deep misery and despair that could be wrought by Evangelicalism often centred on William Cowper (1731-1800). Though acknowledged as the poet of the eighteenth-century Evangelical revival, his verses were still very popular after his death. The publication of Cowper's 'Private Correspondence' in 1824 gave Mrs Lukyn, like many other Othodox Anglicans, opportunity to seize upon the topic of his periodic insanity being tied up with his religious beliefs. In her letter, dated 14 March of that year, she wrote:

> a friend has lent me the private correspondence of

---

79 Rosman, *Evangelicals and Culture*, p.183.

80 Scott turned to Scottish Episcopalianism after abandoning the strict Presbyterianism of his young days: see D. Daiches, *Sir Walter Scott and his World* (1971), pp.10-11; also E. Johnson, *Sir Walter Scott, The Great Unknown*, vol. 1 (1970). pp.30-31. For the good Scott saw in Methodism, see W. E. K. Anderson (ed.), *The Journal of Sir Walter Scott, 1771-1832* (Oxford, 1972), p.74, and for his support of Catholic Emancipation, *ibid.*, p.544.

81 Cited Overton, *English Church in the Nineteenth Century*, p.215.

82 Cited Rosman, *Evangelicals and Culture*, p.186.

83 Cited *Ibid.*, p.182.

Cowper, the Editor his relation[84] is very desirous to persuade the world in his preface that his religion had no part in his melancholic frame of mind, and subsequent derangement. but the arguments he uses confirm I think the contrary. the first letters of the collection possess that playful spirit of humour, so fascinating in his lighter poems. in one he speaks of having settled a plan of lodging and boarding with Mrs Unwin. and here all cheerfulness ceases; another letter at the end of the year, speaks him unhappy as to his hopes of salvation. and after the interregnum of another one, so truly methodistical, as plainly speaks the change those people have wrought in him, but not for happiness. as to those that follow (as far as I have read) one [is] written in a strain of melancholy and despair. it was at this period that he was preparing to publish his 1st Vol. they amuse and interest me extremely.[85]

Certainly, Cowper did suffer deeply from believing he would never be acceptable to God but it has been recognized that his innate disposition was responsible for a history of melancholia that 'sometimes took him over the boundary of insanity'.[86] Seemingly, nothing would have convinced Mrs Lukyn that 'his religion' had no part in causing Cowper's 'melancholic frame of mind' and 'subsequent derangement'. His residence at Huntingdon with Morley Unwin, a retired Evangelical clergyman, and his wife, Mary, was a happy time for Cowper. His mental health improved. However, his life at Olney, where he lived with Mary after she was widowed, brought him in contact with the Rev. John Newton, whose Evangelical 'gloomy piety, imposed on the poet, eventually caused a recurrence of his malady'.[87] Before writing her letter, Mrs Lukyn had probably seen the review of the 'Private Correspondence of William Cowper, Esq.' printed in the *Gentleman's Magazine*, dated March 1824.[88] It included a letter written to Newton in 1783, after his moving to London. Headed 'Cowper's Mental Sufferings', here is an extract from it:

84   i.e. William Hayley; see W. Cowper, *The Letters and Prose Writings of William Cowper*, vol. I, J. King & C. Ryskamp (eds) (Oxford, 1979), p.vi.

85   N.C.R.O., S(T)274.

86   Bebbington, *Evangelicalism*, p.47.

87   *Chambers Biographical Dictionary*, M. Magnusson (ed.), (Edinburgh, 1990 edn), p.356.

88   *Gentleman's Magazine*, XCIV, pt I (1824), pp.243-45.

I have lately been more dejected and more disturbed than usual, more harassed by dreams in the night, and more deeply poisoned by them in the following day...You know not what I have suffered while you were here, nor was there any need you should. Your friendship for me would have increased your inability to help me. Perhaps, indeed, they took a keener edge from the consideration of your presence. The friend of my heart, the person with whom I had formerly taken sweet counsel, no longer useful to me as a minister, was a spectacle that must necessarily add the bitterness of mortification to the sadness of despair.[89]

By this time Cowper had lost his faith.

Undoubtedly, Mrs Lukyn's appetite for prose was even keener than that for poetry. Her letters overflow with authors and titles, but there is no indication that she ever read novels by Jane Austen. This is surprising in view of Mrs Lukyn's likely knowledge that the children of her friends, the Hammonds of St Alban's Court, Nonington, met Jane Austen and her niece, Fanny Knight, socially at some of the great houses in the area.[90] The morals of Jane Austen's fictional characters were shown to be governed more by the customs and manners of the time than conformity to any rigid religious doctrine. Of course, this was not so in the case of Hannah More's exemplary Evangelical heroine at the centre of her popular, didactic novel, *Coelebs in Search of a Wife*, whose religious principles condemned all the fashionable amusements in which most of Jane Austen's characters found great enjoyment.

At the end of the *Edinburgh Review's* uncomplimentary *critique* of the book,[91] this more general comment was made about Hannah More, the most influential female Evangelical within the Anglican Church at that time:

If, instead of belonging to a trumpery gospel faction, she had only watched over those great points of religion in which the hearts of every sect of Christians was interested,

89 *Ibid.*, p.244.
90 For example, see letter to Cassandra Austen, 6-7 November 1813, in J. Austen, *Jane Austen's Letters, 1796-1817*, D. Le Faye (ed.) (Oxford, 1995, 1997 edn), p.252.
91 By Sydney Smith, see W. E. Houghton (ed.), *Wellesley Index to Victorian Periodicals*, vol. I, (1966, Toronto), Item 463, p.445.

she would have been one of the most useful and valuable writers of her day.[92]

Undeterred by such criticisms, with which she and Mrs Strong must have been familiar, Mrs Lukyn did read some of Hannah More's works. Elisabeth Jay has commented, 'From the first, Evangelical publications received attention from a wider circle than the faithful', and even Jane Austen who, despite her declared dislike for Evangelicals, anticipated reading *Coelebs* with some pleasure.[93] As this letter shows, Mrs Lukyn read more than one of More's books and perhaps *Coelebs* was among them:

> I have added little to my stock of literary knowledge during the last 4 months. A little Poetry I fear, with *Practical Piety*, comprises the list of new publications. As for the latter, I was not pleased and am surprised so many *young* people are [reading it]. the work appear'd to me more calculated to *allure* into the narrow path which *she* strews with thorns; the whole work appear'd to me written with the sour spirit of Calvinism, tho' she brought not forward his obnoxious tenet. but if we may judge from its having reached a seventh edition, its an approved work; but to me less beneficial than any of her former ones.[94]

Apparently, Mrs Lukyn had acquired *Practical Piety; or The Influence of the Religion of the Heart on the Conduct of the Life* soon after it was first printed in 1811 for she seems to have read it by August 1812. The work did, indeed, run into seven editions.

It may seem a little suprising that Mrs Lukyn was willing to admit to any of Hannah More's works being 'beneficial'. But the following extract alone might be sufficient to explain why she 'was not pleased' with *Practical Piety*. More's opinion of Orthodox Anglicans was very explicit, and should be quoted at length, for it has illustrated how nearly she described the stance of Mrs Lukyn

---

92 *Edinburgh Review*, XIV (1809), p.151.

93 Meaning *Coelebs in Search of a Wife; comprehending Observations on Domestic Habits and Manners, Religion and Morals* (1809). Jay, *The Religion of the Heart*, p.9, citing *Jane Austen's Letters to her Sister Cassandra and Others*, ed. R. W. Chapman (1952), p.256.

94 N.C.R.O., S(T)240.

and her friends. Such words would probably have struck home with no light impact.

> There are among many others, three different sorts of religious Professors. The religion of one consists in a sturdy defence of what they themselves call orthodoxy, an attendance on public worship, and a general decency of behaviour. In their views of religion, they are not a little apprehensive of excess, not perceiving that their danger lies on the other side. They are far from rejecting faith and morals, but are somewhat afraid of *believing* too much, and a little scrupulous about *doing* too much, lest the former be suspected of fanaticism, and the latter of singularity. These Christians consider Religion as a point, which they, by their regular observances, having attained, there is nothing further required but to maintain the point they have reached, by a repetition of the same observances...These frugal Christians are afraid of nothing so much as superfluity in their love, and supererogation in their obedience...[They] dread nothing so much as enthusiasm.[95]

Like other pious Christians, Hannah More did make Evangelicalism 'alluring'. As Gilbert has said, 'The spectre of terror beyond the grave, and the "[E]vangelical allurements" of justification and eternal life were particularly potent weapons in the religious arsenal' at a time when so many were constantly reminded of the iniquities and general misfortunes of life.[96]

Hannah More addressed her *Practical Piety* to people of all classes and degrees of talent; to those who would be willing to follow as much as to those who saw themselves as leaders:

> Every individual should bear in mind, that he is sent into this world to act a part in it. And though one may have a

---

95 H. More, *Practical Piety; or, the Influence of the Religion of the Heart on the Conduct of the Life*, (1811, 1812 edn, New York), pp.29-30. The 'second class of religion', Evangelicalism, was described in her first two chapters. The 'third class' (ultra-Calvinism) was that of 'the high flown professor, who looks down from the giddy heights of antinomian delusion on the other two, abhors the one, and despises the other, concludes that the one is lost, and the other in a fair way to be so'. *Ibid.*, pp.29-31.

96 Gilbert, *Religion and Society*, p.73, citing J. Wesley, *Works*, vi, p.340.

more splendid, and another a more obscure part assigned to him, yet the actor of each is equally, is awfully accountable...[God] accurately proportions his requisitions to his gifts.[97]

Mrs Lukyn could accept this paragraph, for it expressed ideas that were not precisely against the maxims of unequal talent and birthright by which she, and probably most of those within her social network, judged the individual's suitable place in society. She had friends who held positions of authority in Kent through being born into elite families. Generally, Hannah More did not oppose the prevailing social inequalities, but rather preached in favour of the acceptance of one's lot. That the book appealed to 'so many young people', ought not to have surprised Mrs Lukyn when Hannah More's call disregarded sex and age, as well as class. From evidence given later, it seems likely that those Mrs Lukyn had in mind here were children of local gentry. Perhaps it could be suggested that there was a new undercurrent of sibling rivalry within middle- and upper-class families in the early nineteenth century, when being born male or female and position in the family played such an important part in inheritance. This was not only true of entitlement to property. Individual roles in local religious and social communities also were usually decided by these accidents of birth. The attractions of Evangelicalism for many privileged young people, particularly girls, might have been in recognizing it as a sphere of opportunity for independence of thought and active involvement of a kind normally disallowed within the constraints of familial expectations, and Orthodox Anglicanism.

Hannah More was the innovator of the religious novel. Other Evangelicals were to follow her lead. The Rev. J. W. Cunningham, vicar of Harrow from 1811 until his death in 1861, was an Evangelical clergyman of literary note who moved in elite circles of pious Christians.[98] He was Arminian in persuasion. Yet Frances Trollope, in her caricature of Cunningham as *The Vicar of Wrexhill* (1837), Rev. William Cartwright, described her fictional clergyman

97 More, *Practical Piety*, pp.23-4.
98 See Rosman, *Evangelicals and Culture*, p.83.

as an ultra-Calvinist.[99] Cunningham's *The Velvet Cushion* was a religious novel, published in 1814, which Mrs Lukyn enjoyed and recommended to Mrs Strong in her letter dated 26 December of the same year. Again, she had wasted little time in procuring a new publication:

> of course you have read "The Velvet Cushion" where tho' forewarned of its danger, I scruple not to avow my warm approbation: I am not clear sighted enough to discern the bloom hoof peeping thro' the mild sentiments of liberal candour and that tolerant judgment of those who dissent, which I think our Gospel inculcates. and while it allows all that can be granted to Calvin and ye Church of Rome, fails not to point out the excellence and superiority of our own. I therefore am in no danger of being injured in an amazing and interesting work, where I only find my faith strengthen'd and as I have seen no reviewers know not where to look for what may be thought reprehensible.[100]

This amusing and straightforward novel, was aimed at 'an upper/middle class readership'; its style was neither over-demanding nor condescending.[101] It featured 'The Vicar of a small parish church, whose turrets nodded over one of the most picturesque lakes of Westmoreland'.[102] The narrative revolved around the events in the 'life' of the old and well-worn velvet cushion the Vicar had used in his pulpit for forty-five years. A roll of paper, which appeared mysteriously inside the cushion, bore the inscription, 'My own history'.[103] It recounted 'the cushion's experience in, and opinion of, the various churches and meeting houses in which it [had] passed its long and checkered career'.[104]

99 Jay, *The Religion of the Heart*, p.52. According to Jay, most novelists tended to characterize Anglican Evangelicals as ultra-Calvinist rather than Arminian, 'partly because Arminianism was particularly associated with dissenting Methodism and partly because the hard logic of true Calvinism provided both a clarity of definition and an intellectual position which could easily be shown to be at odds with natural human sympathies', *ibid*.

100 N.C.R.O., S(T)245.

101 Rosman, *Evangelicals and Culture*, p.84.

102 J.W. Cunningham, *The Velvet Cushion* (1814, 3rd edn), p.1.

103 Cunningham, *Velvet Cushion*, p.8.

104 Rosman, *Evangelicals and Culture*, p.83.

Mrs Lukyn was correct in her assessment that Cunningham gave fair consideration to doctrines other than Orthodox Anglicanism in the dialogue between the Vicar and his wife as they read the cushion's story.

The problem of Catholic Emancipation was one of the most contentious to be solved in Britain during the early nineteenth century. Anglicans wrote profusely in arguments on the subject. Cunningham quickly got Catholicism out of the way by allocating some of his first pages in the novel to the subject. Only these short extracts from them will be given here. The cushion's history began in a Catholic church in 'the days of bloody Queen Mary' and it wrote thus of its time there: 'I no sooner heard parts of the Bible than I began to compare them with what I saw and heard around me. And I need not tell you, Sir, that the Bible and Popery do not very strictly harmonize'.[105] This led to the following comment by the Vicar:

> I acknowledge...that Popery has some things in it not likely to inspire loyalty for a Protestant sovereign, or patriotism to a heretical country. But still I believe there are many Papists both loyal and patriotic. Their very refusal to take our oaths, inclines me to hope that they respect an oath. And their refusal to part with any tittle of their own faith for a desirable end, gives some promise, I think that they will not maintain that faith by wrong means.[106]

When referring to Cunningham's 'tolerant judgment of those who dissent', Mrs Lukyn most probably had in mind his opinions of orthodox Dissenters whose preaching style, in the cushion's words, had 'generally avoided disputable ground, and insisted on the fundamental points of religion, in bold, vehement, eloquent, practical, though perhaps somewhat enthusiastic language'.[107] However, the imaginary Vicar expressed Cunningham's view of contemporary Evangelical sectarians in very different terms. These were so representative of Mrs Lukyn's own responses, and probably those of most of her Anglican set, that it is worth quoting much of the relevant passage:

---

105 Cunningham, *Velvet Cushion*, p.18.
106 *Ibid.*, p.24.
107 *Ibid.*, p.125.

I must plainly say, that I have an objection both to the character of their religion, and to a part of their practice. Against their religion, I often find reason to object that it has more of impulse, noise, excitement, of 'fits and frames' than I find either in the Bible or the Liturgy. And to their practice, which is, in many respects, admirable, I have this objection, that they too often teach the people to suspect and under-value their appointed ministers - to love change and novelty - to prefer rash to sober interpreters of Scripture. There was a time, my love, when a good clergyman was regarded as the general father of his flock...when the sheep followed his voice, and the voice of a stranger they would not follow - when, if he kept to his Bible, they would cleave to him. Now...they have shepherds many, and fathers many. The Chapel is erected not always where the duty of the Church is ill, but where it is well performed. The preacher in the church, however unexceptionable, is deserted, at least at one part of the day, for the preacher at the meeting. The people, when they should be learning, are criticising; and refuse to profit from any minister till they have settled which is best.[108]

Cunningham's discussion of Calvinism also unfolds very skilfully in the dialogue:

'The doctrine of *election* has, I think, one merit,' said the old lady; 'it must teach those who believe themselves to be thus elected, to love and honour God.'
'But,' answered the Vicar, 'how will it affect all the rest of mankind? And, surely, I am not likely to love and honour God the less because I believe that he makes to all the offers which others believe he makes only to a few?.
'But', she continued, 'there appears to be much comfort in their other tenet of *final perseverance* - in feeling that 'God will never forsake his true servants'.
'There is indeed,' said the Vicar.[109]

---

108 *Ibid.*, pp.129-30.
109 *Ibid.*, p.119. For '*final perseverance*', see Bebbington, *Evangelicalism*, p.28: Calvinists believed 'that any true believer would remain one until death - the doctrine of the perseverance of the saints. God would guarantee their ultimate salvation'.

As Mrs Lukyn saw, Cunningham had allowed 'all that [could] be granted to Calvin', as well as 'to Rome' (though she always made plain her own firm opposition to the tenets of each). What would have particularly recommended Cunningham to her was that he did 'point out the excellence and superiority of' her own Church through the depiction of the fictional Vicar's predecessor, Berkely. Berkely had not been over-zealous, and he took the part of neither the Calvinists nor the Arminians 'but taught modesty and charity to both'.[110] Though Arminian himself, Cunningham was willing to compromise in order to reach a wider readership. Significantly, this following portrayal of Berkely illustrated that a moderate Evangelical style of preaching and a concerned parochial ministry did have much in common with what might have been expected from an Orthodox Anglican clergyman:

> ...not only did he largely use the language of the Bible – he felt it his duty, as far as possible, to imitate *the style of reasoning* employed in it, and especially in the ministry of Christ. Like him, he endeavoured to seize upon passing events, or objects to illustrate his meaning – like him, to be simple grave, spiritual, touching, tender...He taught the truth – but taught it calmly. He touched the harp of the prophet, but not with that unholy vehemence which snaps its cords.
>
> In general, his manner in the pulpit was rather mild and paternal, than energetic. But there were times, and those not a few, when a new spirit seemed to animate him. His favourite theme was the happiness of the saints in glory...Above all, it was his anxious endeavour to display the character of Christ in his own daily intercourse with his parish. 'The life of Christ', he was wont to say 'was the life of God upon earth; and, therefore the fit model for him who desired to be the representative of God to his parish.' 'Human laws (I have heard him observe) differ from the divine government in three points – they do not pardon the penitent – nor reward the good – nor assist men to discharge the duties, the neglect of which they punish.' 'Now, (he added), in all these points, every man, and especially a minister, should endeavour to supply, to those

under his care, the deficiencies of the laws'. Such therefore, was his rule, and most simply and earnestly did he strive to adhere to it...I have more than once seen him, when some poor offender asked doubtingly, 'whether it was possible *he* could ever be forgiven' point with an eye full of tears, to a fine picture of Mary anointing the feet of Jesus, which hung in his study...As to the remaining duty of assisting his people, in the discharge of their duties, for this he rose early, and late took rest. He built that little school, which you, Sir, so often visit – he enlarged that altar for his increasing flock of communicants, where you so often shed the tears of sacred joy as you dispense the bread of life to hungry souls.[111]

Mrs Lukyn knew that, though she enjoyed the book herself, parts of it were 'thought to be reprehensible'. Interestingly, this ties in with Rosman's statement that 'while evoking the ire of some critics by portraying Anglicanism as the ecclesiastical ideal, Cunningham was far from censorious of other groups'.[112] Some adverse criticisms had come from High Church reviewers, as Mrs Lukyn indicated in her letter dated 14 February 1815:

You flatter me very much, in having read the [Velvet] Cushion on my recommendation it was most illiberally reviewed in the British Critic of Nov. The author in his last edition (ye 5th) has exculpated himself I think very fully from the accusations brought against him.

Discussion of a work by Cunningham can lead back to Lord Byron. Though he admired Byron as an author, Cunningham refused to erect a headstone on the grave of Allegra, the poet's illegitimate daughter, when he buried her in his churchyard in 1822. He feared that a memorial to her might effect a lowering of moral standards on the boys of Harrow School.[113]

Clearly, Mrs Lukyn found stimulation in the religious arguments contained in the printed discourses of prominent

111 Cunningham, *Velvet Cushion*, pp.172-7.
112 Rosman, *Evangelicals and Culture*, p.83.
113 I. Bradley, *The Call to Seriousness: The Evangelical Impact on the Victorians* (1976) p.145. For more Evangelical comments on Byron's works, see: Jay, *Religion of the Heart*, pp.203-4.

ecclesiastics. For example, she had bought those given by Dr. Geoffrey Faussett in his series of *Bampton Lectures*.[114] She had known Faussett from his infancy as he was the son of a family friend, had 'bought the Lectures out of compliment' and 'amply' had she been 'rewarded'.[115] However, she continued, 'I suppose he will be virulently attacked by the Reviewers. the Anti-Jacobin highly commends,[116] but he is too firm a friend to the Church, to be pardon'd by the seceders from it.' No doubt, in discussing this type of literature with Mrs Strong, Mrs Lukyn felt on equal terms with the Archdeacon of Northampton's wife. Although she did not enter into a deep religious discussion of the 'Lectures', she gave the impression that she had grasped their meaning sufficiently to understand the reaction to them by 'seceders'. These discourses had been delivered by an Orthodox Anglican to an audience of some intellectual calibre. Yet, her understanding of the theological arguments was probably far more adequate than that of many women of her time.

During a period of convalescence, Mrs Lukyn wrote in her letter dated May 26, 1832:

> I find what I *call living retired*, is in fact never being alone my kind friends are frequent callers they load me with books I had rather be without and wish to know my opinion. Am obliged to toil thro' them often wishing they had never been published. Another brings me newspapers that contain fuller account of debates than my own paper gives, a third begs I will read some pamphlets or Magazine, which speak exactly my opinions.[117]

It is unfortunate that there is no mention of the titles she wished she had not been lent, for it would have been an indication of the 'books' some of her local friends might have enjoyed. Perhaps they were less educated than Mrs Lukyn, thus

114 The Bampton Lectures were established at Oxford University from a legacy of John Bampton and first delivered in 1780: see L. E. Elliott-Binns, *The Early Evangelicals: A Religious and Social Study* (1953), p.66.

115 N.C.R.O., S(T)266. (March 22, 1821).

116 *The Anti-Jacobin Review*, dated from 1798, aimed at a middle-and upper-class readership. It 'contained numerous articles by the clergy enjoining obedience to civil authority as a religious duty': see Norman, *Church and Society*, p.30.

117 N.C.R.O., S(T)297.

recommending reading material of inferior quality and style. The circulation of literature within this Canterbury women's network has suggested that discussion of shared printed matter, some of which would surely have been on contemporary religious developments and disputes, was an important cultural element of their friendship.

2.3 RELIGION

It is apparent from Mrs Lukyn's letters that many features of the religious and social change taking place throughout early nineteenth-century Britain were appearing within the microcosms of local communities with which she was familiar. Her observations on what was occurring in the religious life of Canterbury, and other parts of Kent that she visited, bore witness to the accumulation of some of the challenges and problems which were to drive the Established Church to reform. Rapid encroachment of Evangelical religion was not the least of its difficulties. Evangelicals were growing ever stronger forces to be reckoned with in parishes, Parliament and the two major universities.[118] Mrs Lukyn's comments on how the surge of popular Evangelicalism touched the religious and cultural lives of herself and people she knew are particularly valuable in adding colour and dimension to the local scene. Extracts from Mrs Lukyn's correspondence quoted in this section contained some of her most subjective remarks, but impartiality was not to be expected from someone whose life had always been bound up with Orthodox Anglicanism. Exaggeration can often accompany emotion when recounting personal experiences, but in Mrs Lukyn's letters embellishment was probably minimal. She would have known full well that Mrs Strong was too close to contemporary ecclesiastical life at the highest levels not to have recognized undue stretching of the imagination. Mrs Lukyn's own attitudes can be assessed as fairly representing those of the older generation of her conservative-minded friends for whom inherited social privilege and allegiance to Anglican Orthodoxy had brought the concomitant authority, benefits and prejudices. For her, and for those who shared her conventional ideas of behaviour and belief, the Evangelical challenges to the established norms of society and religion were seen as a real threat. The fact that most of her evidence has related

118 Walsh & Taylor, 'Introduction', *The Church and Anglicanism*, pp.44-5.

to the Archbishop of Canterbury's own diocese makes it the more interesting. From time to time there may appear to be diversions from my main issues, but any background information included has been thought necessary in order to explain fully the possible interpretation of Mrs Lukyn's observations. For Mrs Strong and others who had been immersed in church life from childhood, such exposition would have been superfluous.

As Frances Knight has pointed out, 'the eighteenth-century mind' realized that a stable society depended on stability at parish level, therefore early in the nineteenth century, when increasing unrest among the British population emitted alarming danger signals for the Establishment, 'legislators and reformers turned instinctively to the parish as the place where the remedy should be sought'.[119]   The Anglican Church and its clergy must be more visibly active in spiritual matters and socially more supportive. Some of Mrs Lukyn's remarks about local conditions will confirm this necessity.   In his article on 'Evangelicalism and the French Revolution', V. G. Kiernan presented his theory that, at about the beginning of the nineteenth century, 'religious enthusiasm was recognised as a possible support for order and stability'[120]. Relations between Church and State were intimate and they needed to stand firmly in support of each other. Around the turn of the century, response came largely through the persistent efforts of William Wilberforce (1759-1833), the Anglican Yorkshire M.P., leading figure within the Clapham Sect and among 'the Saints', as Evangelical Parliamentarians were known.[121] Wilberforce and his friends at Clapham shared fears of disruption but 'felt that it could not be averted by police methods only, or longed for something more idealistic than the existing order.'[122] In 1797, he had published his *Practical View*, which was addressed to his own social class.[123] It was to prove influential during the early nineteenth century. The work claimed 'that Christians would sanctify existing society by their influence rather than escape from it into a subculture of the

119 Knight, *The Nineteenth-century Church*, p.68.
120 V. G. Kiernan, 'Evangelicalism and the French Revolution', *Past and Present*, No.1 (Oxford, 1952), p.44.
121 All were laymen, but they had firm support from John Venn, rector of Clapham: see Reardon, *Coleridge to Gore*, pp.24-5.
122 Kiernan, 'Evangelicalism', p.52.
123 See Reardon, *Coleridge to Gore*, p.25.

elect'.[124] Wilberforce's politico-religious message entreated those with money and authority to exercise the Christian doctrines of moderation and humility, thus 'softening the glare of wealth, and moderating the insolence of power', and rendering the social inequalities 'less galling to the lower orders'.[125]

To Wilberforce's mind, action against existing social evils should not be class-discriminatory. The French elite had 'sadly demonstrated that elegant behaviour and refinement can be consistent with a considerable degree of depravity', and he urged:

> Let us then beware, and take warning from their example...What then is to be done?...The causes and nature of the decay of religion and morals among us sufficiently indicate the course, which, on principles of sound policy, it is in the highest degree expedient for us to pursue. The distemper of which, as a community, we are sick, should be considered rather as a moral than a political malady...Every effort should be used, to raise the depressed tone of public morals. This is a duty particularly incumbent on all who are in the higher walks of life...Let him, then, who wishes well to his country, no longer hesitate what course of conduct to pursue...Circumstanced as we now are, it is more than ever obvious, *that the best man is the truest patriot*. Nor is it only by their personal conduct that men of authority and influence may promote the cause of good morals. Let them in their several stations encourage virtue and discountenance vice in others...But fruitless will be all attempts to sustain, much more to revive, the fainting cause of morals, unless you can in some degree restore the prevalence of evangelical Christianity...The attempt should especially be made in the case of the pastors of the church, whose situation must render the principles which they hold a matter of supereminent importance.[126]

This was a severe indictment of upper- and middle-class lay and clerical morality and an attack on the code by which many of them conducted their private and public lives.

124 J. Wolffe, *The Protestant Crusade in Great Britain, 1829-1860* (Oxford, 1991), p.29.
125 Wilberforce, *Practical View*, p.301.
126 Wilberforce, *Practical View*, pp.308-312.

In rural areas the tithe system had long been a cause of
parochial resentment against the clergy, some of whom were
relentless in asserting their rights to payment. As Parliamentary
enclosure and commutation of tithes extended to increasing
numbers of parishes in the early nineteenth century, many more
clergymen became land-owners with consequential power at grass-
roots level as magistrates and/or administrators of the poor law.[127]
Mrs Lukyn never referred directly to Wilberforce. Nevertheless,
her evidence has indicated that his criticisms were well-deserved by
some, and undeserved by others, in the 'higher walks of life' whom
she knew and among Kentish 'pastors of the church'.[128]

2.3.i Mrs Lukyn and the local context of Evangelicalism

The Clergy

As already indicated, the early nineteenth-century Church defects
were well known. Mrs Lukyn pinpointed a considerable number
of its imperfections in the Canterbury diocese and made her own
assessment of their direct, or indirect, contribution to the growth of
Evangelicalism within local Anglicanism, Methodism and Dissent.
During the early nineteenth century, many of those calling for
Church reform believed that one of the most important reasons for
the spread of Nonconformity was that many parish clergy lacked
enthusiasm and neglected their parochial ministry.[129] The state of
the early nineteenth-century Church has tended to be written
about in general terms and 'to relate to the system rather than to
the individuals', yet of primary importance to parishioners was the
quality of the incumbent and his effectiveness.[130] Fortunately, what
Mrs Lukyn wrote about the clergy was not all generalization. Her
comments on individuals have afforded insight into the ways in
which some local clerics functioned. What is even more
valuable for this present study is that she made reference to
clergymen at all ecclesiastical levels, and has given her assessment
of the contribution they made to the advancement or retardment

---

127 See E. J. Evans, 'Some reasons for the growth of English rural anti-clericalism c.1750-
   c.1830', *Past and Present*, No. 66, (Oxford, 1975), pp.84-109.
128 For more on the importance of control and improvement at parish level, see G. F. A.
   Best, *Temporal Pillars: Queen Anne's Bounty, the Ecclesiastical Commissioners, and the Church
   of England* (Cambridge, 1964), pp.145, 152-53.
129 Gilbert, *Religion and Society*, pp.94-5.
130 N. Gash, *Aristocracy and People: Britain, 1815-1865* (1979), p.60.

of Evangelicalism.

The early nineteenth-century religious revival in Britain came, to the largest extent, from expansion of Evangelicalism within Dissent and growth of Methodist congregations. In her letter of 25th March 1813, Mrs Lukyn wrote of the rising popularity of Methodism in Canterbury and recognized the deficiencies of local Anglican Churches:

> if the industrious poor can be taught the pleasure of saving their earnings, other good habits must inevitably follow. But it is not in large towns, where improved morals can I fear be expected, more especially if that town is a Garrison where the allurements to vice and profligacy of every description are too numerous to meet with much, or long resistance. do not think me tinctured with the preaching fanaticism but the terrific doctrines of the Methodists certainly enforce more external rectitude of conduct than the milder doctrines of the Church of England. and a more favourable spot than this City for its rapid progress, can scarce be found, as our places of public worship from various causes are so ill regulated, its always difficult to find where service will be performed...nor possess we attractive preachers; except our Dean,[131] and a few of our Prebendarys occasionally.[132]

Though their doctrines did not appeal to her personally, Mrs Lukyn realized the power of 'Methodist' preachers to attract congregations, and influence the 'external conduct' of their Evangelical converts. Her experience in Canterbury clearly supports Bradley's statement that, in early nineteenth-century Britain, diminishing congregations had resulted in discontinuance of services in many parish churches, others were often closed on Sundays and, except for some distinguished men, most Anglican clergymen were of low calibre.[133] Mrs Lukyn was being more honest in her criticisms than those who ascribed the rapid expansion of Nonconformist chapels to lack of accommodation in Anglican Churches, 'rather than to any intrinsic merits in Nonconformity'.[134] Over seven years later, in September 1820, Mrs

---

131 This would have been Gerard Andrews, Dean of Canterbury 1809-25.
132 N.C.R.O. S(T)257: (not numbered in correct chronological order by N.C.R.O.)
133 Bradley, *Call to Seriousness*, p.59.

Lukyn was still drawing Mrs Strong's attention to local clergy inadequacies so serious that they were responsible for driving Anglicans to Nonconformist places of worship:

> I sincerely wish your son was here, we have many respectable clergymen and good men, but so deficient in education and delivery that our Churches are empty, and our Meeting houses crowded.[135]

During the early decades of the nineteenth century there was a substantial growth in the number and influence of clergy, as well as laity, who allied themselves to the Evangelical party in the Church of England. According to rough estimates, between 1810 and 1830 the numbers of Evangelical clergy had grown from one in twenty to one in eight.[136] Writing on December 26, 1814, Mrs Lukyn reinforced this statement, and having just reaffirmed the progress of 'Methodism' in the district, she continued:

> I regret to say some of our regularly ordained Clergy have all been added to the strictest of this Sect. earnest in making Converts to their doctrine such is their success, that like an epidemic disease we who still remain firm, tremble, lest we should fall, as not knowing whose turn may be next.[137]

By 'this Sect' she meant 'Anglican Evangelicals', and she often called them 'Methodists'. This analogical use was quite common because, to many people's minds, the latter term had an historic connection with John Wesley's Methodism and the Evangelical Revival of the previous century.[138] Wesley had remained an Anglican clergyman until his death in 1791. By then the 'Methodists' had become a strong body within the Established Church and it was not until 1795 that they broke away to set up their own separate organization.

The most Orthodox clergyman could be classed 'zealous' if he

134 Knight, *The Nineteenth-century Church*, p.63.
135 N.C.R.O., S(T)264.
136 See E. Jay, 'Introductory Essay', in E. Jay (ed.), *The Evangelical and Oxford Movements* (Cambridge, 1983), p.5.
137 N.C.R.O., S(T)245.
138 See Ditchfield, *The Evangelical Revival*, p.57; Bradley, *Call to Seriousness*, p.58.

worked assiduously for his parish. Orthodox members of the laity and the Church Establishment disapproved strongly of the unconventional methods and irregularities of their Evangelical clergy, 'who were perennially referred to as Methodists.'[139] Despite the ambiguity of terms, Mrs Lukyn knew exactly the type of parson she had in mind when she mentioned 'Methodists', 'the strictest of this Sect' and 'Converts'. Those who, like herself and Mrs Strong, had been brought up under close church influences would have known full well what she meant. Nevertheless, as has been illustrated, Mrs Lukyn also used the term 'Methodist' in the denominational way. In the nineteenth century, Skeats claimed that whatever the various proponents were called, 'the high character of the arduous labours of the evangelical section of the Established Church was as conspicuous as were the negligence and the laxity of the majority of their brother clergymen'.[140] This was a very extreme opinion, and obviously biased. Although she severely criticized some Church of England clerics, Mrs Lukyn did recognize that there were ones known to her who were not Evangelicals and yet were able and conscientious. Ian Bradley's twentieth-century judgement was that 'although there were notable exceptions the general calibre of Anglican clergymen was low', but many of them were from landed families and had chosen what they saw as a not too demanding career in the Church.[141] However, as Gerald Parsons has pointed out, it is inaccurate to describe the great majority of late eighteenth-century Anglican clergy as lacking in a sense of vocation and devotion to their parishes. Not all clergymen had been 'pastorally lax, worldly, and void of a sense of vocation', though early nineteenth-century reforms in 'pastoral discipline and ideals' were considered urgent.[142]

Close hierarchical scrutiny was difficult in the ecclesiastical system of pluralities of livings and non-residence of clergy. The Church itself was largely to blame for the growth in Protestant sectarianism because it failed to ensure its traditional local ministry in all parts of the country.[143] In the early years of the nineteenth

---

139 *Ibid.*, p.58.

140 H. S. Skeats, *A History of the Free Churches of England from A.D.1688-A.D.1851* (1869, 2nd edn), pp.528-9.

141 Bradley, *Call to Seriousness*, p.59.

142 G. Parsons, 'Reform, Revival and Realignment: The Experience of Victorian Anglicanism', in G. Parsons (ed.), *Religion in Victorian Britain, I, Traditions* (Manchester, 1988), p.23.

century over twenty-five per cent of all parish clergy were non-resident and ten per cent of parishes were without any Anglican minister at all.[144] Furthermore, within the new squire-parson relationships that generally developed in parishes affected by Parliamentary enclosure, when many clergy became landowners, much of the clerical week was spent enjoying favourite leisure activities - hunting, racing, drinking and playing cards. Parochial duties were often neglected and ineffective ministry presented opportunities for Evangelical clergy and Dissenting preachers to come into their own.

In her letter of December 1818, Mrs Lukyn was still reporting a great increase in the number of Evangelical clergy in the area, and it was not only at parish level that reform was necessary. She suggested that at least one member of the Canterbury ecclesiastical hierarchy, as well as two of his underlings, were lax in carrying out their duties, which only added further to the poor image of the Anglican Church:

> the [Evangelical] Sect make rapid strides among us and I am sorry to say the conduct of two of our Clergy (not in this place) has been such, as calls for severe reprehension. am told the Parishioners of one have addressed the Archdeacon on the subject, but he will go to sleep and forget it. the other largely prefer'd, is the Counterpart of Crabbe's Village Curate, and proves the character was no fiction of the Poet's brain; these instances and their being unnoticed gives great cause for triumph to the enemies of the established church.[145]

The Archdeacon's inertia may partly have been due to the amount of time and travelling entailed in parish visitations, as well as lack of monetary incentive. Insufficient funding caused most problems for archdeacons in their attempts to carry out their duties efficiently.[146] Perhaps Archdeacon Strong's reaction to recalcitrant clergy would have been different, but Mrs Lukyn showed distinct absence of sympathy for the Archdeacon of Canterbury. She might have been expected to know that the disciplinary powers of bishops and

143 Gash, *Aristocracy and People*, p.63.
144 Bradley, *Call to Seriousness*, p.59.
145 N.C.R.O., S(T)258.
146 Knight, *The Nineteenth-century Church*, p.167.

archdeacons were limited, and court proceedings could be expensive. The curate in the Reverend George Crabbe's poem, *The Village* (1783), probably fairly represented the local character Mrs Lukyn wished to portray as his 'counterpart':

> A jovial youth, who thinks his Sunday's task
> As much as God or man can fairly ask;
> The rest he gives to loves and labours light,
> To fields the morning and to feasts the night;
> None better skilled, the noisy pack to guide,
> To urge their chase, to cheer them or to chide;
> Sure in his shot, his game he seldom missed,
> And seldom failed to win his game at whist;
> Then, while such honours bloom around his head,
> Shall he sit sadly by the sick man's bed
> To raise the hope he feels not, or with zeal
> To combat fears that even the pious feel?[147]

A curate was usually understood to be the clergyman 'in whom was vested sole charge of a parish in the absence of a non-resident incumbent'.[148] Thus, it was possible for him to find considerable freedom in the way he conducted his personal life and parochial duties. In 1833, William Howley, Archbishop of Canterbury from 1828 to 1848, revived the office of rural dean in his diocese.[149] Through this arm of informal supervision, he had better prospects of gaining knowledge of any clergy indiscipline and other matters directly affecting parochial ministry.

Though bishops held a significant share of patronage and often gave preferments to relatives, lay individuals formed the largest category of private patrons.[150] Some of them were women. The system allowed freedom of choice so there were opportunities for members of the laity to offer livings to Evangelicals. To reduce the chances of this, some Bishops adopted their own methods when selecting incumbents or choosing candidates for ordination. In two

147 G. Crabbe, 'The Village' (1783), in G. Edwards (ed.), *George Crabbe, Selected Poems* (1991), pp.11-12.

148 Knight, *The Nineteenth-century Church*, p.116.

149 R.A. Burns, 'A Hanoverian legacy? Diocesan reform in the Church of England c.1800-1833' in Walsh, Haydon, Taylor (eds) *The Church of England*, pp.268.

150 M. J. D. Roberts, 'Private Patronage and the Church of England, 1800-1900', *Journal of Ecclesiastical History*, vol.32, no.2 (1981), p.201.

of her letters Mrs Lukyn commented on the procedures devised by Bishop Marsh of Peterborough and other prelates. On August 14, 1823, she put matters very succinctly, but Mrs Strong would have been so well-informed about current arguments concerning ordination of Evangelicals that a detailed clarification would have been superfluous:

I felt a most lively indignation at the illiberal attack on your good Bishop, not quite so easy a one as Norwich, who ordain'd any who offer'd. equally inimical to Church and State and who meant to replace the good Archdeacon Gooch, if he survived...by a notorious radical. I *think* of the name Harrison. I regret (to *you* I may venture to do so) the in-efficiency of many of our Clergy. providing too often unworthy relations, and servile dependants, makes merit in the profession of little avail. our Archbishop had sent us too many, whom he felt obliged to provide for, as relatives. his two sons in law Percy and Crofts are amiable and bright exceptions.[151]

With the increasing supply of Evangelicals coming out of the universities, particularly Cambridge, ordinands were subjected to thorough questioning by some bishops. Mrs Lukyn no doubt echoed the Strongs' admiration for Marsh, their 'good bishop' at Peterborough from 1819 to 1839. He had been appointed Lady Margaret Professor of Divinity at Cambridge in 1807, and was one of the ablest prelates of his day.[152] Marsh was at the centre of controversies over ordinating and appointing Evangelicals. He was attacked from many quarters for devising his '"celebrated trap for Calvinists"', the eighty-seven questions he put to candidates for ordination, institution, or licences within his diocese.[153] These were questions which 'no Evangelical could possibly answer to the bishop's satisfaction' without renouncing his principles.[154] Marsh's objective was to stop the supply at source so that there would be no successive Evangelicals to go into the system. Other bishops might have been pleased to accept the candidates he had rejected.

151 N.C.R.O., S(T)272.
152 Overton, *The English Church*, p.187.
153 Best, *Temporal Pillars*, p.243.
154 Moorman, *A History of the Church in England*, p.316.

Marsh's test was unlawful, and there were strong objections from Evangelicals everywhere, not least from those in Parliament. On June 14, 1821, Marsh found it necessary to deliver a speech to the House of Lords in answer to a petition presented by Lord King. The grounds for the petition were that the Bishop had refused a Licence, in summer 1820, to a person whom the Petitioner had nominated to the Curacy of Burton Latimer, Northamptonshire. Marsh defended his questions thus:

> For though they are disliked by the Petitioner, and by others who think like himself, I can confidently assert, that they are approved by the great body of my Clergy; approved, my Lords, because they are a check on fanaticism, from which the Church, in this country, has more to apprehend, than from any danger that now besets it.[155]

Mrs Lukyn's less-favoured 'Norwich' was Henry Bathurst (1744–1837), nephew of the first Earl Bathurst. A Whig Liberal, he supported Catholic Emancipation in the Lords' vote of 1828, and in 1831 was one of only two Bishops who did not oppose the Bill for Parliamentary Reform.[156] As Mrs Lukyn commented, Bathurst in this context was probably 'an easy one' in comparison with Bishop Marsh, and was prepared to appoint 'a notorious radical'. For 'Norwich', the Evangelicals were probably best left to go their own way. Norwich was a diocese whose problems Bathurst never managed to control.[157] Mrs Lukyn's evidence of the Evangelical Bishop Ryder's mode of questioning ordinands was minimal and unattributed, but there is every reason to believe that it contained a strong element of truth. This is what she wrote on May 15, 1824:

> Ryder I fancy is not changed; a young gentleman who had gone thro' the University with great credit applied for Ordination. when the Bishop put the puzzling question "at

---

155 'A speech delivered to the House of Lords on Tuesday, June 14, 1821, by Herbert, Lord Bishop of Peterborough; in answer to a petition presented to the House of Lords respecting his examination questions', in Anon., *Tracts on the Bishop of Peterborough's Questions* (1821), p.28.

156 Norman, *Church and Society*, pp.81 & 85.

157 Best, *Temporal Pillars*, p.202, n.1.

what time he felt the call to the Ministry?" the young man was dumb, and I believe drew back. however the Bishop refused to Ordain him. perhaps if many of them were a little more strict, it would be for the advantage of the National Church, but while Livings can be purchased, and families must be provided for, qualified or not qualified, worthy or unworthy, we must not expect a change. but many of our Clergy do honor to their profession, and devote their time and talents to the sacred cause, and to counteracting the dangerous tenets of Methodism.[158]

The Hon. Henry Ryder was appointed Bishop of Gloucester in 1815 (to Lichfield in 1824). He was the first Evangelical to be raised to such high office.[159] But, despite his Evangelicalism, Mrs Lukyn seemingly thought Ryder's selection methods preferable to any that were not truly discriminating.[160]

Mrs Lukyn was not alone, by any means, in denigrating patronage. 'The more intelligent thinkers about church reform' recognized it as the dominant cause of clerical inefficiency and occasions of scandolous behaviour; advowsons were valuable monetary property but meant more in terms of social standing or family advantage.[161] Reformers could only urge patrons to take their responsibilities seriously: they should make appointments on professional worth and what was best for the Church, rather than for convenience of their own relatives or political interests.[162] However, the Bishops were accountable for distribution of great numbers of the most lucrative preferments, the majority of which they bestowed on friends and relatives, or on themselves. The 'venerable fathers' of the Church were 'at once the objects and the dispensers of the most important patronage which our constitution [knew]'.[163] Nepotism was rife but had to be accepted. Mrs Lukyn saw that current procedures at Canterbury could place incompetent Orthodox men in posts for which they were unfitted,

158 N.C.R.O., S(T)274.

159 Bebbington, *Evangelicalism*, p.107; Reardon, *Coleridge to Gore*, p.24; Moorman, *History of the Church*, p.316.

160 See Knight, *The Nineteenth-century Church*, pp.112-13, for other Bishops of the time who did examine ordination candidates thoroughly.

161 Best, *Temporal Pillars*, p.189.

162 *Ibid.*

163 Anon., 'The state of the Established Church', *Christian Observer*, X (1811), p.719.

to the detriment of both the Church's image and its efficiency. This could generate attraction to any local Anglican or Dissenting places of worship in which congregations were led by more able and zealous Evangelical ministers.

Charles Manners Sutton was Archbishop of Canterbury from 1805 to 1828. Mrs Lukyn's letters were written during nineteen years of that period and she had a good deal to report on the Archbishop's self-interest and nepotism. There was no mincing of words in what she wrote on April 24, 1822, soon after the death of their Archdeacon:

> he was largely and richly prefer'd; and as the Archbishop has the disposal, he is as usual, loading his relatives with all they can grasp, without too much attention to their merits. the Prebendary to one of his sons in law, Mr Crofts, of whom we know nothing. the Archdeaconry [£]400 a year and the patronage of 13 Livings to his other son in law, Mr Percy, a most amiable man, of whom I have never heard censure, but has already a Church preferment to the amount its said of £5,000 a year. 2 valuable Livings, Ickham, and Gillingham, not yet given; one hoped for by a dashing extravagant Nephew, who cannot live as he likes on a Living of [£]1500 a year, and a Prebendary of Lichfield; some Cousins too of a similar description, think they have not quite enough. am persuaded this indiscriminate appointment of improper Clerical characters does as much injury to Religion as blasphemous publications.[164]

Most of Mrs Lukyn's statements were probably true. Though we do not know the sources of her information, it can be assessed that she had close contacts with the Cathedral. Three months later she observed:

> the Archbishop gave Radcliffe Prebendal to one son in law and the Archdeaconry to the other; both respectable but very discouraging to those men of talent and merit who happen not to be allied to him.[165]

164 N.C.R.O., S(T)269
165 N.C.R.O., S(T)270.

As Mrs Lukyn said, the Archbishop's son-in-law, the Hon.
Hugh Percy was made Archdeacon of Canterbury in 1822. He was
promoted Dean of Canterbury in 1825, consecrated Bishop of
Rochester in 1827, and a few months later became Bishop of
Carlisle. Her letter of Jan. 15, 1824, was in similar vein. Here she
went so far as to say that she saw nepotism as directly responsible
for the Church's inability to stem the tide of 'Methodism' in the
area:

> its long since the exertion of our Orthodox Clergy has
> been so essentially necessary. the progress of Methodism is
> rapid in this neighbo'ro'hood among the higher ranks, and
> we are unfortunate in having few who take the trouble of
> counteracting them. but this must be the case, where
> interest and family connections decide, instead of merit of
> the individual.[166]

Nowhere, it seems was reform more necessary than among
members of the Canterbury Cathedral Chapter. In her letter of
July 23, 1826, she had this gossip to pass on to Mrs Strong:

> We have been most unfortunate in our Minor-Canons. 3
> disgraced themselves by various misconduct; and now a
> 4th has taken himself off to avoid a less agreeable abode;
> having left a large amount of debt, shamefully contracted
> by every specie of ostentations, vanity and folly; and a wife
> who brought him a handsome fortune, which he has
> spent, and one child destitute...but he was very handsome,
> master of Music, with a very fine voice. and the folly of
> some foolish woman here turned his head; if he
> returns not by the November Audit...the Chapter
> will elect another in his place...the Church stands in
> need of firm supporters. Happily many do honour to
> their sacred function.[167]

Apparently, the Archbishop's son-in-law, Percy, soon began to
exercise considerably more authority at Canterbury than his
predecessors. By November 1826 Mrs Lukyn was able to write:

166 N.C.R.O., S(T)273.
167 N.C.R.O., S(T)280.

'Our Dean is much and deservedly esteem'd but he is not a "King Log" and where he saw reform wanted, he has effected it'.[168] This evidence suggests that Dean Percy was endeavouring to bring about change some years before the Ecclesiastical Commission was set up in 1835. However, it appears that stricter interpretation of rules was not altogether popular among the Canterbury clergy and when writing six months later Mrs Lukyn observed:

> [Our Dean] is losing a little of his popularity with a few of the old members of the Church; by enforcing regulations strictly proper but which through the ease, perhaps indolence of his predecessors have fallen into disuse, till every man did what best suited his own convenience and inclinations.[169]

Clearly, changes had taken place, and were continuing to do so under Percy's successor, the Hon. Richard Bagot, Dean at Canterbury from 1827 to 1845, but not without further contention, according to Mrs Lukyn's letter of February 1828:

> Our once peaceful Chapter is divided by faction. some new comers wish to rule alone, the old ones mortified at being set aside before their time, oppose what they call innovations, and certainly the air oftenest repeated during the Audit was 'When the Stormy winds do blow'. the loud roaring has ceased, the hoarse sullen murmur is still heard.[170]

Precise interpretation of 'divided by faction' is not easy, for there may have been disagreement on diverse matters of reform. Assuredly, Evangelicals and Orthodox clergymen had their own axes to grind. 'Innovations', too, could have taken many forms. Whether some of them were of an Evangelical nature is difficult to establish. From 1800 to 1830 there was much diocesan reform throughout England. Reform at Canterbury in 1828 probably included more conscientious and thorough archidiaconal and episcopal visitations to provide stricter supervision of clergy and

168 N.C.R.O., S(T)281.
169 N.C.R.O., S(T)282.
170 N.C.R.O., S(T)285.

detailed reporting of what was occurring in individual parishes.[171] Richard Bagot retained his position as Dean at Canterbury, even though promoted Bishop of Oxford in 1829. He also remained rector of Blinfield, Staffordshire. This was Mrs Lukyn's short, sharp remark about him in her letter of July 1829: 'our Dean is a Bishop, but we do not get rid of him. He keeps every thing he has. so much for reducing pluralities'.[172] Perhaps she was aware that some ecclesiasts were clamouring for action on plural livings, even before June 1831 when Archbishop Howley's 'modest' bill to limit them failed in Parliament because it was thought insufficient.[173]

It can be acknowledged that the standards set by Evangelicals inside and outside the Church had played no small part in bringing the necessity for reform to the forefront of discussion among churchmen and parliamentarians. Though Mrs Lukyn was very critical of Anglican clergy, it must be remembered that she was writing to an intimate friend at a time when much was being voiced publicly, and even more printed, on the controversies within the Established Church. The national call for positive action in Church matters was answered when the Ecclesiastical Commission was set up in 1835, which happened to be the year of Mrs Lukyn's death. The Commission's aim was to produce reports for improving the state of the Church. Their observations soon became enshrined in Acts of Parliament.[174] The Pluralities Act of 1838 did much to bring about more effective parochial ministry. It restricted the holding of plural livings, thus reducing the number of non-resident incumbents, and revised the regulations concerning the employment of curates.[175] The Church Discipline Act (1840) gave bishops, themselves, direct recourse to the law if it was deemed necessary to suspend dissolute clergy.

Churches, chapels, and meeting houses

One may reasonably assume that exigencies of war with France during the early years of the nineteenth century delayed Government expenditure on church buildings, even though it was recognized that accommodation for worshippers in expanding towns and cities was inadequate. Furthermore, the Church of

171 Burns, 'A Hanoverian legacy?', pp.270-4.
172 N.C.R.O., S(T)289.
173 See O. Chadwick, *The Victorian Church*, Pt 1 (1966, 1971 edn), pp.38-9.
174 Knight, *The Nineteenth-century Church*, p.11.
175 *Ibid.*, pp.116-22.

England was competing on unequal terms with Dissenters because
the law made it difficult to create new ecclesiastical districts.[176] A
few years after the war substantial plans were made to relieve the
situation and to meet the increasing challenge from Evangelical
Dissent. Church building in the early decades of the nineteenth
century has been called a 'popular panacea' for contemporary 'social
evils'.[177] The Society for Promoting the Building and Enlargement
of Churches and Chapels was established by laymen in February
1818 (renamed the 'Incorporated Church Building Society' in
1828). Its role was to co-ordinate donations from members of the
public and to allocate aid to parishes that did not fulfil the
qualifications for help from parliamentary funding.[178] In March
1818 the Government allocated one million pounds for building
churches in centres of increased population, and this was followed
by a further half a million pounds in 1824.[179] According to Mrs
Lukyn, there was no necessity for additional Anglican churches in
Canterbury, though the population was increasing.[180] She wrote in
1813, 'our Churches are ill attended while every meeting-house is
crowded, and every accidental dropper-in instantly, and
comfortably accommodated with a seat'.[181] The Methodists and
Dissenters seem to have had little difficulty in filling the ever-
increasing numbers of new local chapels and meeting houses. Mrs
Lukyn's experience of the situation in Canterbury did nothing to
encourage her wholehearted support for the massive programme of
building new churches throughout England. She made her feelings
obvious when writing in November 1828; by this time the I.C.B.S.
was showing signs of falling into severe financial difficulties and
Anglicans were having to shoulder the burden themselves:[182]

> [I am not] bit with the fashionable mania of Missionary
> societies, and building Churches. but I think an immense
> sum will be raised for the latter purpose, if in proportion
> to what was collected in this place and neighbo'ro'hood. I

176 Norman, *Church and Society*, pp.51-2.
177 *Ibid.*, p.53.
178 Knight, *The Nineteenth-century Church*, p.64.
179 Norman, *Church and Society*, pp.53-4.
180 W. Page (ed.), *Victoria History of the Counties of England: Kent, III* (1974), pp.368-9 show
    increase of 4,077 between 1801 and 1831.
181 N.C.R.O., S(T)257.
182 Knight, *The Nineteenth-Century Church*, p.65.

gave to both, because our excellent Clergyman, Mr Pellow, one also of our Prebendaries, wished it. he is just made Dean of Norwich, and will do honour to any station.[183]

Mrs Lukyn openly admitted that her contribution to the local collections was out of respect for the collector, rather than approval of the specified causes. Her negative response to mission was probably directed at The Church Missionary Society which had been launched in 1799. This was an Evangelical initiative not well-favoured by Orthodox Anglicans.[184]

A letter dated 13 November 1827 has indicated that Mrs Lukyn gave contributions to other charitable enterprises with whose work she did not wholeheartedly agree. She saw Canterbury as a magnet for the poor at that particular time. Significantly, it was late autumn when demands for labour in all kinds of Kentish agriculture would have been low. Many of the City's charities were probably connected with local Evangelical organizations and their mission to gain allegiance from the poor through temporary relief. Such philanthropy required extra funds to be collected without delay. This was Mrs Lukyn's comment:

> In truth my dear Madam my spirits are depressed with the distress hourly arising: from the numerous charities of this place, the poor with large families have pour'd in, *in such abundance* we seem become a *City of paupers*. I *really* dread a low tap at the door, lest it should be some fresh application, I can only give a temporary relief to. and even friendly callers generally have some benevolent purpose in hand, for which they are soliciting subscription. while our streets swarm with prostitutes, too often so, I fear from the superior education given by our National Schools, which make them feel superior to the *humbler* stations of servitude.[185]

'A low tap at the door' might signify that callers knocked quietly with some trepidation, or that some of them were small children.

---

183 N.C.R.O., S(T)286.
184 See Elbourne, 'The foundation of the Church Missionary Society', pp.247-64;
    Moorman, *A History of the Church*, p.321.
185 N.C.R.O., S(T)284.

Certainly, there had been an increasing number of Evangelical places of worship registered in Canterbury during the early decades of the nineteenth century and a growth in their congregations. A new Methodist Chapel had been opened in St Peter's Street, Canterbury, on 1 January 1812 in order to accommodate the large number wishing to attend. Three services were held each Sunday (morning, afternoon, and evening).[186] Membership rose from 227 to 248 in that year and was to increase dramatically a few years later when, 'during the winter of 1820-21, a revival broke out;...between fifty and sixty conversions were reported in a month.'[187] Between January 1813 and July 1824, the Consistory Court of Canterbury registered another 415 chapels and meeting houses in the diocese for use by congregations of 'Protestant Dissenters'.[188] Only occasionally was the denomination specified. In addition to the buildings registered for religious purposes in Canterbury itself, several applications were approved for premises situated in villages where Mrs Lukyn was entertained by friends, or in seaside resorts that she visited for holidays. By no means were the majority of new registrations for 'chapels'. Often a licence was issued for 'a certain building' or 'a dwelling house'. During the month of February 1817 alone, there were seven registrations of properties in Margate. But the successful outcome of an application dated 1st February 1823 submitted by 'William Lyle of the Precincts of the Archbishop's Palace', for the use of 'a Chapel in Graveas Lane near the Old Castle, Parish of St Mildred's in the City of Canterbury the property of Mr Smith...as a place of religious worship by an Assembly or Congregation of Protestant Dissenters', could have been particularly upsetting for Mrs Lukyn.[189] St Mildred's had been her father's parish.

This increasing number of buildings being registered in the Canterbury diocese followed national trends.[190] New confidence appears to have followed the repeal of the Five Mile and Conventicle Acts passed in 1812.[191] Thereafter, everyone had liberty

186 N. Yates, R. Hume, & P. Hastings, *Religion and Society in Kent, 1640-1914* (Canterbury, 1994), p.46.

187 J. A. Vickers, *The Story of Canterbury Methodism* (Canterbury, 1961), p.21. The Chapel still stands today, is well-maintained and has an active congregation.

188 Registration certificates, Canterbury Cathedral Archives, H/A/185-600.

189 Canterbury Cathedral Archives, H/A/535.

190 Table 2.3, 'Dissenters' places of worship certified by Registrars-General, 1691-1850', Gilbert, *Religion and Society*, p.34.

191 Repeal by 52 Geo.III, c.155 (1812).

to worship God according to personal beliefs and to preach or teach if registered. Furthermore, *bona fide* religious gatherings were legally protected from interference. Alan Everitt's comment that, by 1851, 17 parish churches in the city of Canterbury had been closed and amalgamated with those adjacent, is striking.[192] There is every reason to suppose that diminishing Anglican congregations in the city, witnessed by Mrs Lukyn between 1809 and 1835, made some of these closures inevitable.

The Anglican problems in Canterbury, it seems, were increased by the inability to provide comfortable surroundings for their worshippers. There were probably others who, like Mrs Lukyn, could not remain strictly loyal to their parish churches because the fabric was so poor. As already shown, she recognized that the local meeting houses were making better provision for their congregations, and this had become an added Evangelical attraction. Undoubtedly, Mrs Lukyn and her friends were accustomed to their creature comforts and in January 1824 she had this specific complaint to make:

> my own Parish Church is so damp and unpleasant in all respects, I regularly pay for a seat in another, where I'm certain of being edifyed by one of the first *Preachers* and *Readers* of the present time; but on sacramental days attend my own. as has happen'd before at this Season, the damp of the Church and pew lining were like a wet blanket thrown o'er me.[193]

It can be assumed that Mrs Lukyn had recently attended a Christmas celebration in her own parish, which she considered had little to offer. As well as the implied drier conditions of her favoured Church, the preacher there was also an attraction. She mentioned him in another letter, dated 16 November 1822, and clearly she found him more inspiring than her own local clergyman:

192 Everitt, *Pattern of Rural Dissent*, p.84.
193 N.C.R.O., S(T)273.

I have the happiness and hope advantage of hearing twice
every Sunday, one of the best preachers that can be heard;
a Dr Birt, Head Master of the Kings School; unfortunately
not my Parish Priest, who poor man cannot benefit any
who hear him.[194]

Mrs Lukyn saw nothing wrong in paying rent for a seat in two
churches. She occupied the one in her own parish church only on
'sacramental days'. This probably meant her attendance once a
quarter, on Sacrament Sundays when Holy Communion was
celebrated – at Easter, Whitsunday, Michaelmas and Christmas.
There were usually large congregations in both town and country
on these occasions. It is possible that for these special celebrations,
even in Canterbury, the poor were driven, through lack of church
accommodation, to join the Evangelical chapels and meeting
houses. Mrs Lukyn's pew in her parish church may well have
remained empty for the rest of the year.

The pew rent system was flourishing almost everywhere and
Mrs Lukyn's evidence revealed one of its abuses. Such a practice
was mainly the privilege of upper- and middle-class families with
money to spare. Perhaps the position was not so dire in Canterbury
for most of the time. However, this dog-in-the-manger attitude
could only contribute further to the already severe problem of
insufficient church accommodation in some towns and cities, and
to the popularity of Evangelical places of worship. Clearly, the
responsibility lay at the ecclesiastical authorities' own door and the
large number of privately appropriated pews was seen by some as
an embarrassment to them.[195] High pew rents were beyond the
means of the impoverished, and the number of cheap or free seats
in most parish churches was an inadequate resource. However,
some Evangelical clergymen on arriving to take up incumbencies
abolished the pew rent system and 'literally opened the church to
the people'.[196] One such was John Bird Sumner who, as a young
vicar, saw rented pews empty and locked whilst the poorer
worshippers had to stand in the aisles.[197] Sumner became the first

194 N.C.R.O., S(T)271. A desire to compete with Nonconformity seems to have been the
    reason for two services on a Sunday but the practice did not become the norm until
    after 1830, see Knight, *The Nineteenth-century Church*, pp.76-79.
195 Norman, *Church and Society*, p.55.
196 Bradley, *Call to Seriousness*, p.64.
197 *Ibid.*

Evangelical Archbishop of Canterbury in 1848, only thirteen years after Mrs Lukyn's death. However, 'most Church leaders were opposed to pew rents, and episcopal *Charges* [to the clergy] had inveighed against them since quite early in the century...By the 1890s, most seats were free'.[198]

Holidays on the Kentish coast over many years provided opportunity for Mrs Lukyn to observe the development of seaside resorts as they expanded to accommodate the increasing numbers of visitors arriving by road, rail and steamboat. A passenger train ran from Canterbury to Whitstable for the first time on 3rd May 1830 and the first steamboat arrived at Herne Bay on 12 May 1832.[199] No longer were such places exclusively for the enjoyment of fashionable society. Archdeacon and Mrs Strong preferred Broadstairs to the other nearby coastal resorts. In her letter of July 1813, Mrs Lukyn explained why she had not stayed there recently herself: 'I do not feel quite your attachment to Broadstairs. am told last year it was occupied chiefly by Methodists, who thought it wrong to frequent the Libraries'.[200] The libraries were some of the chief attractions for most people who visited Broadstairs and other Kent coastal resorts. No further explanation of why the Methodists 'thought it wrong to frequent' them is necessary when, apart from condemning much of the literature that would have been available, the libraries were undoubtedly seen by serious Christians as centres for undesirable social activities. They were places for gambling, musical concerts, and evening assemblies. They advertised and sold tickets for other forms of entertainment, including the local theatre or playhouse.[201] That the expanding seaside resorts of the Kent coast were popular summer *venues* for Evangelical assemblages, is more than likely. Further evidence can be seen in the following lines written by Mrs Lukyn on 2 March, 1814, after a visit to Margate. 'Mrs Townsends sons were continually preaching there. whether the Mother converted them or they her, is differently reported, but all I think alike now.'[202] It was not revealed who Mrs Townsend was.

In a letter to Mrs Strong written in November 1822, Mrs

198 Norman, *Church and Society*, p.163.
199 T. A. Bushell, *Barracuda Guide to County History: I, Kent* (Chesham, 1976), pp.84 & 86.
200 N.C.R.O., S(T)242.
201 J. Whyman, *Kentish Sources: the Early Kentish Seaside, vol. VIII* (Gloucester, 1985), p.266.
202 N.C.R.O., S(T)243.

Lukyn indicated that she considered the Evangelical movement partly responsible for the planned building of boarding houses at Herne:

> its quiet and simplicity of manners in the few inhabitants are rapidly [being broken] in upon by a rich Dissenter, who finding few cou'd attend Church at two long miles distance, has got subscription from all classes of Sectaries, and built a Meeting House, to the displeasure of every family in the neighbo'ro'hood; who tho' they may annoy, cannot prevent the numerous Itinerants from hence, from preaching in it, or their making converts of a class, little inform'd beyond the leading truths of our Church. in consequence of this supposed attraction to numbers, Speculating Builders have purchased land, for more commodious lodging houses, and soon it will be a second Broadstairs.[203]

The 'rich Dissenter' had seized a valuable opportunity. Herne Bay was only a short distance from Canterbury by land. The newly-built meeting house would have been a welcome facility for itinerant preachers in their efforts to gain proselytes from among the many weekend or holiday visitors free from the demands of the normal working day.[204] Apparently the Evangelical gatherings had become an 'attraction to numbers', and certainly Herne Bay did expand in the 1820s. How much this was in order to accommodate Evangelical visitors is difficult to assess, but research has shown that there was usually a strong element of truth in Mrs Lukyn's evidence.

A long letter 'To the Inhabitants of Herne' signed by 'A Churchman' and dated 22 February 1823, has confirmed that there was indeed considerable discord between some local Anglicans and those responsible for the new 'Meeting-house'.[205] Evidently, a little

203 N.C.R.O., S(T)271.

204 Reg. certificate, 2 December 1822, was for 'a certain building or premises at Hearn Bay', applicant 'B. Baines, St. Alphage, Canterbury', Canterbury Cathedral Archives, H/A/525. The Union Chapel was officially opened on that date, but had probably already been in use for a short time (Herne Bay Historical Records).

205 G. May, Strode Park, Herne, Circular letter (printed, Canterbury). I am grateful to Mr H. Gough, Hon. Curator, Herne Bay Historical Records Society, for this document. A Wesleyan Chapel was erected in 1823, Canterbury Cathedral Archives, Reg. Cert. H/A/542.

book entitled *An Account of the Introduction of the Gospel at Herne Bay, in Kent* had been distributed by zealous Dissenters and accused 'the regular Clergy of not preaching the Gospel' in the parish. This extract from the Churchman's letter suggests that some Anglicans were showing double-allegiance:

> My friends, we are all members of the Established Church; not one Dissenter, I believe, is to be found amongst us. Is it therefore to be wondered that we should be jealous of this interference on the part of Dissenters? The Meeting-House has evidently been built in opposition and hostility to the Church, which therefore it becomes us, as Churchmen, to unite more firmly than ever to support, by a frequent and regular attendance. Let us not attempt the impossible task of serving two masters, by going sometimes to the one, and sometimes to the other.

Having spent a holiday at Herne Bay in August 1833, Mrs Lukyn gave some further interesting evidence:

> At the place I have just left the nearest Church is 2 miles. but there is a neat Methodist Chapel to which many not Sectaries went, and all freely accommodated. they talk of a Church, but cannot settle how the Clergyman is to be renumerated. The ground given by the Lord of the Manor, Sir Henry Oxenden.[206]

By 'not Sectaries', she probably meant Anglicans. This type of double allegiance to Methodism and Anglicanism was not uncommon, and the above extract gives reasons for it at Herne Bay. Evangelicalism was always a beckoning force, and free seats were an added attraction for the poor.[207] In June 1827 Mrs Lukyn had visited Broadstairs and noted, contrastingly, that there was 'a beautiful new Church' but 'it ha[d] been productive of fierce factions among the inhabitants'.[208]

Mrs Lukyn's account of the problems of another local church

206 N.C.R.O., S(T)303. A new Church (Christchurch) was built in 1840: see Bushell, *Barracuda Guide to County History: I, Kent*, pp.86 & 88.
207 However, seating was by no means rent-free in all Nonconformist chapels.
208 N.C.R.O., S(T)283.

has presented what was perhaps an unusual case. In November
1828 she wrote: 'As the roof of Mr Farbrace's church has fallen in
and in the country Churches are not to be borrow'd, and as the
distance is only 7 miles he drives over whenever necessary'
[presumably to Canterbury].[209] Almost certainly this was the Rev.
G. H. T. Farbrace, rector of Eythorne (Kent).[210] As Mrs Lukyn was
a regular visitor to Nonington, which is only about two miles from
Eythorne, she probably knew Mr Farbrace quite well. It is an
interesting anomaly that another church in the locality was not
made available for him, but Anglican ruling did not normally allow
the crossing of parish boundaries. Furthermore, itinerant
clergymen smacked too much of Evangelicalism. By 1828 there
were many more young Evangelicals amid clergy ranks. It can be
understood that some Bishops and Archdeacons, as well as lay
patrons, made every effort to avoid the risks entailed in sanctioning
the occasional intrusion of an 'enthusiastic' parson into a parish of
one who was High Church. This cautionary approach might have
been Canterbury's general policy, but perhaps the rule was relaxed
slightly in circumstances such as those prevailing at Eythorne, a
parish not too far from the ecclesiastical centre. To speculate
further, the permission to use a city Church 'whenever necessary'
might be seen as a pragmatic solution to enable Mr Farbrace at least
to continue conducting the rites of passage for his own
parishioners. Nonconformist families, too, could still call upon the
services of their parish priest for baptisms, marriages, and burials.
Maybe it was thought that the close eye of the Cathedral hierarchy
would reduce the risk of controversy between incumbent and
visiting clergyman. Nevertheless, some of Mr Farbrace's
congregation could well have found their way to nearby Dissenting
places of worship on Sundays, instead of attending another
Anglican church. Local Evangelical Nonconformists would have
been speedy to take advantage of the situation. A close
investigation might reveal specific trends in Eythorne at that time.

2.3.ii Evangelicalism and local society
The Evangelical movement as the instrument of change in early
nineteenth-century parish life was the stuff of novels, and it was this
that provided 'the backdrop' of 'Amos Barton' and 'Janet's

---

209 N.C.R.O., S(T)286.
210 Venn, *Alumni Cantabrigienses*, pt II, II, (1944), p.458.

Repentance', two of George Eliot's *Scenes of Clerical Life*.[211] The intrusion of Evangelicalism on the rural area around Nonington evoked Mrs Lukyn's most passionate responses. Evidence will show that her reports were not fictional. Writing on December 26, 1814, she had this to say about the ways in which Evangelical religion was expanding locally:

> Methodism which tho' rapid in its progress, was confined to a Class, supposed rather to take on trust than investigate, has taken on a higher flight in worldly rank; two families of consequence, young, beautiful, rich and rationally enjoying amusement, [and] nearly the whole Regt. of Artillery quartered here...a kind of Holy War is introduced to common conversation, where prejudice and bold assertion, sometimes take a lead.[212]

There are various points to bring out from these comparatively few lines. Mrs Lukyn appears to have thought the tenets of Evangelicalism readily acceptable to the lower 'Class', who were willing to believe without questioning. Certainly, Evangelical religion was considered by many to be intellectually narrow.[213] Large numbers of converts from the lower classes had been and still were turning to 'Methodism' during the early nineteenth century and Evangelicalism was 'taking on a higher flight in worldly rank' within the Anglican Church.[214] Seemingly, Mrs Lukyn was shocked at recent developments because one of the two families 'of consequence' that she mentioned were probably the Plumptres of Fredville, Nonington, who feature more specifically in the next extracts quoted from her letters.

Clearly, heated arguments had developed when the subject of Evangelicalism had been discussed within what can be taken as local social groups of which Mrs Lukyn was part. Perhaps some of her middle- and upper-class friends were responding directly to what Hannah More had advocated in her *Practical Piety*.[215] They

---

211 Jay, *The Religion of the Heart*, p.223.

212 N.C.R.O., S(T)245.

213 See Reardon, *Coleridge to Gore*, p.29: 'The wider problems of faith and reason did not trouble it and in philosophical theology it had no interest'.

214 See Bradley, *Call to Seriousness*, p.37.

215 See More, *Practical Piety*, pp.149-55.

were bringing religious matters into 'common conversation'. However, More had been sufficiently shrewd to warn that discussion of religion might lead to dispute and altercation if the social setting and moment were not chosen with discretion. Mrs Lukyn's experience must have typified the controversy that could arise within circles such as her own. George Eliot depicted a similar *milieu* in 'Janet's Repentance' which was set in the 1820s but written in 1858. In this story, one of her *Scenes of Clerical Life*, Eliot wrote of Tryan, the 'first Evangelical clergyman who had risen above the Milby horizon'. He could be 'treated as a joke' so long as his 'hearers were confined to Paddiford Common'...

> Not so when a number of single ladies in the town appeared to be infected, and even one or two men of substantial property...seemed to be 'giving in' to the new movement...Evangelicalism was no longer a nuisance existing merely in by-corners, which any well-clad person could avoid; it was invading the very drawing-rooms, mingling itself with the comfortable fumes of port-wine and brandy.[216]

The metaphorical likening of Evangelicalism to a bodily infection, or some kind of malady, was not unusual when its adversaries wished to imply its potential for causing spiritual sickness. Epidemics were part of everyday experience and probably such analogies came easily to the tongue. In one of her letters Mrs Lukyn used the term 'epidemic disease' with regard to Evangelicalism,[217] and in another remarked, 'Methodism spreads like canker, here we have little to counteract it.'[218] Responses were undiluted in such contexts; Eliot's term 'invading' has the same belligerent ring about it as Mrs Lukyn's 'Holy War'.

Canterbury barracks, too, had apparently become a centre of Evangelicalism, but where large numbers of men were quartered together a new religious excitement was likely to spread rapidly. It must be remembered that there was continuing uncertainty about Napoleon, who was in exile on Elba when this letter was written. Soldiers were only too aware of recent war casualty rates, and

216 G. Eliot, *Scenes of Clerical Life* (1858), D. Lodge (ed.) (1993), p.263.
217 N.C.R.O., S(T)245.
218 N.C.R.O., S(T)307.

Evangelicalism offered a firm hope of salvation should they soon be brought face to face with death in some conflict or other. Waterloo was yet to follow in June 1815.

This long extract from her letter of January 5, 1818 is one of Mrs Lukyn's most revealing about life in Nonington at the time when Evangelicalism there was becoming a force to be reckoned with. That it was sufficiently powerful to instigate social change in the local community is evident.

> The Holy War is commenced in this neighbo'rohood on the subject of the Bible Society and I fear as much gall, as ink, will flow but pleased am I to find that many of our excellent Clergy are rousing themselves to the Combat. Never were their efforts more necessary, for the progress of Methodism in all ranks is rapid, beyond what I had any idea of till lately on a visit to St. Albans Court. my old and most excellent friends, the benefactors of all around them lamented their inability to stem the torrent. 6 accomplished sons and daughters of a neighbouring family, their nearest, and most intimate friends, have all taken this turn, and devote their whole time to making converts, in which their zeal knows no bounds. as they visit Mr. Hammond's more immediate Cottagers and dependants, who from cheerful, happy, industrious peasants, who by the judicious distribution of employment, and benevolence, from *this* family know [n]either care [n]or want are transformed into miserable, defected *terrified* beings, who spend their whole time in praying with the Miss Plumbtrees[219] by reading the books they give them. as these young people have hitherto been unable to convert their Parents they make them miserable by losing all respect for their opinions and treating their rational mode of life with contempt; never speak at table,[220] or accompany

219 Clearly she was spelling the name as it is still pronounced today but meant 'Plumptres', as shown in the next quotation.

220 The girls' Evangelicalism may well have been criticized by family and friends on occasions when they gathered round the table for meals. The young women were perhaps following Hannah More's instruction that, in situations where others might challenge their beliefs, it was better to keep silent than prejudice their own cause by 'fiery defence' of it; and 'though "to keep silence from good words" may be pain and grief, yet the pain and grief must be borne, and the silence must be observed': *Practical Piety*, p.137.

them on any occasion, but to Church, where unfortunately they contrive that two ordained Calvinists occasionally shall officiate. I suppose it cannot be remedied...while however I may disapprove the tenets of the Evangelicals candour obliges me to respect and admire their conduct. while I see them free from all indecorum, giving up the allurements of the world, readily attending the sick, and bestowing their alms. The young people I have already named confine not endeavours to the poor, and have been eminently successful among their young friends of their own ranks, who naturally religious and good, are desirous.of attaining greater perfection.[221]

It was of great regret for Mrs Lukyn that her close friends were affected by these events. The Plumptres' '6 accomplished sons and daughters' lived with their parents at 'Fredville', another mansion in Nonington.[222] Like the Hammonds, the Plumptres were a family of traditional power and influence as members of the landed gentry.[223] Though the Hammonds themselves had two sons and five daughters, Mrs Lukyn does not indicate that they were then among the Miss Plumptres' proselytes. It has been recognized that 'the most important agents in spreading Evangelical religion among the upper classes seem to have been the female members of their families'[224]. Mrs Lukyn's evidence of this is more definite. Of special local historical interest here is that the Plumptre girls had been very successful in their efforts to convert the poor of their parish. Between 1811 and 1821 Nonington was an expanding village. During that period the population had grown from 566 to 730, the number of families from 112 to 129 and the total inhabited houses from 91 to 129. Families employed in agriculture increased from a total of 73 in 1811 to 101 in 1821.[225] The Hammonds and the Plumptres were the predominant agricultural employers in Nonington.

It might be argued that, as Mr Hammond's 'more immediate cottagers' and 'dependants' were being led by young women from an exalted local family, they felt reasonably secure in their challenge

---

221 N.C.R.O., S(T)256.
222 Nonington was one of the parishes in Canterbury diocese which were exempt from the Archdeacon.
223 See Burke, *Landed Gentry*, II, p.1683.
224 Bradley, *Call to Seriousness*, p.40.

towards the established religious and social norms of their community. Furthermore, a certain degree of anti-clericalism may already have developed among Nonington's labourers.[226] Only a closer study of the parish is likely to reveal the presence of a resident incumbent. However, from what Mrs Lukyn has written, one can sense an atmosphere of changing circumstances in the village. January 1818 was a particularly difficult time for the poor as the cost of bread was rising towards famine prices.[227] Mrs Lukyn wrote of Mr Hammond's 'employment' of the cottagers, which was probably waged labour and only seasonal. Undoubtedly, Mr Plumptre also employed local labourers. Mrs Lukyn was writing after her visit to St Alban's Court in the previous November when agricultural unemployment in the community was likely to have been on an upward curve towards a winter maximum. Thus, though perhaps she meant it figuratively, it could have been true that many of the cottagers were spending 'their whole time in praying with the Miss Plumptres'. And here was one of Mrs Lukyn's most biassed responses – the 'cottagers' had been 'transformed into miserable, defected terrified beings', whereas beforehand they had been 'happy and cheerful'. Many Orthodox Anglicans held this view of the effects an ever-present fear of not being in a state of grace had on Evangelical minds. Mrs Lukyn, like many other critics, failed to acknowledge the spiritual joy and hope that converts might experience.

It can be argued that, by establishing Evangelical religion within their parish church, the Miss Plumptres were alleviating the necessity for a separate Nonconformist group to be formed. Most 'pious' Anglicans tried to avoid breaking away from their own churches and Evangelical clergymen encouraged such fidelity. Surely the young Plumptres were of so high a status that every effort would have been made not to lose them from the congregation of the local parish church with which the family had

225 *Abstract of Answers and Returns 1811,* p.139; and *Abstract of the Answers and Returns pursuant to an Act, passed in the First Year of the Reign of His Majesty King George IV intituled "An Act for taking Account of the Population of Great Britain, and of the Increase or Diminution thereof" 1821* (1822), p.139. The increase in local agrarian employment is noticeable, but over the ten years there were likely to have been greater demands for agricultural products from the region to feed expanding populations of Canterbury, Kentish seaside resorts and even London.

226 See Evans, 'Some reasons for the growth of English rural anti-clericalism', pp.84–109.

227 Gash, *Aristocracy and People,* p.77. The number of 'poor constantly relieved [by the four charities in Nonington Parish were] about thirty, casually forty': see Hasted, IX, p.259.

been so long associated. Perhaps in their newly-formed alliance with Evangelicalism the cottagers found a sublimation of inclinations towards more extreme forms of protest, and the Miss Plumptres were instrumental in saving the parish from violent manifestations of discontent similar to those in other counties two years earlier.[228] Mr Hammond's 'benevolence' towards his cottagers signified his wish to alleviate their distress. In 1800, the number of 'poor constantly relieved' by the four charities in Nonington Parish had been about thirty, casually forty'.[229] Probably Mr Hammond was one of the charity administrators but his personal generosity might have been other than monetary. Nevertheless, despite his kindness and authority, he was 'unable to stem the tide' of Evangelicalism. Here we have evidence of an elite landowner who, at the hands of local Evangelicals enjoying similar status, was in the process of losing considerable traditional power in his parish community. This must have been an unsettling experience for him and for other nearby privileged members of society likely to suffer similarly from the same causes. Furthermore, the 'cottagers' were literate, and it can be suggested that, through their Evangelical unity with the Miss Plumptres, they had taken on a shared identity with members of a much higher social class, a relationship they had probably never previously experienced. Perhaps the Hammonds 'lamented' what could be interpreted as disloyalty to themselves more than the infidelity being shown to Orthodox Anglicanism.

Mrs Lukyn saw the Plumptre parents as beyond reproach, leading a 'rational mode of life' with opinions to be respected, and their children 'naturally' born with good impulses. But the sons and daughters had shown great independence of thought and spirit. They constituted a formidable army of newly-converted Evangelicals in one household. According to Mrs Lukyn, they were guilty on several counts, but what she implied as disobedience to their parents was, in reality, a manifestation of their Evangelical religion and this sometimes required such defiance. They would 'never speak at table, or accompany them on any occasion, but to church'. Hannah More endeavoured to inculcate such extreme behaviour into her readers, and almost certainly the Miss Plumptres read some of her works. It seems the young people had 'given up

---

228 See J. L. & B. Hammond, *The Village Labourer, 1760-1832: a Study of the Government of England before the Reform Bill* (1911, 1987 edn), p.177.
229 Hasted, *Kent*, IX, p.259.

the allurements of the world', which probably meant largely that they refused to accompany their parents to balls, the theatre, private parties, and to play cards. Undoubtedly, they considered these entertainments too frivolous and wasteful of precious time that could be devoted to Evangelical activism. And such levity was seen as detrimental to the Evangelical image of seriousness.[230] Hannah More would have considered the young Plumptres exemplary in their changed attitudes and mode of life. However, even Mrs Lukyn admired the young women's decorum and their good works among parishioners. But this is how, in 1826, she remembered the early period of their conversion and activism:

> you mistake my amiable friend Mrs Hammond for their nearest and most intimate neighbo'r Mr. Plumptre of Fredville, whose Methodistical daughters were a sad annoyance to my friends at St. Alban's [Court] by praying and turning the heads of all the Villagers. and making home miserable to their parents and relatives who visited in the house. never were members of the Church of England more truly what they ought, than the Hammonds. more charitable, more justly beloved.[231]

Clearly, Mrs Lukyn still looked upon Evangelicalism as irrational and a 'turning' of 'heads', but it seems that the Plumptre girls had been eminently successful in converting 'all the Villagers'.

In Mrs Lukyn's eyes, and in those of many who shared her social rank and Orthodox beliefs, the likes of Mr and Mrs Hammond remained the epitome of Christian philanthropy and Anglican Church allegiance. Further on in the letter just quoted she described their family thus: 'all Mrs Hammond's children except the oldest daughter, the best of human beings are married, and settled in distant Counties, except the elder son [William Osmund], who resides at the family seat'.[232] In 1815, Mrs Lukyn had seen the marriage of William Osmund (1790-1863) to Mary, eldest daughter of Sir Henry Oxenden. Evidence given below will reveal that at least one of the Oxenden daughters became Evangelical. From memorials in Nonington Church, there is every

230 See Rosman, *Evangelicals and Culture*, pp.71, 120.
231 N.C.R.O., S(T)279.
232 *Ibid.*

indication that Mary and William were both converted at some
time. Mary's memorial is inscribed 'She sleeps in Jesus' and, like her
husband's, ends with a biblical quotation. Tablets in memory of
three of their daughters are situated above those to the parents and
it is significant that each inscription ends with words from the
Bible. The family at Fredville were not alone in suffering domestic
disharmony after the conversion of its young members. Such
disagreements occurred within many English upper-class families
of the time.[233]

It has already been mentioned above that Jane Austen knew the
Hammonds and her correspondence is particularly useful in
confirming what Mrs Lukyn said about the Plumptres. However,
Mrs Lukyn's letters may be one of the few extant primary sources
that can give added meaning to what Jane Austen wrote
concerning the Fredville family. In a letter to her sister written in
November 1813 after attending a 'Concert', probably at one of the
mansions near Nonington, the famous author commented: 'the
Hammonds were there, Wm Hammond the only young Man of
renown...I was just introduced at last to Mary Plumptre, but should
hardly know her again. She was delighted with *me* however, good
Enthusiastic Soul!.'[234]   No doubt this was a sarcastic reference to
Mary Plumptre's Evangelical 'enthusiasm'. However, Jane Austen's
remark was made about five years before Mrs Lukyn's comment.
The Plumptres were probably already progressing towards
conversion but were not yet leading so serious a life as later on.
John Plumptre, the family's heir to Fredville, had wished to marry
Jane Austen's niece, Fanny Knight, and she had nearly become
engaged to him. Jane wrote at length about the matter in a letter
of 20 November 1814, apparently responding to Fanny's concern
about John's diffident character and his Evangelical inclinations:

> If he were less modest, he would be more agreeable, speak
> louder and look Impudenter;-and is not it a fine
> Character, of which Modesty is the only defect?...And as
> to their being any objection to his *Goodness*, from the
> danger of his becoming even Evangelical, I cannot admit
> *that*. I am by no means convinced that we ought not all to

233 See Bradley, *Call to Seriousness*, p.38.
234 Le Faye, *Jane Austen's Letters*, no.96 to C. Austen, p.252.

be Evangelicals, & am at least persuaded that they who are
from Reason & Feeling, must be happiest & safest & don't
be frightened by the idea of his acting more strictly up to
the precepts of the New Testament than others...and if his
deficiencies of Manner &c &c strike you more than all his
good qualities, if you continue to think strongly of them,
give him up at once.[235]

When writing again to Fanny ten days later, her Aunt Jane's
opinion was somewhat altered: 'The risk is too great for *you*, unless
your own Sentiments prompt it.-You will think me perverse
perhaps...I am at present more impressed with the possible Evil that
may arise to *You* from engaging yourself to him...than with
anything else'.[236]   On 13 March 1817, Jane asked of Fanny, who
lived at Godmersham Park about twelve miles from Canterbury,
'Do none of the Plumptres ever come to Balls now?-You have
never mentioned them as being at any?'.[237]

Mr John Plumptre married Catherine Methuen in 1818 and
inherited the Fredville estate after his father's death (1827). He
became a barrister and in the 1832 General Election stood for East
Kent. Writing to Mrs Strong just before the poll, Mrs Lukyn
referred to him as

a Reformer but a gentleman of fortune and great
respectability. but so evangelical that the whole body of
dissenters, a numerous class are for him. his family decided
Methodists tho' they forsake not the Church. believe he is
secure.[238]

John Plumptre and his family had remained faithful to
Evangelicalism. It is noticeable that Mrs Lukyn saw him as 'a
Reformer' who had the support of many dissenters. That a man's
religious and political affiliations were dual considerations in
elections of the day was confirmed in what Mrs Lukyn wrote on
23 January 1833, soon after he was elected:

235 *Ibid.*, no.109 to F. Knight, p.280.
236 *Ibid.*, no.114, p.286.
237 *Ibid.*, no.153, p.332.
238 N.C.R.O., S(T)298.

Mr Plumptre a gentleman of most amiable private character, a reformer and methodist. he boasted in his speech that he had not been supported by the gentry, or clergy, he might have added or yeomanry, but the reformers, radicals, and dissenters all for him to a man.[239]

Thus, the relationship between Church and State was accentuated in parliamentary elections. Clergy support for a candidate could be significant, but John Plumptre had won the election without their backing. However, his majority was only 334 above his nearest rival, Sir E. Knatchbull (3,574 to 3,240).[240] A whig government was returned. Of the opposing tory candidate, Mrs Lukyn had this to say:

Sir E. Knatchbull an avow'd Orange has served us faithfully a friend to Agriculture, and farmers. his Cavalcade was the most numerous and highly respectable I ever saw, all the gentlemen, Clergy, and yeomanry nearly of the County. The show of hands decidedly in his favour. but this we know goes for nothing.[241]

Mrs Lukyn would have agreed with Knatchbull in his 'avow'd Orange' sympathies and she had this to say in an undated letter, probably written a short time before the Catholic Emancipation Bill was passed in 1829. 'Methodism increases rapidly around us. if Catholic Emancipation takes place we cannot expect their Priests will be idle, and our Churches will be still more deserted'.[242]

Mrs Lukyn made it clear that Evangelicals in Nonington maintained their close association with Anglicanism. The Plumptre sons and daughters, along with the cottagers, still attended their local church in 1818, though converted to Evangelicalism. Of particular interest is that the Plumptres were able to 'contrive that two ordained Calvinists occasionally officiate[d]', which Mrs Lukyn termed 'unfortunate'. Perhaps this was because Nonington's own clergyman served in more than one parish. Clearly, Mrs

239 N.C.R.O., S(T)300.
240 Sir H. Knatchbull-Hugessen, *Kentish Family* (1960), p.211. Mr Plumptre was returned as M.P. for East Kent until he resigned in 1852.
241 N.C.R.O. S(T)298.
242 N.C.R.O., S(T)315.

Lukyn thought a certain amount of scheming had taken place but, here again, the power of manipulation would have been strong in the Plumptre sons' and daughters' hands. In 1832, John Plumptre and his family were still 'Methodists' but had not forsaken their Parish Church. Did the Evangelical arrangements in Nonington serve as an example of what might have developed in other parishes? Has Mrs Lukyn's evidence cast some light on Everitt's inability fully to account for the fact that 'Nonconformity in Kent was...a far more urban movement than in...Leicestershire, Lindsey, and Northamptonshire?'[243] His investigation has shown that, in these three counties, the ratio of Nonconformist chapels in rural parishes to those in towns was roughly two-thirds to one-third:

> In Kent the position was reversed. Out of 500 chapels in the county only about 36 per cent were in the countryside, whereas 64 per cent were in urban areas. No doubt this was partly because the urban population was larger in Kent, in absolute terms at any rate. This cannot be the only reason for the disparity.[244]

I suggest a further explanation. Everitt also said that there could be 'little doubt...that the weakness of rural Nonconformity in much of Kent was largely due to the remarkable strength of the old squirearchy of the county in [the] downland and chartland areas'.[245] This was probably so, but perhaps not in the sense that he meant it. Clearly, 'Nonconformity' did exist, but in the shape of Evangelicalism accommodated within rural parish churches through the influence mostly of female members of the 'squirearchy'.

On 7 August 1834, Mrs Lukyn named more women from among local gentry 'united by ties of marriage in [the] single great county cousinage',[246] who were caught up in the Evangelical movement. Apparently, they were effective and assertive in their endeavours:

> Methodism in all ranks in this neighbo'ro'hood spreads rapidly, scarce a family where one, chiefly the daughters are

243 Everitt, *Pattern of Rural Dissent*, p.57.
244 *Ibid.*
245 *Ibid.*, p.60.
246 *Ibid.*

not of that persuasion. and they are indefaticable [sic] and generally from perseverance successful. Sir H. Oxenden goes to a neighboring friend Sir H. Montresor, to beg a dinner on Sunday, as his daughter[247] will not allow any to be dressed on that day and he likes a hot one. and his equally near neighbor on the other hand, Sir F. Mulcaster, has a wife of an equally religious character who tho' not possessing power for a similar prohibition, would look very coldly on him on that day. on giving you this enumeration, I really recollect only 2 families in that populous district, free from this taint. and you seem to be annoyed by similar efforts, of your Bible ladies.[248]

Sir Henry Oxenden owned Broome House, 'a magnificent Elizabethan mansion' in the Parish of Barham, set in parkland eight miles from Canterbury,[249] and Deane Park, Wingham, about ten miles from Nonington. General Sir Henry Montresor, resided at Denne Hill, a mansion with extensive grounds in the Parish of Kingston, about seven miles from the city.[250] Both were widowers but later remarried. Sir F. Mulcaster lived in nearby Charlton Park, Bishopsbourne, and his wife was General Montresor's sister. Undoubtedly, Evangelicalism had become widespread among upper-class women of the area and they were proving powerful not only in the locality, but in their own homes. The dominating influence of the Oxenden daughter and of Lady Mulcaster on the Sunday routine of father and husband, respectively, reflected their Evangelical Sabbatarianism, and the subtle changes that belief in strict Sunday observance could bring about in domestic power relationships between men and women within elite families.

It was through Evangelical persuasion that George III had made his 'Proclamation Against Immorality and Profaneness' in 1787, which included profanation of the Lord's Day in its catalogue of offences punishable by law.[251] William Wilberforce and others attempted to reinforce the Sabbatarian code by setting up a society to enforce the King's Proclamation. In 1802 this became known as the Society for the Suppression of Vice which, as part of its work,

247 Possibly the one who had married William Osmund Hammond.
248 N.C.R.O., S(T)306.
249 Greenwood, *Epitome of County History*, p.402.
250 *Ibid.*, p.404.
251 Bradley, *Call to Seriousness*, p.95.

continued the Evangelical fight for strict Sabbath observance.[252] Although the existing laws were regarded by some as limiting pleasurable activities of the poor, others thought they protected employees from Sunday labour. It was the obligation of their social superiors, also, to respect the Lord's Day, as Hannah More pointed out in her *Thoughts on the Importance of the Manners of the Great*.[253]

For Evangelical families and their servants Sunday should be a day for public worship and private prayer, with no unnecessary work and no recreations.[254] Sir Henry Oxenden's having to beg a hot dinner at his friend's home and his daughter's not allowing 'any to be dressed on that day' probably meant that she would not permit their servants to dress game or cook any meal on Sundays. Their Sunday fare most likely consisted of cold collations and cold sweets to allow all members of the household freedom to attend church.[255]   As for Sir F. Mulcaster, his wife was probably so Evangelical that she considered any pleasurable indulgence on the Sabbath contrary to her strict Sunday observance, and would 'look upon him very coldly on that day' if he did not practice self-denial of any recreational activities. There can be little doubt that these two Evangelical women from the landed gentry still attended their parish churches, accompanied by male members of their families. If they were also Bible ladies they unavoidably had contact with the local poor, who probably joined them in worshipping at the Anglican church. As already indicated, there were many other elite members of society living in that 'populous district', and according to Mrs Lukyn there were only '2 families' in which the girls had not been converted. The accumulative results of their unflagging perseverance in the area must have been considerable.

The extracts from Mrs Lukyn's letters have been worthy of more than cursory attention. Expansion of Evangelical religion in Kent was of such concern to her that she mentioned it on several occasions. The nature, causes and effects of early nineteenth-century Evangelicalism were complex and numerous. Examination of what Mrs Lukyn expressed, often so succinctly, has revealed that she and her Anglican friends witnessed aspects of 'vital religion' to

252 Norman, *Church and Society*, p.25.
253 H. More, *Thoughts on the Importance of the Manners of the Great* (London, 1788), p.97, quoted in Norman, *Church and Society*, pp.25-6.
254 D. Englander, 'The Word and the World: Evangelicalism in the Victorian City', in G. Parsons (ed.), *Religion in Victorian Britain, II, Controversies* (Manchester, 1988), pp.21-2.
255 *Ibid.*, p.22.

some extent and responded to them in their own way. This was true of other women, but her letters prove extremely valuable in giving an unusual female perspective on a social and spiritual movement itself much associated with countless wives, daughters, and sisters of her time. That she disapproved of early nineteenth-century Evangelical revival in her own area is clear. There were probably many other women in England whose responses were similar and are yet to be discovered. In September 1828 Mrs Lukyn declared, 'Methodism makes so rapid a progress as makes us fear *we* of the National Church shall be consider'd as Sectaries'.[256] This was the view of numerous clergymen in the first decades of the nineteenth century.[257] Probably their concerns were shared by not a few of their womenfolk.

256 N.C.R.O., S(T)287.
257 Walsh & Taylor, 'Introduction', *The Church of England*, p.19.

Chapter 3

THE BOSWORTH FAMILY AND
THE REV. THOMAS JONES
(CREATON, NORTHAMPTONSHIRE)

Among the cleanly rain-washed, slate memorials heading many of the graves in the country churchyard of St Andrew's Church at Spratton, Northamptonshire, are those bearing the following inscriptions:

In memory of
Two daughters of Thomas and Ann Bosworth
Matilda died Feby 26th
1816 aged 14 years.
Maria died Jany 27th
1821 aged 17 years.

These gentle Sisters grew up side by side,
Lovely in life, in death too near allied.
Their mould'ring ashes share an early grave
God has recalled the life which first he gave:
But Jesu's death a glorious hope supplied
Who sleep in Jesus shall in Jesus rise,
In him shall triumph in the realms of light,
Where glory shines without the shades of night.

Here
LIE THE REMAINS OF SELINA
daughter of Thomas and Ann Bosworth.
She was married to the Revd. John Owen.
And after a happy union of
two years within a day, departed this
life May 9th 1822 aged 22 years
"Her sun went down while it was yet day."[1]

Also Clara daughter of Thomas and Ann Bosworth
who fell asleep in Jesus, Feby 7th 1848 in the 50th year of
her age.
1 Thes.IV.xiiii

---

1   Jeremiah, 15:9, 'Her sun is gone down while it was yet day'.

The two double graves of the four Bosworth sisters lie east to west adjacent to each other, and their parents are buried nearby.[2] Reference to the atonement at line 5 of the rhyme on the first memorial, and adaptations of biblical references in both epitaphs give indication of Evangelicalism. The connotation of 'sleep in Jesus' is more easily understood if verses 13 and 14 from chapter 4 of 'The First Epistle of Paul the Apostle to the Thessalonians' are quoted in full:

> 13 But I would not have you to be ignorant, brethren, concerning them which are asleep, that ye sorrow not, even as others which have no hope.
> 14 For if we believe that Jesus died and rose again, even so them also which sleep in Jesus will God bring with him.

St Paul was reassuring the Thessalonians that believers who had died should not be lamented. When Christ returned, he would be accompanied by those who had fallen 'asleep' trusting in him and unite them with their loved ones.[3]

The above memorial inscriptions have confirmed the Bosworth family's biblicism, the ardent belief in biblical truths, which Bebbington identified as one of the defining attributes of Evangelicalism. Quotations from several handwritten primary sources used in this chapter support his claim that biblicism, along with crucicentrism, conversionism and activism were the four main elements central to Evangelical doctrine. Biblicism and crucicentrism are evidenced most frequently in the extracts quoted in this chapter. A few instances of conversionism and activism have also been apparent in the letters and are noted in my text, but the correspondence has been particularly important for illustrating how often verses from the Bible, or their adaptations, could appear with regularity in communications between Evangelicals. It will be shown that the Bosworth children growing up between 1800 and 1850 were taught doctrines of Evangelicalism from their earliest days. The only evidence of a conversion experience in the family has been given by the Rev. John Owen, husband of Selina, whose name appears on the memorial inscription given above. Her final

---

2   The ledger is encrusted, only the names are visible.
3   J. Denney, 'The Epistles to the Thessalonians', pp.170-3, in Rev. W. Robertson Nicoll (ed.), *The Expositor's Bible* (1909).

conversion has been described in a lengthy obituary written by him that included the scene of her death. This document has provided the original source for part of the chapter. Diverse positive responses to Evangelical religion that came from other individual women in their own personal circumstances are also revealed in the following pages.

The four Bosworth daughters named on the two churchyard memorials and their one brother were brought up at Highgate House which was situated on the outskirts of Little Creaton, a hamlet contained within the parish of Spratton.[4] Their widowed grandmother, Elizabeth Bosworth, had owned the premises at the end of the eighteenth century and had run the house as a coaching inn providing short-stay accommodation, particularly for those travelling long distances. However, for the Evangelical Rev. Thomas Jones, bachelor son of a Welsh farmer, it became a permanent residence through the response of successive generations of Bosworth women to his need for a home. This chapter will illustrate and explain how, with Thomas Jones sharing day-to-day existence at Highgate House, his Evangelical influence on the lives of the Bosworth women and many others in Creaton, Spratton and the surrounding area was profound.

3.1 Mrs Elizabeth Bosworth and the arrival of Thomas Jones

In the first instance, the Rev. Jones's accommodation at Highgate House had been a matter of expediency. In 1785 at the age of thirty-two he arrived to take up the curacy of the Church of St Michael and All Angels in the neighbouring parish of Great Creaton (usually known as merely 'Creaton'), but no home could be found for him there. Highgate House stood just outside his parish boundary, in 'a beautiful part of the County...adjoining the high Road between Northampton and Leicester through Welford',[5] about seven miles from Northampton and nearly nine from Market Harborough. It was a farmhouse more than an inn, as there was a large farm connected to it.[6] To say the least, it was unusual for a clergyman to adopt a permanent home in an inn for there was a

---

4   The present Highgate House, on the same site, is now a conference centre, though largely rebuilt since the Bosworths' time.
5   *Sale catalogue* (1858), N.C.R.O., D1562.
6   Rev. J. Owen, *Memoir of The Rev. Thomas Jones* (1851), p.144.

canon which forbade it.[7] Then how did the situation arise, when
there was a parsonage at Creaton? More than one historiographer
of Evangelicalism has found a place for Thomas Jones's name.[8]
Though his residence at Highgate House has sometimes been
mentioned, no explanation for it has been given, yet the factors
which governed the decision made at this time can be considered
important in their effects. The following sequence of late
eighteenth-century events were instrumental in bringing Thomas
Jones to Highgate House, and consequently in his playing a
significant part in the lives of four generations of the Bosworth
women and girls during the next sixty years or so. In addition,
Jones was to make Creaton an important Midland centre for
Evangelicalism.

It was through the persuasion of the Rev. Charles Simeon, one
of the most influential Evangelicals of the time, that Jones had gone
to Creaton after being 'driven from parish to parish because of his
hated "enthusiasm"'.[9] Simeon was 'the man who did more than
any other for the cause of Evangelicalism in both the university and
town' of Cambridge.[10] He was Vicar of Holy Trinity, Cambridge,
from 1783-1836 and mentor to generations of Evangelical
ordinands,[11] but his influence spread far beyond the local sphere. In
1785, Jones attended a meeting in Birmingham at which leading
Evangelicals were present, among them Simeon and William
Romaine (1714-1795).[12] At that time Jones was looking for a
living and, as there was a vacancy at Creaton upon the recent death
of the parish's Evangelical minister, the Rev. Abraham Maddock,
Simeon urged him take up the curacy there.[13] Simeon had himself
preached at Creaton the Sunday before, 'to a very nice people'.[14]
Members of the Bosworth family must surely have been present. As

7   Ibid., p.147n.
8   For example, Bebbington, Evangelicalism, p.72; E. Evans, Daniel Rowland and the Great
     Evangelical Awakening in Wales (Edinburgh, 1985), pp.1,4,360; M. M. Hennell, John Venn
     and the Clapham Sect (1958), p.84; G. R. Balleine, A History of the Evangelical Party in The
     Church of England (1908), pp.122-3,168.
9   J. Wesley Bready, England: Before and After Wesley; The Evangelical Revival and Social Reform
     (New York, 1938, 1971 ed,), p.57.
10 Elliott-Binns, The Early Evangelicals, p.284.
11 Bebbington, Evangelicalism, p.31.
12 Romaine had been Lady Huntingdon's senior chaplain. See Elliott-Binns, Early
     Evangelicals, pp.116- 142.
13 Owen, Memoir, p.76.
14 Ibid.

Evangelicalism was already established in the parish, Simeon was probably eager to do all he could to ensure that it continued there.[15] Like Simeon,[16] Thomas Jones was a moderate Calvinist. His connections with prominent pious clergymen continued and several of his religious works were published.[17]

The patron under whom Jones first served as curate at Creaton was the Rev. Christopher Davenport, who had been instituted to the Rectory there in 1773.[18] Davenport had held the curacy at Creaton since 1760, and he then either inherited or bought the advowson in 1773, whereupon he appointed Maddock[19] as his own curate. In acquiring a benefice, a clergyman had maximum opportunity of achieving independence both of clientele and of professional colleagues and superiors.[20] It seems that Davenport took full advantage of these liberties in different ways. There are two documents, dated 5 January 1785, leasing church buildings and land from him to Mrs Elizabeth Bosworth of Highgate House.[21] Davenport had sufficient confidence in Mrs Bosworth to give her tenure and certain responsibilities regarding church property, and this may well explain why Jones was first accommodated at her inn. The Leases were for

> the Parsonage House, Orchard and Premises belonging, the Church Yard, and Two Plots of Land containing 10 Acres in Great Creaton for 19 years at the yearly rent of £16. and Part of the Rectorial Allotments on Creaton Inclosure containing 123 acres 1 Rood 28 perches for 19 years at the yearly rent of £129. a close in the Great West Field of 1a.2r.13p, and a parcel of land in the same field, of 8a.1r.27p., part of an allotment at inclosure to the Rev.

---

15 In 1817 the Simeon Trust was created to purchase rights of patronage: see Roberts, 'Private patronage and the Church of England', pp.209-10.

16 Balleine, *History of the Evangelical Party*, p.135; Walsh & Taylor, 'The Church and Anglicanism', p.57.

17 For example, his *Scripture Directory: or an Attempt to assist the unlearned Reader to understand the General History and Leading Subjects of the Old and New Testaments*; for a review, see Anon., *The Evangelical Magazine and Missionary Chronicle* (1813), p.305.

18 Peterborough Diocese, *Institutions Book* (1764-1839), N.C.R.O., ML733, p.45.

19 Sometimes spelt 'Maddocks', or 'Maddox', but he signed the parish registers 'A. Maddock'.

20 Roberts, 'Private Patronage and the Church of England', p.206.

21 *Leases*, C. Davenport to E. Bosworth, 5 January 1785 (also signed by the Bishop), N.C.R.O., Bos. Coll.

Davenport, in lieu of his glebe lands. All tenanted by Mrs
Bosworth.[22]

Possibly the lease of the parsonage and churchyard was an
unusual arrangement, especially as it was for nineteen years, but by
canon law the incumbent owned the herbage of the churchyard
and was responsible for mowing the grass or grazing it, preferably
with sheep as these were normally considered less offensive than
other animals.[23] Perhaps the Rev. Maddock had lived in the house
and it had been leased to another tenant before Thomas Jones's
arrival. Of course, the building might have been in a bad state of
repair, but the lease stated that Mrs Bosworth must insure it. This
indicates her personal interest in the property and maybe she
accommodated some of her day labourers in it.[24] Most certainly,
her rental of church property confirmed an alliance between
Elizabeth Bosworth and Davenport. When Jones arrived at
Creaton, Elizabeth's willingness to accommodate him at Highgate
House solved the immediate problem, and it can be assumed that
she was happy for Evangelicalism to continue in the parish. Vital
Christianity had expanded in the local Anglican Church under
Maddock between 1773 and 1785, for 'when he arrived at Creaton
the congregation numbered only twenty; but it soon increased so
rapidly that a gallery was built; even that could not contain all those
who wished to hear, and many stood outside to listen as best they
could.'[25] Undoubtedly, as patron, Davenport approved the
extension of accommodation, thus gesturing tangible support of
Evangelicalism. Unfortunately, but not unexpectedly, no figures
can be found to indicate the relative numbers of females to males
who made up the congregation at any stage in the ministry of
Maddock or Jones.

Elizabeth Bosworth and successive members of her family
witnessed many events in Mr Jones's ministerial life. It was not only
his residence at Highgate House that caused him to be a

22 The award was about 22 acres for glebe, and 123 acres for tithes; *Reconstruction of Map
from Award Document, Great and Little Creaton Parishes Inclosure Award, 1782-3* (1978),
N.C.R.O., Map 5498.

23 D. Dymond, 'God's disputed acre', *Journal of Ecclesiastical History*, L, no.3 (1999), p.469.

24 See V. Barrie-Curien, 'London clergy in the eighteenth century', in Walsh, Haydon,
Taylor (eds), *The Church of England*, p.94. Some dilapidated parsonages accommodated
the poor: see Knight, *The Nineteenth-century Church*, pp.139-40.

25 Elliott-Binns, *Early Evangelicals*, p.291.

controversial figure in the diocese of Peterborough. He was firmly committed to Evangelical religion. 'In his youth' Jones had been 'greatly affected by the preaching' and personal friendship 'of Daniel Rowland, the famous vicar of Llangeitho', one of the itinerant fathers of Calvinistic Methodism in Wales.[26] Jones, too, became well known in Evangelical circles, not only locally but nationally, through his many contacts and his published tracts and sermons. In his first years at Creaton he often crossed local parish boundaries to preach, and people from other villages became members of his congregation. We have Jones's own evidence that women were among those who responded by travelling some distance to attend Creaton Church. This is part of a letter written by Jones to a friend, Mr. Charles of Bala, about two years after he had taken up the curacy at Creaton:

> Last Sunday se'night we were honoured with a carriage at Creaton from beyond Northampton, that is, a cartful of old women: which pleased and diverted me much. God be praised for the great simplicity I see among the poor people at Creaton. I have found none in England who so nearly resemble my countrymen as they. Their singing sometimes moves even my hard heart.[27]

One might conjure up a picture of a jolly Sunday night out for these 'old women' at a time when other ways of spending the Sabbath in any sort of convivial manner were very limited for the poor. The whole nation was subject to George III's 'Proclamation Against Immorality and Profaneness' (1787) which restricted Sunday amusements.[28] Jones has confirmed here that many of his congregation were poor and they enjoyed expressing their simple faith through singing, probably hymns. Congregational hymn singing had been introduced into the Church of England by Evangelicals. Up to 1820 some bishops still acted upon it as a legal offence.[29]

Jones's itinerant activities were not confined to his own diocese. In a letter to a friend, the Rev. Griffin of Shrewsbury, dated 6

26   Ibid.
27   Quoted in Owen, Memoir, pp.104–5.
28   Bradley, Call to Seriousness, p.95.
29   S. S. Tamke, Make a Joyful Noise unto the Lord: Hymns as a Reflection of Victorian Social Attitudes (Athens, Ohio, 1978), p.27.

November 1799, Jones reported that he had been 'called upon' to
account for his 'conduct at Chester', and was asked by Bishop
Robinson, 'How can you reconcile such proceedings with your
profession of regularity?'[30] Jones went on to tell Griffin that he was
to 'take [his] trial in form, before a Clerical court at Highgate
House' the following Easter, and he expected that they 'must all be
very careful in future to commit not one act more of irregularity'.
It would be surprising if emotional involvement in such a censorial
incident on their own premises did not serve to increase the
Bosworth women's support of Jones, and help to cement family
relationships with him that were to prove enduring. However, the
rural remoteness of Creaton and Spratton, and the structure of
authority in both parishes aided his more local autonomy. This will
be dealt with later.

3.2 Mrs Ann Bosworth, her family, Thomas Jones and letters
By the time Elizabeth Bosworth died, her son Thomas had married
Ann Wright on 8th June 1796 in her Parish Church at Holdenby,
about two miles from Spratton.[31]   The couple became fully
responsible for running the business at Highgate House. Thomas
was a man quite superior to his station;[32] and he and Mr Jones were
very intimate and became like brothers.'[33] After only eight years of
marriage, Thomas Bosworth died.[34] By then their family consisted
of the four young daughters whose epitaphs introduce this chapter,
and a son named Thomas Wright Bosworth. From that time the
Rev. Jones became even more influential within the domesticity of
Highgate House, particularly with regard to the girls.

> Towards this young family Mr. Jones discharged all the
> duties of a kind parent, not merely from the great love and
> regard he entertained for the father, but also from the great
> affection he had for the children themselves. He became
> their teacher; and no children could have loved their own
> father more, and no father could have felt more love and

---

30 Jones, *Letter* to Rev. Mr. Griffin, Shrewsbury (6 Nov. 1799), N.C.R.O., ZB1052/2.
31 N.C.R.O., microfiche 171p/4.
32 He was a member of the Lamport and Highgate House Agricultural Society, see his
    experimental result, *The Particulars of an Experiment respecting Smut in Wheat*
    (Wellingborough, 1798). N.C.R.O., Bos. Coll.
33 Owen, *Memoir*, p.144.
34 Buried at Spratton, 9 October 1804, N.C.R.O., microfiche 295p/6.

affection for his own children.[35]

Jones would have been reluctant to leave after the death of his landlord and close friend. Furthermore, his accommodation at Highgate House freed him from concerns about the upkeep of a home of his own, leaving more time and energy for ministry. The ecclesiastical ideal was for a clergyman to be married, with children,[36] but if Jones had no wish to marry, his life with the Bosworth family provided a loving, domestic alternative for him.

Jones's affection and practical care for the children is illustrated in the first paragraph of a letter he wrote to Clara Bosworth on 14 May 1813, when she was about fifteen. By then she was attending Mrs Grigg's School at Bedford, which was probably chosen as suitably Evangelical. The literary style of Jones's personal correspondence was that usually adopted by Evangelicals when writing to each other, whether clergy or laity. Biblical messages were interwoven with news of day-to-day domestic events and local gossip. His letter ran as follows:

> My dear Clara,
> Tho' I have nothing particularly to communicate, I can't but write a line by Mr Dunilo to say that we are all well, only Mrs Bosworth's having suffered from a pain in her head for a day or two, and is now getting better. Your brother and sisters are as usual with me at this time of the morning, 8 o'clock. The two eldest are together in grammar and get on very fair. Tommy is very inattentive to his book, and of course makes no rapid progress. We do not know when or where he is to go to school, it is however designed that he shall go somewhere at Midsummer, if a proper school for him can be found near. My dear girl let me cherish the comfortable hope that you attend seriously to your best and highest concerns. That you constantly remember that you are a lost sinner without Christ that union of heart with the blessed Jesus is absolutely necessary to salvation; to be one with Christ and Christ with us is life eternal. Pray much for his Salvation. You know that I do not even wish to see you

35 Owen, *Memoir*, p.145.
36 Davidoff & Hall, *Family Fortunes*, pp.122-3.

with all the solid sedateness of an aged person, for I like
nothing unnatural, I therefore say to you, retain and
cultivate the spritely vivacity becoming your age.

Live in love with all, be sensible of kindness, and make
a grateful acknowledgement for every attention shewed
you. The new gig is now to be entered, and to be used as
soon as a proper horse can be found to draw it. At
Midsummer you will see it at Bedford coming to wheel
you to Highgate House. I hope, in company with Selina
and myself. All things future are to us uncertain, let us
always do the duty of the day, and leave tomorrow till it
arrives. Mr Dunilo is come into the room, and I must
conclude with saying, that I wish you every blessing and
comfort.
Yours affectionately
Thos. Jones.

P.S. A bundle of love from all here to Clara.[37]

Clara did not escape Jones's indoctrination during their
temporary separation, nor would she have expected otherwise. It
was probably the first time she had been away from home for any
length of time. He was urging her not to become lax in her
spiritual life and never to forget that she was 'a lost sinner without
Christ'. Crucicentrism can be detected here.[38] However, Jones
tempered his message with understanding. Though his wish was
for Clara to 'attend seriously' to what should be her 'highest
concerns', her Evangelical response must not quash her natural
sense of fun and *joie de vivre*. This might seem a contradiction of
the seriousness usually associated with Evangelicalism, but it
appears that for the young Bosworths there was still a place for
natural high spirits and frivolity.[39] Jones's instruction to 'Live in love
with all' echoed the 'new commandment' Christ gave to his
disciples at the Last Supper: 'That you love one another'.[40]

It is likely that Thomas Jones's domestic role at Highgate House
satisfied paternal affections in him which living elsewhere in the
usual style of a clerical bachelor of his time probably would not

---

37 Jones to C. Bosworth, 14 May 1813, N.C.R.O., Bos. Coll:
38 See Bebbington, *Evangelicalism*, pp.15–16.
39 As for the Clapham Sect families: see Tolley, *Domestic Biography*, p.8.
40 John, 13:34.

have fulfilled. Selina joined Clara at school in Bedford when she was about fifteeen. This undated letter was sent to them by Jones a few months before Clara was to return home for good at around the age of seventeen.

My dear Clara and Selina,
I can't let your box come without sending you a few words, though I have nothing very particular to communicate more than what Matilda informs you respecting the indisposition of your Grandmother. She certainly is very much reduced in strength, though she may live a while longer, yet there is at present no great prospect of her recovery.

On this occasion you must learn submission to the will of God, and pray for grace to submit and say, 'The judge of all the earth will do right'. You will, I trust, give thanks, when you hear, that your pious Grandmother is very happy in her soul, and saith continually, 'The will of the Lord be done. He will not leave nor forsake me in life or death. If I die I shall go and be with him in glory, which is far better than to continue here in a world of sin and suffering.' Such is her language day by day. If God spares her life, I shall be highly gratified and if he take her away to himself, I shall rejoice over her, having no doubt respecting her everlasting felicity. She had long served the Lord, and believed in his name. All the rest of your family are in health, and Tommy seems to be quite at home at Guilsboro' where he has 14 boys to keep him company. I hope my dear Selina enjoys Bedford and rejoices that she has in prospect to spend two happy years there to her improvement and edification in every useful way, when my dear Clary's tears flow now and then in thinking that she must stay at home after a few months more, free from labour and sorrow from cares and anxieties. I would say to you both, forget not your God, he does not forget you. In all your ways acknowledge him and he will direct your step. May his blessing descend and rest upon you both.
I am, my dears,
Your affectionate friend,
Thos Jones.   Friday, 18th.[41]

Again, this is typical of the way in which Jones always included some Evangelical message, but we shall never know the real responses of the girls to these parts of his letters. Nevertheless, continual indoctrination during their early years had lasting effects and Evangelicalism formed the central principles of their faith throughout the rest of their lives. The first quotation marks here indicated Jones's extraction from Genesis, 18:25, but he had turned the question 'Shall not the Judge of all the earth do right?' into a positive statement. In telling the girls that their grandmother[42] was 'happy in her soul' at the prospect of her impending demise, Jones probably hoped to ease their concern and soften the blow of bereavement if it came. It was a particularly appropriate moment for sermonizing. This pious woman's supposed words reflected the 23rd Psalm, as these three verses alone from it indicate:

1.   The Lord is my shepherd; I shall not want.
4.   Yea, though I walk through the valley of the shadow
      of death, I will fear no evil; for thou art with me;...
6.   Surely goodness and mercy shall follow me all the days
      of my life; and I will dwell in the house of the Lord
      for ever.

The evidence here confirms that Evangelicalism could offer a simple, comforting panacea for bewilderment in the face of death, but we might question whether expressions of faith entered into the grandmother's ordinary everyday speech when she was well. The example set by someone dear to them, who 'had long served the Lord, and believed in his name', must have been of significant influence on the girls' own lives. Biblicism can be noted again in Jones's penultimate sentence, which was almost word-for-word from Proverbs 3:6 - 'In all thy ways acknowledge him, and he shall direct thy paths'.

Ann Bosworth continued the running of the inn and farm after her husband died. Clearly, she managed affairs at Highgate House successfully and was the second widow in the family to do so. Though, as already pointed out, Evangelicalism upheld the middle-class woman's dependence on, and subordination to man, there was 'some ambiguity among [E]vangelicals as to the strict definitions of

---

41   Jones to C. and S. Bosworth, c.1815, N.C.R.O., Bos. Coll.
42   This must have been on their maternal side, for the letter was written some years after
     Elizabeth Bosworth's death.

male and female responsibilities.'[43] Women's subordinate role did not always preclude their influence in society. The home was considered their proper sphere, but sometimes they needed to enter the man's world of work to partially, or fully support a family.[44] So, Evangelicalism allowed that it was acceptable for a woman to take an active part in business life after the death of her husband. However, a growing social disapproval of public drinking places could present difficulties for a widow running an inn.[45] Locally, Ann Bosworth and her family may well have gained added status from their close association with Jones, but she herself must have commanded respect in both the commercial and parochial life of the neighbourhood. Though her business assets had been built on those accumulated by at least one generation of her husband's family during the previous century, could she have been suitably placed among the female members of the new middle class, many of whom conspicuously embraced Evangelicalism in the early years of the nineteenth century? Certainly, if property and wealth were the criteria, she could. The Probate of her Will, proved on 20th July 1833 in the Prerogative Court of Canterbury, showed the extent of her pecuniary and proprietary assets.[46] She left £1,000 each to her surviving children, Clara and Thomas; the same amount was to go to her two granddaughters, Matilda and Selina Bosworth Owen, the children of the deceased Selina. In addition, she devised and bequeathed to Clara and Thomas, 'as tenants in common' her

> All and every Messuages Cottages Closes Lands Grounds Hereditaments and Real Estate whatsoever and wheresoever. And also all and singular Household Furniture Goods Chattels and implements of Household Stock Trade Corn Grain Hay Malt Book Debts ready money securities for money Government Stock Mortgages in fee or for years and all other personal Estate and Effects whatsoever and wheresoever.

The valuation of her personal estate and effects included livestock, crops, machinery, harness, etc., and malt, all to the value of

---

43 Davidoff & Hall, *Family Fortunes*, p.117.
44 *Ibid.*
45 J. Rendall, *Women in an Industrializing Society: England 1750-1880* (Oxford, 1990), p.52.
46 *Probate of the Will of Ann Bosworth deceased*, 20 July 1833, (Will dated 3rd December 1824), N.C.R.O., Bos. Coll.

£3,146.[47] The livestock totalled 492 sheep and lambs, 87 calves, beasts and cows, 35 pigs, and 18 horses. In addition, Highgate House itself was a valuable asset for it contained '13 Bedrooms furnished, Travellers' Room, Sitting Room, Dining Room, 2 Passages. 2 Store Rooms, Hop Room, Cellar and Brew House, Ware House, Tap Room, Saddle House, Kitchen, Dairy'; the contents of which were valued at £824.[48] It is small wonder that the Rev. Jones found comfort and space for quietude at Highgate House. Furthermore, Mrs Bosworth must have employed a fair number of servants and labourers, and it is very likely that their allegiance to her led some of them to Jones's congregations. In 1829, she was elected one of the two Overseers of the poor for Spratton.[49] Though she served for only a month, and it may have been a temporary appointment until a male successor could be found, she was the only female recorded as overseer in the extant vestry minute books for this parish, dated, 1811, 1827, 1829-32, and 1842.

His comfortable, supportive home among the Bosworth family at Highgate House, and his ministerial success in both parishes probably dismissed any serious thoughts from Thomas Jones's mind of ever moving permanently to another area. However, it cannot be expected that all the laity in the neighbourhood gave Jones support, and some of the local clergy 'often attempted to prejudice his Bishop against him...particularly on the ground of his living at an Inn'.[50] This was merely a pretext for getting him removed from Creaton. At one visitation Bishop Marsh 'very unexpectedly and publicly lectured' Mr Jones for residing at Highgate House, but 'when the case was explained' to him, he allowed the curate to remain there, a permission already granted by his predecessor.[51] Mrs Bosworth's hostelry was respectable, and there was plenty of room for Jones to escape from its day-to-day public business. Nevertheless, over the years Marsh still censured him from time to time. This is obvious from two of Jones's letters to Clara, the first

47   Knight and Clarke, *The Valuation of the Personal Estate and Effects of the late Mrs A. Bosworth of Highgate House* (1833, though undated), N.C.R.O., Bos. Coll.

48   *Ibid.*

49   *Spratton Vestry Minute Book* (25 March 1829), N.C.R.O., 295p/11.

50   Owen, *Memoir*, p.147. Thomas Sikes of Guilsborough, a neighbouring parish, was one of the strongest contemporary opponents of Evangelicalism, see Reardon, *Coleridge to Gore*, pp.34-7.

51   Owen, *Memoir*, p.147.

written in 1821:

> I did not attend the Bible Society yesterday at
> Northampton which I hear went off very well. Lord
> Althorp in the chair. Neither did I go today to make my
> bow to the sour Archdeacon at his Visitation at
> Northampton but wrote to say that I had various
> hindrances and dated my note at Highgate House; because
> I strongly suspected that he was my accuser to the surly
> Bishop.[52]

Addressing the letter from Highgate House clearly had
significance. Perhaps the censure had been for holding meetings of
Evangelical clergy there, but regular gatherings were important for
them as a means of support in what could be a hostile Anglican
arena.[53] Coincidentally, the 'sour Archdeacon' and the 'surly Bishop'
were William Strong and Herbert Marsh, respectively, who feature
so prominently in the second chapter of this book. That the
personal religious biases of Mrs Lukyn and Thomas Jones could
create such differing views of these men, shows the potential
divisiveness of Evangelicalism. No doubt, by this time, Clara and
her relatives had all accepted Jones's opinion of these divines.
A second illustration of his discord with Marsh appeared in
Jones's letter to Clara Bosworth dated 10 May 1823, when she was
staying at Kennington Cross, Surrey. It is worth giving space to his
full account of the contention:

> You doubtless know before this that I was lately there [in
> London] and under the necessity of hastening home;
> especially as war was proclaimed between Peterboro' and
> Creaton. A most unequal contest between a Gigantic
> Bishop and a dwarf of a Curate. He wrote four letters about
> my employing Bugg to officiate for me during my illness.
> The first two received mild answers; but his third called
> forth the Welshman to the field. To which he replied in a
> very angry tone; but he evidently writes cowardly. I do not
> expect that any more letters will pass on the subject. The
> Bishop wrote once to Mr. Bugg, and demanded to know

52 Jones to C. Bosworth, 6 June 1821, N C.R.O., Bos. Coll.
53 M. M. Hennell, *John Venn and the Clapham Sect* (1958), p.84.

by what authority he officiated in his Diocese for Mr.
Williams of Barby and for Mr. Jones of Creaton, and said
that he had no licence nor authority from him to do so;
that he should put him in the Court of abuses for his gross
offence, and had taken prepary [sic] steps for that purpose,
and that if Mr. Bugg did not ask his pardon for his past
offences, and promise not to offend in like manner again,
that he should proceed. Mr. Bugg sent for me in haste, and
we construed a letter of this sort. Bugg pretended that his
offence consisted only of *informality*, and in order not to
transgress a second time, proposed himself to be licensed
regularly to a Curacy in this diocese, and begged that his
Lordship would have the goodness to inform him what
steps were necessary for him to take for that purpose. He
had not lately answered Mr. Bugg, and probably will not,
and I expect that the whole business is for the present at an
end. But he is like the restless sea whose waves by nature
toss and roar, beat against the rocks, and die away in foam.[54]

Such intimacy was important in the relationship between Jones and
Clara, and he possessed a light-heartedness which he could share
with her. Jones obviously felt secure in his position at Creaton and
Spratton if he was prepared to challenge Marsh as he did, and to
influence his fellow Evangelical, George Bugg, to call the Bishop's
bluff. Surely, Marsh was aware of Bugg's reputation as a
controversial figure in other dioceses.

Rosemary Dunhill's article has very fully chronicled George
Bugg's 'Fortunes' as an Evangelical curate; minimal facts from it will
be given here.[55] First, in 1802, Bugg had been dismissed from a
curacy in Lincolnshire after only eleven weeks because of his
Evangelicalism. From 1803, as curate at Kettering in the
Peterborough Diocese under Marsh's predecessor, various
controversies led to a request for him to leave in 1815. Seemingly,
a move to a curacy at Lutterworth, Leicestershire, in 1817 was an
unwise step. The Bishop of Lincoln, who had dismissed Bugg from
his first curacy, gave him notice to quit after only ten months.
According to Dunhill, not much is known about his activities
during the next twelve years, but apparently he was living at

54 Jones to C. Bosworth, 10 May 1823, N.C.R.O., Bos. Coll.
55 R. Dunhill, 'The Rev. George Bugg: the fortunes of a 19th century curate',
    Northamptonshire Past and Present, VII, No.1 (1983-4), pp.41-50.

Kettering for part of that period, and this present investigation has also located him at Spratton at different times. There were the occasions mentioned in the above letter, and he had conducted the funeral services for two of the Bosworth daughters, Maria in 1821, and Selina (Owen) only a year later.[56] No doubt he and his wife were frequent visitors at Highgate House. In his very long letter to Clara dated 29 August 1821, when she was still away from home, Jones mentioned that Mrs Bugg had been with them for three weeks; Mr Bugg and the children were expected from Kettering that day, and 'all [were] to march home well soon'.[57] Mrs Bugg's frailty is evident. She died at the age of twenty-eight leaving her husband with four daughters under seven. One of them, Eliza, remained in touch with the Bosworths for many years. It can be expected that Mrs Ann Bosworth held Bugg in special affection. Very surprisingly, Bishop Marsh allowed him to return to the Peterborough Diocese in 1831 as curate of Desborough. By this time Marsh had probably come to terms with the fact that he could be opposed at parish as well as Parliamentary level. Another petition had been brought against him in the House of Lords in June 1822 for adding a further thirty-six questions to the eighty-seven he already put to all clergy before he licensed them.[58]

Jones's letter to Clara just quoted began with much local news and this extract is lengthy. Not only has it confirmed that she was always subject to a doctrinal message from him, but also that he could share confidences with her. There is interesting evidence concerning development of Evangelical religion within another local family and at some Northampton churches. Biblicism, conversionism and activism are apparent.

29 August 1821
My dearest Clara,
I could hardly tell how it gladdens my heart to hear of your improving state of health. May God perfect what he has so mercifully begun, and incline our hearts to render unto him, who is indeed the fountain of all goodness, and the God of all consolations. It is a great favor to be taught to see that every good and every perfect gift come from the

56 N.C.R.O., microfiche 295p/4.
57 Jones to C. Bosworth, 29 August 1821, N.C.R.O., Bos. Coll.
58 *Northampton Mercury*, 7 June, 1822.

father of lights, and a greater gift still to apply to him full
of faith in his promised grace, under a dire sense of *intire
dependance on God*. This last point is of prime importance
to believe; yet ill understood, and seldom studied by
professed believers. It is now strongly recommended to
dear Clara...Having finished my short and hasty sermon, I
shall next relate a few particulars that my dear girl will be
interested in. And first of all, Frank Lucas is become
decidedly serious. Spends the greatest part of his time in
studying Scriptures, in praying, and trying to bring his
relations and friends to seek the Salvation of God. He told
me that he owed much to the early instruction which he
received of his mother, and mentioned Creaton church.
His concern for the Salvation of his relations is remarkable.
His poor father was greatly alarmed and outraged at what
had taken place in him; conceiving that he would no more
attend to business, and would ruin all his wordly prospects.
Young Lucas and his sister came to me to go and dine with
them and to talk to their father, in which I succeeded
wonderfully, removed his fears, and brought him into good
temper, now all is smooth and pleasant. Sarah is also, as far
as now appears, as decided as her brother. I had hopes of
her for some considerable time back.

Thanks...The gospel is now faithfully preached in two
of the Churches at Northampton [All Saints' and St.
Sepulchre's]. Mr Butcher the Attorney purchased St.
Sepulchre, presented his son, who appointed one Moses
Marcus, a converted Jew,[59] to the curacy, and allowed him
£50 for his salary. But in the Licence the Bishop allowed
him the whole emoluments of the Living being under
£150 a year, the house is also given him free of a rent.
Injoining him to have two services, one at 11, the other at
6 in the evening for the convenience of *other parishes.*[60]
Butcher enraged at this, gave the Curate notice to quit in

59 The London Society for Promoting Christianity among the Jews, established in 1809,
    was an interdenominational missionary body. Leading Evangelicals, including Simeon,
    were among its enthusiastic supporters.

60 Jones's underlining most likely signified that he saw cunning in the Bishop's motive,
    which was probably to organize a 6 p.m. service for Anglicans from local parishes where
    the only opportunity for evening worship was provided by Nonconformists, who
    usually held two services each Sunday.

one month. The parishioners to the number of 500 sent a petition to the Bishop, requesting that the Curate might be continued. The Bishop confirmed the licence for three years. Bishop Marsh forever! Ho ra Clara...
Your true and affectionate friend,
Thos. Jones[61]

Adapted scriptural phrases strung together created the short 'sermon' at the beginning of the letter. Jones's second sentence appears to have been constructed from two different texts - Joshua, 24:23 and Romans, 15:5. A Bible concordance will show that 'fountain' and 'goodness' occur several times in both the Old and the New Testaments. His third sentence was based on another two biblical passages - James, 1:17, 'Every good gift and every perfect gift is from above, and cometh down from the Father of lights', and Ephesians, 2:8-9, 'For by grace are ye saved through faith; and that not of yourselves; *it is* the gift of God. Not of works, lest any man should boast'. This confirmed that salvation could not be won by good works alone. The 'point' that Jones saw as 'ill understood and seldom studied by professed believers' was probably the Gospel message that salvation depended entirely on God's gift of grace through the atonement. Humans contributed nothing to their own redemption. To God alone was the praise.

Jones's account of the Lucas household is particularly useful in illustrating how Evangelicalism expanded within a middle-class family. It was the mother who had been converted first and Creaton Church had played a significant part in this. Mrs Lucas showed an independent spirit, as her religious views were not shared by her husband. Their son acknowledged that his mother's 'early instruction' had sown the seeds of his adult conversion. Sarah had eventually responded to her brother's activism. Seemingly her change of heart had been gradual, but Anglican Evangelicals, 'commonly more educated, sober and respectable than their brethren in other denominations', easily accepted that gradual conversions might occur.[62]

Ann Bosworth ran Highgate House for another twenty-nine years after her husband's death. She died at the age of sixty, and was buried at Spratton on 7 July 1833.[63] Domestic harmony among all

61 Jones to C. Bosworth, 29 August 1821, N.C.R.O., Bos. Coll.
62 Bebbington, *Evangelicalism*, pp.7-8
63 N.C.R.O., 295p/4.

inhabitants of Highgate House must have depended on a mutual Evangelical religiosity. Probably most of Mrs Bosworth's employees there were female and she would have tried to ensure that those who lived in were of the same faith as her own. Evangelical servants, themselves, preferred to be employed within a pious household. In such a milieu they would have been expected to accompany the family to church at least once every Sunday, thus satisfying their serious need to worship regularly on that day. Furthermore, Evangelical employers might be willing to give servants time to be involved in some form of local activism. A Miss Cole assisted Mrs Bosworth as housekeeper and she shared the domesticity of Highgate House for many years. As can be gathered from Jones's letter to Clara, dated 10 May 1823, Ann Cole carried a certain degree of authority and responsibility, for she was left in charge when Clara and her mother were away:

> Tell Mrs Bosworth I went down into the house to enquire how things went on in the Kitchen, and Miss Cole said, all move in very regularly, and nothing in the house is out of place: not many travellers lately, they all ride by on the coach, and do not look in.[64]

When Mrs Bosworth and Clara were absent for a few days or more, Miss Cole would have supervised the other domestic staff in their work and made sure they kept to their religious duties. Despite her busy life at Highgate House, as my next chapter will show, Miss Cole was able to perform an active Evangelical role in Spratton as a penny collector for the Church Missionary Society. Jones mentioned their housekeeper again when he wrote to Clara at Kennington Cross in January 1825: 'Your Mother and Miss Cole join me in all affection to you and dear Tommy'.[65]

Some sixteen years later, on 10 June 1841, Thomas, married Matilda Bosworth Pearson in London.[66] They were probably cousins. Thomas had left Highgate House before his marriage, and he took Jones to live with him in his new home at Spratton. Their extended household also included Ann Cole as housekeeper, and a

---

64 Jones to C. Bosworth, 10 May 1823, N.C.R.O., Bos. Coll.
65 Jones to C. Bosworth, 28 January 1825, N.C.R.O., Bos.Coll.
66 *Certificate of Marriage*: Thomas Wright Bosworth to Matilda Bosworth Pearson, 10 June 1841, N.C.R.O., Bos. Coll.

female farm servant.[67] Matilda had responded positively to Jones's need for a home, thus continuing the family's care for him, but Miss Cole remained with them for only a few months after the wedding. The advisability of her staying was discussed between Clara and her brother. In a letter of reply, Clara wrote, 'You asked what I thought of Miss Cole staying with you. I can scarcely judge but fear it would not answer.'[68] Perhaps Thomas thought his wife might not feel mistress in her own home so long as the family's housekeeper was there. The rather sad tone of a short, undated letter written by Jones to Clara recorded his sincere affection for Miss Cole.

> I shall try to pen a few lines to you, tho' I have now but little sight left. While we are on the earth, our trials may change but they shall [not] come to an end till we go to the rest. A rest remaineth of a nature which is far beyond our comprehension while here...Yesterday, Miss Cole left us, I shall miss her not a little tho' Mrs Bosworth is as kind as can be. I always feel it very backward to part with those I have been long with, and Miss Cole had been here for nearly forty years.[69]

Miss Cole was a devout and active Evangelical, who had formed a close personal and religious relationship with Thomas Jones. As usual, there was a biblical element in his letter. The second sentence echoed belief in the transitory nature of this life, with its changing scenes as man travelled on a roller platform of inescapable trials. Freedom from earthly tribulations came only in death's blissful 'rest'.[70]

At various times, Thomas Jones had baptized all the Bosworth daughters and their brother at Creaton Church.[71] But the funeral service for each of the girls was conducted at Spratton by one or other of his local clergy friends.[72] Jones's place would have been among the family mourners. Officially, his ministerial appointment at Creaton had begun in September 1785, and ended in December 1833, a term of forty-eight years and four months, though his

67 *Census Enumerators' Returns* (1841), N.C.R.O., microfilm M348.
68 C. Bosworth to T. Bosworth, 'Saturday' 1841, N.C.R.O., Bos. Coll.
69 Jones to C. Bosworth, (undated, c.1841), N.C.R.O., Bos. Coll.
70 Probably taken from Job, 3:17.
71 N.C.R.O., microfiche 90p/5.
72 N.C.R.O., microfiche 295p/4.

memorial puts his ministry at fifty years. As he had requested,
Thomas Jones's memorial on the wall inside Spratton Church bears
the stern message he regularly proclaimed:

On the outside of this wall
lie interred the remains of
The Rev. Thomas Jones,
who was officiating minister
of Creaton for fifty years,
and for eighteen of that time
the curate of this parish,
he departed this life
on the 7th day of Jan. 1845,
Aged 92.
A sinner saved by grace! reader farewell;
Time is short, the salvation of God shall
be for ever. Sinner mind eternity, and
prepare to meet thy God.

Alongside is the stone in memory of the only son and youngest
member of the Bosworth family. The last sentence of his epitaph
echoes the wording on his sisters' memorials. It confirms their
shared Evangelical beliefs, something of great significance in their
relationships with each other:

Sacred
to the memory of
Mr. Thomas Wright Bosworth,
more highly gifted than others and trained
under the fatherly care of the Rev. Thomas Jones.
He was made an instrument of much good
to this place and neighbourhood.
Influenced by Christian principles he was
always lowly in his own eyes, knowing in
whom he had believed.
After a brief illness,
He fell asleep in Jesus, 31st May 1856,
Aged 51 years.[73]

---

73 Thomas and his wife, Matilda, are buried alongside his parents and sisters in Spratton
    Churchyard.

3.3 Evangelicalism as expressed in other correspondence

The Rev. John Owen was lent much personal correspondence when writing his *Memoir* of Thomas Jones. Some of the letters had passed between Jones and the Bosworth family, but those quoted above do not appear to have been included in Owen's work, nor do the others that are used here. In the Bosworth Collection there are just a few letters exchanged between Clara, her brother, or his wife. When writing to her new sister-in-law, Matilda, in August 1841,[74] soon after the wedding, Clara remarked with some humility: 'Though mine are very small insignificant letters I believe my dear sister will like to receive one from me'. She goes on to ask, 'How did you like the gaze of the people on Sunday?...Lady brides are a novelty and rarity at Spratton'. Presumably, this related to the newlyweds' first attendance at Spratton Church after their marriage in London. Clara expected that the other worshippers had been unable to subdue their curiosity with regard to the recently married young 'lady' who had come to live among them. This might confirm that most of the congregation were working-class women and their keen interest in the bride from a higher social circle than their own was a likely reaction.

Two letters from Clara to Thomas were requests for money. Very small, and written in pencil, they are now difficult to read and will not be included here. For some years before her death Clara stayed in Cheltenham and was 'wholly confined to her bed',[75] therefore she probably found ink less convenient to use. This next extract from a tiny letter, also in pencil, to her 'Dear Brother' and dated merely 'Wednesday' 1842, is a rare, personal confirmation of Clara's Evangelicalism:

> I was truly grieved to hear so painful an account of dear Matilda and sincerely do I hope that by now she has succeeded in gaining her strength. These things are great trials to our patience. I do trust that patience will achieve perfect work and that afterwards affliction may yield the free pardonable fruit of righteousness in things that are endured hereby. When we look not at the things that are seen but them that are unseen, we should bear in mind that God doth not willingly afflict or grieve the Children

74   C. Bosworth to M. Bosworth, August 1841, N.C.R.O., Bos. Coll.
75   Owen, *Memoir*, p.165.

of man.[76]

One should not underestimate the significance of Evangelicalism in Clara's life. In this short extract alone there are adaptations of several biblical verses. A high religious tone appears to have come naturally to her, as with other female Evangelical letter-writers.[77] No doubt the phrases used here and numerous others were imprinted on her memory from long familiarity with the Bible. Her second sentence and the beginning of her third were based on James, 1:3-4: 'Knowing this, that the trying of your faith worketh patience; But let patience have her perfect work, that ye may be perfect and entire, wanting nothing'. Clara's next phrase was seemingly borrowed from Ephesians, 5:9: 'For the fruit of the spirit is in all goodness and righteousness and truth.' Her last sentence began with an almost direct quotation from the first part of 2 Corinthians, 4:18, 'While we look not at the things which are seen, but at the things which are not seen'. It ended with something almost word-for-word from Lamentations, 3:33: 'For he doth not afflict willingly nor grieve the children of men'. However, many Christians have found it difficult to reconcile personal affliction and mass suffering from catastrophic so-called 'acts of God' with the professed Divine love of humanity. For amplification of the way in which Evangelicals might come to terms with this anomaly of suffering, we can turn to Hannah More again:

The reflecting christian will consider the natural evil of sickness as the consequence and punishment of moral evil. He will mourn, not only that he suffers pain, but because that pain is the effect of sin. If man had not sinned he would not have suffered. The heaviest aggravation of his pain is to know that he has deserved it. But it is a counterbalance to this trial to know that our merciful Father has no pleasure in the sufferings of his children, that he chastises them in love, that he never inflicts a stroke which he could safely spare; that he inflicts it to purify as well as to punish, to caution as well as to cure, to improve as well as to chastise.[78]

76 C. Bosworth to T. Bosworth, 'Wednesday', 1842, N.C.R.O., Bos. Coll.

77 As Tolley has claimed for Mary Babbington, daughter of Thomas Babbington and niece of Zachary Macaulay, Clapham Sect members: see Tolley, *Domestic Biography*, p.9.

78 More, *Practical Piety*, p.225.

A quite different letter was written by Clara to her brother on 12 July 1847, only seven months before she died. Written in ink and formal in its language, there is a legal ring about it. By now Thomas had a family of his own and Clara, remembering her late sister's children, asked this of him: 'In the event of [her] dying Intestate [her] property consisting of land' would become his. But 'in that event', as a proof of his 'love' to her, and 'justice', she requested that he would give to her nieces, Matilda and Selina Owen, the sum of £350 each, and £20 each to two of her friends.[79]

The selection of correspondence here should include one of the only three letters there are to Clara from her brother. That Evangelicalism was a bond between them and that he, too, was able to express his spirituality freely is obvious from this one dated 12 March 1840. It was written by Thomas soon after hearing about the death of his brother-in-law, George Pearson, 'at San Lucar, 20 miles from Cadiz, on 21st February'. He shared the bereavement experience with Clara and his expressions of mutual faith probably helped to assuage the sense of deep grief felt by both:

> I know you will grieve. To me the loss is great. My bosom friend and companion is gone. 'Know that I am God' is loudly spoken by this dispensation of the Almighty. Yet was there great mercy in the judgement, and we have in our sorrow good reason to hope that our dear departed friend was led by the warning voice of affliction to Look to Jesus, the sinner's refuge ere the close...Mr Jones feels acutely. George was one of his favorites, especially of late...
> We unite in love My ever dear Sister,
> Yours,
> Thomas[80]

The words in quotation marks were taken from Psalm 46:10, 'Be still, and know that I am God'. Thomas seems to indicate that George Pearson had been ill for some time and God had been merciful in letting him die. Yet there was cause for optimism in that, at the prospect of death, George had most likely affirmed his faith in Christ's salvation of the self-acknowledged sinner.

79 C. Bosworth to T. Bosworth, 12 July 1847, N.C.R.O., Bos. Coll.
80 T. Bosworth to C. Bosworth, 12 March 1840, N.C.R.O., Bos. Coll.

Further confirmation that Thomas's wife, Matilda, was part of
an Evangelical extended family can be found in this
communication to her from her cousin, Mrs Ann White, writing
from London on 4 October 1841:

> I suppose now you are sole housekeeper if Miss Cole has
> left, how do you like your new engagement?...I was quite
> pleased with your account of Mr Jones. I am sure I should
> both love, and admire him, and would almost *envy you the
> privilege* of living with that venerable character. Who can
> wonder if he does long to join his Saviour and be ever
> blest? in that world 'where the wicked cease from troubling
> and the weary are at rest'. May we all through the merit of
> Him who died that *all might* live obtain an entrance into
> His glorious Kingdom.[81]

Ann White quoted from Job,3:17 for her penultimate sentence.
Although apparently she had never met Thomas Jones, an idolized
figure of him had been presented to her by others. Maybe there
were several women among his parishioners and friends who
elevated Jones practically to divine stature.

Women's susceptibility to the charisma of pious ministers was
only too well realized. Charismatic clerical figures often appeared
in novels by Evangelical female writers, whose works George Eliot
described as 'silly novels' of the 'white neck-cloth species, which
represent[ed] the tone of thought and feeling in the Evangelical
party'.[82] This is part of Eliot's comment on such literature: 'In the
ordinary type of these novels, the hero is almost sure to be a young
curate, frowned upon, perhaps, by worldly mammas, but carrying
captive the hearts of their daughters, who can "never forget *that*
sermon";...'[83] Women's emotional response to Evangelical clergy
was also exploited by satirical female novelists. This can be seen in
the fictitious Helen Mowbray, who later did not fully understand
her previous naive admiration of Mr Cartwright, the Evangelical
Vicar of Wrexhill in Mrs Trollope's novel:

81   A. White to M. Bosworth, 4 October 1841, N.C.R.O., Bos. Coll.
82   G. Eliot, 'Silly Novels by lady novelists', (*Westminster Review*, October 1856) in *Selected
     Essays, Poems and Other Writings*, A. S. Byatt & N. Warren (eds) (1990), p.156. It is
     interesting to note that George Eliot, herself, created a young charismatic curate, the
     Revd. Edgar Tryan, in 'Janet's Repentance', the last of her stories in *Scenes of Clerical Life*.
83   *Ibid.*, pp.156-7.

I cannot explain even to myself what species of feeling it was which took possession of me when first I became acquainted with Mr Cartwright. Of this, however, I am quite sure, that I believe with all the simplicity of truth and innocence, that all I felt proceeded from the immediate influence of the Deity working within me to secure my eternal salvation. Had I seen the Holy Ghost descend bodily upon Mr Cartwright, I could not more firmly have believed that he was God's appointed agent on earth and everything he did and everything he said appeared clothed in a sort of holiness in my eyes which would have rendered it impious to judge him as another would have been judged.[84]

Clara Bosworth still kept in touch with friends she had made at school in Bedford. Soon after her sister, Matilda, died at the age of fourteen, she received a letter of condolence from a young woman named Fanny, who was newly-married and employed at the school. Very lengthy, and interspersed with biblical quotations, its contents were almost entirely devoted to illness, or death, and fully confirm to what extent Evangelical beliefs centred on the sinner's hope of heavenly bliss. Fanny and the 'ladies' she mentioned may have been less directly influenced by domestic association with an Evangelical clergyman than the Bosworth girls. In this they were more typical of the majority of pious women. Though the following extract is long, it is only a small portion of the whole letter. It can be recognized as a classic Evangelical response to a friend's bereavement:

I can hardly say I was sorry to hear of the death of your dear sister Matilda, what reason have we to grieve? Should we mourn because she has left a world of sin and sorrow to be translated to one where she will enjoy *perfect* happiness for ever, where she will know nothing of sorrow, temptation, sin, affliction, and all the trials and dangers we are exposed to in this vale of tears. Happy soul. She now beholds her redeemer face to face, she now knows what perfect happiness is. She loved her God and Saviour while on earth, she sought him and she found him

---

84 Mrs F. Trollope, *The Vicar of Wrexhill* (1837), pp.155-6.

willing to hear and answer her prayer, and now she does
not repent of her search, she is praising in the halleluyas of
Paradise...O my dear Clara, may we once join that blessed
glorious company. Let Matilda's happy death be an
example to you and me dearest Girl to 'remember our
creator in the days of our youth', to seek the Lord while
he may be found...I am happy to inform you that several
of the Ladies are much altered, and have lately devoted
themselves to Christ, finding no *real* happiness but in
him...Ann Palmer, whom you may remember was quite
the reverse of everything relating to serious things, she has
undergone a great, a great change, she is now a humble
and devoted follower of the Lamb, and writes me very
beautiful letters which really delight me. She seems so
sincere and devoted to lead a new life and to gain eternal
happiness. Miss Buxton, whom you do not know but
who is a great favourite with Selina, is really in a most
beautiful frame of mind, she is in a consumption aware she
has not long to be in this world, but death has no horrors
for her, she can look on it with confidence and is waiting
in the joyful expectation of being freed from this tenement
of clay to enjoy eternal felicity, and happiness in the
mansion of bliss and glory.[85]

Fanny had no doubt whatsoever concerning Matilda's piety
during her short life. To contemporary Evangelicals, 'happy death'
was a familiar term, much used when recording the last moments
of relatives or friends.[86] In this letter, also, we have examples of
biblicism and conversionism. The quotation marked by Fanny was
from Ecclesiastes, 12:1, 'Remember now thy Creator in the days of
thy youth', though she adapted it to suit her context. Her account
has indicated a wave of conversions among women at the school.
They were committed in full devotion to Christ.

However, letters were written by Evangelicals to mark happier
occurrences within this network of family and friends. One sent
to Matilda and Thomas a few days after their wedding came from

85 Fanny to C. Bosworth, 12 March 1816, N.C.R.O., Bos. Coll.

86 According to Hannah More, not all reported 'happy deaths' should have been termed as
    such. 'Nothing is more suspicious than a happy death where there has neither been
    religion in the life nor humility at its close, where its course has been without piety, and
    its termination without repentance': see *Practical Piety*, pp.198-9.

their cousin, Elizabeth Bosworth, writing from North Bridge. It ran as follows:

> June 19th 1841
> My dear friends,
> In our progress through life various scenes present themselves, and a diversity of duties devolve upon us, some of a painful, others of a pleasurable nature, of the latter kind is the one now before me, namely to congratulate you upon your union, which I trust will be long and happy, free from trials and blessed with a large portion of domestic comfort. May the Father of mercies and giver of all good[87] pour upon you His choicest favors, and may you be the means not only of promoting each others happiness in this world but above all, may you assist one another in your journey Zionwards; that whenever it shall please God to call you away from sublimary pleasures, toils and cares, Heavens portals may open to receive you and 'come my blessed of my Father' may be the welcome summons.[88] Love to dear Mr Jones, Miss Cole, Joseph Henry,
> believe me to be your affectionate cousin
> Elizabeth Bosworth.[89]

The Evangelical tone throughout this letter is unmistakable. Here again, the writer adapted biblical quotations to fit in with her message. The Bible proclaimed 'the ransomed of the LORD shall return, and come to Zion[90] with songs, and everlasting joy upon their heads...sorrow and sighing shall flee away'.[91] In today's context, it seems extraordinary that any allusion to their deaths should be made in a congratulatory letter to newly-weds. Evangelicals faced up to mortality and Elizabeth was urging her relatives to encourage each other in their spiritual journey through this transitory life to eternity.

It is likely that the following letter, written to Clara at Highgate

---

87   2 Corinthians, 1:3, 'the Father of mercies, and the God of all comfort'.
88   Matthew 25:34, 'Then shall the King say to them on his right hand, Come ye blessed of my Father, inherit the kingdom prepared for you from the foundation of the world'.
89   E. Bosworth to M. and T. Bosworth, 19 June 1841, N.C.R.O., Bos. Coll.
90   See 1 Kings, 8:1, 'the city of David, which is Zion'. The latter was one of the hills of Jerusalem.
91   Isaiah, 35:10.

House in April 1830, was composed with some difficulty by
Harriett Middleton, a domestic servant in Barnsley. Obviously,
Harriett had been well-known to the Bosworth family at some
stage and, in contrast, was a working-class Evangelical:

> Madam I should be truly oblig'd to you if you would have
> the goodness to ask Mrs Ramsden if she should hear of a
> situation for me or any other friends of yours. I have not
> left my situation but shall as soon as I can hear of one that
> will sute me. I should very much wish to get into a pious
> Familey witch as not been the case since I left Mr Owen.
> should very much like to come to live in your part if divine
> Providence should order it so...I hope Mr Jones his in good
> health. I heare he is been at Quinborough how I should
> like to hear him Preach once agane. I have heard not a
> sermon Preached since I left Quinborough.[92]

Clearly, Evangelicalism was a very important element of
Harriett's life and she hoped to find an employer who shared the
same faith. Her belief in 'divine Providence' conformed to the
Evangelical notion of placing one's life in God's hands. That she
had 'heard not a sermon Preached since [she] left Quinborough'
probably did not indicate her non-attendance at any religious
establishment. It can be assumed that she had been required to
accompany her present 'Familey' to worship in an Orthodox
Anglican Church where the liturgy, not the sermon, was central to
the service. Undoubtedly, there was nothing artificial about any of
the correspondence quoted in this section; they all knew each other
too well for that.

3.4 Parish Structure

Evangelicalism was unlikely to win converts to an Anglican or a
Dissenting religious community and maintain their loyalty if the
parochial structure was unfavourable. During the ministries of both
Maddock and Jones, Creaton exemplified an ideal rural community
in which 'vital' Christianity could flourish in the parish church.
The following characteristics made it so. It was a fairly remote
parish within which enclosure allotments had been made to several
different landowners, and those with the largest acreage were

---

92 H. Middleton to C. Bosworth, 20 April 1830, N.C.R.O., Bos. Coll.

Evangelicals who resided within the parochial boundaries. There existed a diverse pattern of employment. This tended to lower the concentration of working-class dependence on employers, with concomitant freer choice of religious allegiance. The advowson of Creaton passed continuously from one Evangelical patron to another and, when one of these was the incumbent himself, he appointed a curate of like faith and gave him autonomy. The clergyman responsible for the cure of local souls was domiciled within or just outside the parish boundaries. Furthermore, he conducted a committed and effective ministry which bode well for local Anglican allegiance and religious uniformity. A similar parochial structure appertained at Spratton when Jones was curate there from 1810 to 1828, and some of the larger landowners held property in both parishes. More detailed reference to the above characteristics is given below. However, it must be remembered that, although men were usually the main breadwinners in English families at this time, women of all classes tended to guide the internal dynamics of day-to-day domesticity, which might include some form of religious education for their children and attendance at a place of worship.

3.4.i Landowners and patrons: Creaton and Spratton

The following 1981 descriptions of the main physical features of Creaton (now comprised of the former Little and Great Creaton) and Spratton are still applicable, and probably there has been little change in the undulating landscape of this area since the early nineteenth century:

> [Creaton] parish lies mainly across the valley of a small S.E.-flowing brook...In the S.W. the land rises to a flat-topped ridge...and falls again into the...valley of another small S.E.-flowing stream which forms the parish boundary there. Both Great and Little Creaton lie on the steep hillside of the main stream.[93]

> Spratton parish, bounded by two small S-flowing streams which meet in the S.E. corner, occupies a S-facing spur.[94]

---

93 Royal Commission on Historical Monuments, England, *An Inventory of the Historical Monuments in the County of Northampton*, III, (H.M.S.O. 1981), p.58.
94 *Ibid.*, p.172.

Though consisting of only 790 acres, (Great) Creaton was a
very 'open', mixed agricultural parish, enclosure awards in 1782-3
having been made to twenty-three individual persons, as well as to
Queen's College.[95] There was no large country estate at Creaton,
or at Spratton; in neither parish had landowning power been in the
hands of one particular dynasty. There was a mansion at Spratton,
which stood west of the church, but it had not remained in one
family's ownership, and by 1822 it had been reduced to a small
farm-house.[96] A freer choice of religious allegiance was more likely
to have prevailed in these two villages than in the nearby estate
communities of the Spencers at Althorp, and the Ishams at
Lamport.

> Parishes in which there was a significant incidence of
> freehold tenure, or in which smallhold farming was
> prevalent and the ratio of labourers to farmers relatively
> low, were unamenable to the kind of influence possible in
> 'closed villages' (sometimes called 'squire's villages' or
> 'manorial villages') where the entire population was more
> or less directly dependent on the economic power of a
> single landlord.[97]

Both Creaton and Spratton can be classed as 'areas in which a
significant proportion of the population had achieved
emancipation from the "system of dependency"'.[98] Here Gilbert
was writing about Dissent, and this had existed in these parishes
from the seventeenth century. Independents (Congregationalists)
had first gathered together at Creaton as early as 1688 and a
Meeting House was built in 1694; there was also a dependent and
associated chapel at Spratton.[99] It was not until about 1840 that a
Baptist Church was formed at Creaton. No record can be found
of a Methodist meeting house existing at Creaton or Spratton and
this may well be because Evangelicalism was enthusiastically
practised in a local parish church.[100] Evidence has already been

95 *Inclosure Award, 1782-3*, N.C.R.O., Map 5498.
96 G. Baker, *The History and Antiquities of the County of Northampton*, pt 1 (1822), p.68.
97 Gilbert, *Religion and Society*, p.104.
98 *Ibid.*, p.97.
99 *Creaton Church Book*, N.C.R.O., Creaton Congregational 5, dorse of title page.
100 According to Gilbert, 'the most important reason for the spread of Nonconformity...was
    the "lukewarmness" and negligence of many parish clergymen'. See *Religion and Society*,
    pp.94-5.

given that Evangelical clergy were appointed at Creaton from the middle of the eighteenth century. Therefore worshippers from that village and from nearby Spratton, who were inclined towards Evangelicalism, might have found their spiritual needs supplied by a serious, active ministry in at least one of the two local Anglican places of worship, thus feeling no necessity to form a breakaway Methodist meeting.[101]

Though they can be classed as open villages with landownership in several hands, evidence shows that significant areas of Creaton and Spratton and the private patronage of their churches were owned by Anglican Evangelicals. Private patrons, some of them women, were instrumental in the appointment of successive Evangelicals to the living at Creaton. The Queen's College enclosure award, mentioned earlier, consisted of two allotments totalling just over one hundred acres, forming its College Farm.[102] This may have given Charles Simeon some leverage in the appointment of Jones; perhaps Davenport knew Simeon personally for they had both been students at Cambridge University, though at different times.[103] When Davenport died in 1796, the advowson passed to his widow, who presented the Rev. Robert Young to the living.[104] Both she and Young were willing for Jones to continue as curate of Creaton. However, after the death of Young, Jones himself was instituted to the Rectory of Creaton on 21 January 1829, on the presentation of the Rev. Edmund T. Beynon and Martha, his wife, 'the Patrons in true right'.[105] Mrs Davenport had perhaps sold the advowson to them. Jones resigned as curate of Spratton just before becoming Rector of Creaton

---

101 The situation at Creaton and Spratton was different from the one at Nonington (Kent), mentioned in the previous chapter. That was a close village with large estates owned by two separate families of the landed gentry, who were Orthodox Anglicans. It will be remembered that daughters from one of those families were the first to bring Evangelicalism to Nonington parish church. In so doing they challenged established local traditions of power firmly held in the hands of High Church Anglican landowners. No Dissenting chapel or Methodist meeting house had been registered at Nonington, probably because it was a close village. In the early nineteenth century, when Evangelical religion was expanding rapidly and confidently in other agricultural areas of Kent, the young Plumptre women's success in the Anglican Church at Nonington provided a centre for serious Christianity in the locality.

102 *Inclosure Award, 1782-3*, N.C.R.O., Map 5498.

103 Venn, *Alumni Cantabrigienses*, pt II, II, p.232. C. Davenport, Trinity B.A. 1760. He had been at school in Guilsborough (Northants).

104 *Institutions Book* (1764-1839), N.C.R.O., ML733, p.164.

105 *Ibid*. p.303.

having been a pluralist for eighteen years, from 1810 to 1828, when he held the curacies at both Creaton and Spratton. Significantly, after Jones's resignation in 1833 (also the year of Mrs Ann Bosworth's death), his successor at Creaton was Edward Francis Beynon.

'Francis Beynon' also appeared in the name of the patron of Spratton vicarage, Francis Beynon Hackett. He had inherited the advowson through his grandmother's line.[106] Among the marble memorials in the chancel of Spratton Church are those to his parents, Elizabeth and Andrew Hackett, and his grandparents, Elizabeth (nee Okell) and Francis Beynon. The latter, through his marriage, 'and by successive small purchases,' had 'acquired a considerable estate' at Spratton, which by 1822 was vested in his grandson, Francis Hackett.[107] It can be judged from wording on Elizabeth Beynon's memorial, especially the capitalized 'FAITH' and use of 'assured expectant through Christ', that she was an Evangelical:

> Sacred to the memory of
> Elizabeth Beynon, wife of
> Francis Beynon, esq., of Spratton
> Only daughter of Benjamin and
> Elizabeth-Dorothy Okell
> who after a long Confinement by Unremitted Illness
> Which a true *Christian* FAITH supported her through
> with *Resignation* and *Fortitude*,
> *departed* this life *April* 22nd 1770. Aged 53
> A well assured expectant through CHRIST
> of exchanging it for a *Blessed Eternity*.

Francis Hackett's connection with Mrs Ann Bosworth is mentioned below.

By far the largest enclosure allotment at Creaton went to Robert Andrew, who lived at Harlestone Park, a few miles away. Andrew's awards at (Great) Creaton totalled 334 acres, and at Little Creaton, just over 44 acres. He held the advowson of Harlestone, and also that of nearby Dodford. In addition, he was lord of the manor at Harlestone, and in the early 1830s his Park, which

---

106 G. Baker, *The History and Antiquities of the County of Northampton*, pt.1 (1822), p.68.
107 *Ibid.*

adjoined the Althorp estate, was purchased by Lord Spencer.[108] Andrew was one of the two 'executors of Francis Beynon' who presented 'Robert Crowther, chaplain to the 4th dragoons', to the living at Spratton in 1794.[109]   Beynon's land at Creaton and Spratton was sold to Mr Robert Ramsden who, around 1822, purchased Spratton Place [Hall] and made it his residence; the house had been built by Francis Beynon, no doubt, for his wife and himself.[110] Later evidence here will show that Mr Ramsden and his wife were landed gentry, firm Evangelicals, and played an active part in parochial life until they removed from the parish.

At the time of her death in 1833, Mrs Ann Bosworth had been keeping stock on farms belonging to 'Creaton Rectory, Wills, Mr Ramsden, Mr Hackett, Spratton Vicarage', as well as on her own land at Highgate House.[111] Unlike his forebears, Francis Beynon Hackett was an absentee landlord, and lived at Moor Hall, Sutton Coldfield, in Warwickshire. Francis had inherited the Manor of Spratton,[112] and the advowson of the Parish Church from his mother, and, possibly through the same line of inheritance, he also owned the Manor of Creaton.[113] When enclosure came in 1782-3, the 'Trustees of Eliz. Hackett' were awarded about 98 acres of land at Little Creaton, in the parish of Spratton, adjoining the 62 acres that went to the Vicar.[114] Elizabeth had died by the time Jones was given the curacy of Spratton in 1810, and it was probably Andrew, her eldest surviving son and heir at that time, who agreed Jones's appointment. This generation of the Hackett family might have known him and the Bosworths personally, for Highgate House would have made a convenient place to stay on occasional visits to the parish. A continued family allegiance to Evangelicalism can be safely assumed, for they manifested their support, not only in allowing Thomas Jones to become curate of Spratton, but also in a willingness to lease land to Ann Bosworth. Undoubtedly the Hacketts, and others who held power of freehold in Spratton and Creaton, acknowledged Mrs Bosworth's integrity. The Hackett land, also, was later sold to Mr. Robert Ramsden, who continued

108 J. A. Gotch, *Squires' Homes and other Old Buildings of Northamptonshire* (1939), p.36.
109 Baker, *County of Northampton,* pt 1, p.69.
110 *Ibid.,* p.68.
111 Knight and Clarke, *Valuation.*
112 L. F. Salzman (ed.) *Victoria History of the County of Northampton,* IV (Oxford, 1937), p.104.
113 *Ibid.,* p.106.
114 *Inclosure Award, 1782-3,* N.C.R.O., Map 5498.

the lease with her. Some time before 1820, Francis Hackett sold the advowson of Spratton to the Rev. John Bartlett, of Buckingham.[115] Bartlett became incumbent of Spratton himself in 1823 (to 1861). However, Jones continued as curate there until 1828. As will be shown, Ann Bosworth's granddaughters, Matilda and Selina Owen, were still visiting their relatives at Spratton in the 1840s, and were on friendly terms with the Rev. Bartlett.

3.4.ii Demography of Creaton and Spratton

Apart from the larger landowners, what type of local people were they among whom Thomas Jones conducted his ministry so successfully from his base at Highgate House? The Creaton Militia List for 1819 has supplied the earliest, extant nominal and occupational source for the parish. Of the seventy names contained in it, forty men were labourers or servants, nine were farmers, eight were in trade, twelve were village craftsmen and one was an excise officer.[116] If it can be assumed that several of these men and their families belonged to the Parish Church, then Evangelicalism traversed social divisions within the community. It is likely that females predominated in the congregations of both Maddock and Jones. We have Jones's own evidence that many of his Creaton congregation were poor. Reference will be made to Government Population Returns which confirm that, during Jones's earliest years in the parish, several villagers were agricultural labourers, but also a significant proportion of the population of both parishes were employed in trade, manufacture and handicraft. This three-fold category would have partly comprised small-scale production and an artisan domestic industry in which women's involvement was significant, for they were often important contributors to cottage economy. Trade, manufacture and handicraft brought a degree of economic independence. 'In the early nineteenth century it was the skilled who were overwhelmingly attracted to Evangelical Nonconformity', and the suggestion is that Evangelicalism in the Church of England also brought in artisans: they 'were commonly to be found in church'.[117]

However, Jones left the following useful evidence of two working-class female members of his congregation who were

---

115 Salzman, *V.C.H.*, IV, p.106.
116 *Constable's list of the Parish of Creaton in the Division of Daventry in the County of Northampton* (1819), N.C.R.O., D2837.
117 Bebbington, *Evangelicalism*, p.111.

connected locally with occupations of a different kind.[118] The first concerned 'this daughter of Abraham',

> a good woman, who for many years kept a Turnpike Gate, and who was constantly speaking to all, who came fairly in her way, about redemption, and mercy, Salvation and immortality; and God blessed her faithful exertions to many a poor sinner.

The second was about the wife of a horse-dealer. Her husband, a man 'of the wildest cast, was persuaded one Sunday by some of his neighbours to come to Creaton Church: he was brought to the knowledge and love of God, and became a devoted servant of Christ'. However, it was not until two years later that his wife, 'after having persecuted him' for that length of time because of his Evangelical enthusiasm, decided to accompany him to Church; she 'returned home weeping, and a penitent'. From then on they worshipped there together and 'lived and died most happy in the Lord'. At the end of these anecdotes Jones acknowledged that the laity as well as ministers, 'may win souls to Christ'.

Jones had already been at Creaton Church for fifteen years when he took up the curacy of Spratton, a parish of 2,810 acres. As already suggested, the demography of both parishes can be considered favourable for the growth of Evangelicalism during the early decades of the nineteenth century. Only by giving details can this be confirmed. Unfortunately, there is no extant Militia List for Spratton. The 1811 and 1821 Government Returns for Creaton and Spratton have revealed that there were more women than men in the parishes.

In 1811 at Creaton the total population of 345 contained 161 males and 184 females.[119] There were 75 houses, and of the 87 families occupying them, only 38 were employed in agriculture. Exactly the same number of families worked in trade, manufacture, or handicraft, and 11 were in neither of these categories. By 1811, Jones was also curate of Spratton, and at that time the population there was 896, consisting of 467 females and 429 males. There were 192 inhabited houses, and 89 families employed in agriculture, 82 in trade, manufacture or handicraft, and 34 in neither of these

---

118 In a Manuscript found after his death, quoted in Owen, *Memoir*, pp.87-9.
119 *Abstract of Answers and Returns of Population, 1811*, p.224.

categories.[120] There was a carpet factory within Spratton parish.

During the next ten years of Jones's ministry at Creaton the population increased considerably by 147, to 492, with 257 females and 235 males. The village had expanded by 33 houses, to 108, and their occupying households to 111.[121] Of the 73 additional females in the parish, surely some of this large number would have swelled Jones's congregation. But the pattern of employment also changed significantly. By 1821, 68 families were employed in agriculture, 30 more than in 1811, but there were now only 25 in trade, manufacture or handicraft. In Spratton the trend was similar. There were 20 more houses in the parish, and the population had increased from 896 to 945, with 464 males and 481 females; 115 families were employed in agriculture, which was 32 more than in 1811; a much reduced number of 48 were in trade, manufacture or handicraft, and 51 in neither of these two classes.[122] The growth in population followed the national trend, and the larger number of families in agriculture in both parishes came before innovations in farm machinery produced a tendency towards reduction some twenty or thirty years later. Increased production of home-grown food had been necessary during the war with France, but the local agricultural industry was probably expanding even further to satisfy requirements of developing towns in the county, especially Northampton itself. In both Creaton and Spratton, the number of families in trade, manufacture or handicrafts had reduced perhaps because advancing industrialisation was undercutting some of them. Yet it seems that established loyalties to Jones were so strong that change in employment patterns did not affect his popularity.

The 1841 Census figures show that very little demographic change had occurred in these parishes since 1821. Creaton contained 124 households, with 243 males, and 251 females; the total population had increased by only 2. There was scarcely a household in which one of the men was not an agricultural labourer. A few were carpenters, blacksmiths, brickmakers, or tailors. In Spratton parish, there had also been minimal change; the population had increased by only 11. The number of women had reduced by 5. Of the 490 males, agricultural labourers predominated, and a very small number were farm servants.

120 *Ibid.*, p.228.
121 *Abstract of Answers and Returns, 1821*, p.223.
122 *Ibid.*, p.227.

Among the comparatively few artisans, shoemakers were conspicuous, and probably represented what was still a local cottage industry. By this time, Spratton Parish Church was in the hands of the Rev. Bartlett. It was eight years since Thomas Jones had resigned the living at Creaton.

Despite his growing reputation in wider Evangelical circles, Jones's over-riding ministerial work and care were local, in the parish of Creaton and then for eighteen years as curate for Spratton. In addition to his curate's stipend of £20 a year at Creaton, a supplement of £40 was allowed to him by the Parish.[123] Most of the extra money he earned from his writing was given to further the Evangelical cause or to help people in his community. It can be assumed that, having no upkeep of church accommodation, no wife or family of his own to support and the domestic benefits of living at Highgate House, he could manage on a small income. From his base in the Church at Creaton, Jones;

> transformed the surrounding community, and threw out influences which affected the nation; he was a founder of Sunday Schools, 'Dame-Schools', Sick Clubs, and Clothing Clubs; with the profits from his devotional books, published both in English and Welsh, he built six almshouses for aged widows; through the efforts of the Creaton Clerical Education Society, which he founded, he enabled fifty Evangelical laymen to enter the Ministry; and during the first eighteen years of its work, the Society for Poor Pious Clergymen, which also he created, distributed more than £35,000; while besides all this, he established a post-Easter spiritual Retreat to which for prayer, Bible-study, fellowship and consultation earnest clergymen from several surrounding counties annually repaired.[124]

The 'six almshouses for aged widows' were built in 1825 on waste land overlooking the village green at Creaton.[125] They were later replaced but the original date stone can still be seen as it was incorporated in the brickwork at the front of the new buildings.

123 Longden, *Northamptonshire and Rutland Clergy*, VIII (1940), p.55.
124 Bready, *England Before and after Wesley*, pp.57-8, citing Balleine, *A History of the Evangelical Party*, pp.122-3.
125 Kelly, *Northamptonshire Directory, 1847*, p.2064.

The only reference to local clothing clubs we have in Jones's own hand is contained in his letter to Clara, dated 28 January 1825, when he wrote: 'The clothing business gave more than usual satisfaction this year in all the neighbourhood'.[126]   As already mentioned, Highgate House was the venue for clerical gatherings; its size and position as a coaching inn in the Midlands made it admirably suited for the purpose. Apart from any incentives of increased business, Mrs Bosworth and the other women in her household would have wished to provide a comfortable and congenial atmosphere on these occasions to show their loving support of Jones. He and Evangelicalism were of great significance in all their lives. Chapter 4 will show that many other women in Creaton, Spratton and nearby parishes also played a vital part in the success of Jones's ministry.

3.5 Evangelicalism and Marital Choice

That Evangelicalism could be a strong influence on the choice of a marriage partner is evident in the lives of the only two Bosworth daughters who survived beyond their teens. For an Evangelical in the Anglican Church to marry a Dissenter was considered an infidelity, and even for someone like a Bosworth daughter to wed an Orthodox Anglican would probably have been seen as a betrayal.

Clara Bosworth

Though Clara never married, the letters quoted below indicate that she had two suitors at differing stages of her life. The first was when she was about eighteen. The evidence is that domestic pressure was brought to end the relationship because of the clash between her Evangelicalism and her lover's Dissent, or perhaps his less pious Anglicanism. About ten years later Clara declined the marriage proposal of another suitor, even though he was an Evangelical clergyman. By this time she was twenty-eight and able to decide her own future.

The following two letters were undated but can be estimated to have been written to Clara in about 1816, when she was in her late teens. They were from a Thomas Peck and there is clear evidence of mutual love between them. The letters were well-written and the first was very long. In order to show the full depth of emotion shared by the couple and the unhappiness they suffered

126 Jones to C. Bosworth, 28 January 1825, N.C.R.O., Bos. Coll.

because of Clara's selfless response to her Evangelicalism, it is best to quote them in full.

                                    Northampton, Tuesday night
My dear Clara
Convinced of your attachment to me, in spite of circumstances, I am happy. But I am apprehensive that it would be more prudent, instead of rushing headlong into all the perplexities and sorrows attendant on clandestine affection, to defy the sometimes over-whelming attacks of feeling, and - disclose our love. I leave it however entirely to your determination. If you could be happy in the arms of another, hate your too fond T.P. But if *not*, despair shall henceforth never be an inmate of this bosom! We *may* be happy. This, instead of we *are* completely miserable, is now my Motto. Your attachment to Mr J[ones] I admire. Gratitude demand it. Love him as a Christian, as your friend, as your minister, but especially love him as an adopted father! Could I bear to wound the feelings of such a man? - no! rather let me endure all the agonies of disappointment through life. Oh! Clara! rather than incur the displeasure, perhaps the hatred of your *tried friends - forget, despise* your untried, and comparatively *worthless* admirer. - At all events, never act but in perfect coincidence with their wishes. Your strict adherence to filial duty will throw a lustre upon your character, which will ever render you increasingly dear to me.

If your opinion should agree with mine respecting a discovery of our *mutual affection*, it is my wish that it should be done on the eve of my journey to Town. If a prospect of future comfort succeeds, my Studies will be pursued with avidity and delight, whilst I occasionally steal a glance from my '*cottage maid*'. If on the other hand, the flowers of hope that bloomed but to day, are withered by the blast of morrow - distance will preclude the possibility of seeing you often, and - no! I cannot forget you! my love has become constitutional so that, whilst existence continues, my attachment to my Dear Clara must constitute a part of it. But let me guide my straggling thoughts 'hope sat buoyant on my heart', 'and very pulse beat joy' - *once* I was happy in the possession of every good wish - but now the

morning light gleams upon my joyless pillow and the
bright orb of day declines beneath the western hills,
without yielding a ray of hope to my cheerless bosom. You
too, my dearest Clara, perhaps passed the morning of your
life almost without a sigh; - but you are disconsolate - you
weep, and 'tis for me! Oh! this heart can never be that of
a wretch who could slight love like yours. The sky of my
future life must ever be over-cast with clouds, unless gilded
by a Smile from - *you*.

I should very much like the *pleasure* of anticipating the
pleasure of your company at Guilsboro in the School
Room. I wonder whom I should choose for my partner
in the two first dances. I leave you to occupy half a
moment in considering. Forgive my haste if I expect a
letter from you (as usual) by return of post, wherein I beg
of you to fix a day, *an early day*, when you will see me.
I remain
Your very affectionate - lover
Thomas Peck.[127]

It appears that Clara had already warned Thomas of Jones's
likely reaction to their association and knew full well what the
response of all at Highgate House and her friends would be at the
prospect of their romantic attachment. Thomas's letter was a
heartfelt expression of devotion. Yet, though a secular declaration
of love written in the Romantic style, it was coloured by what
might be seen as language of 'the religion of the heart'. It was full
of passion, with use of terms such as 'overwhelming attacks of
feeling', 'despair', 'love becoming constitutional'. Similar words
often appeared as connotations of Evangelical conversion.
Furthermore, Thomas's sentence 'Oh! this heart can never be that
of a wretch who could slight love like yours' would have fitted well
into an Evangelical sermon acknowledging the love of God.
'Heart' and 'wretch' were very familiar words in the highly
emotional vocabulary of Evangelicalism. Thomas has left us with
no doubt as to the 'circumstances' likely to bar his future life with
Clara. He was fully aware that Jones held a prominent place in her
admiration, loyalty and affection. The problems of the young
couple's differing religious allegiances, which Thomas specifically

127 T. Peck to C. Bosworth, undated, c.1816 (watermark 1813), N.C.R.O., Bos. Coll.

mentioned in his next letter, probably were insurmountable. Clara already knew in her own mind that those to whom she was closest would regard Thomas as an unsuitable match, and she had told him of her misgivings. His own selfless good sense and understanding portrayed a genuine, honourable character and it can be imagined that he might have offered Clara much. Noticeably, Thomas made no specific appeals to God for guidance. This has surely indicated a lesser religious enthusiasm than Clara's, but it is interesting to note that her seriousness did not preclude her dancing, as it did for many Evangelicals. Their romance had been clandestine so far and, unfortunately, Clara's reply must be imagined. It drew this response from Thomas:

> Northampton Monday evening
> Truly sorry am I, my dear Clara, that *you* have felt a pang on *my* account. But I know not how to address you - a strange union of determination and indecision swelled my bosom almost to madness - The storm has however partially subsided, and my mind has relapsed into a kind of habitual melancholy, somewhat perhaps resembling the gloomy appearance of the heavens after a hurricane.
>
> 'Religion is' indeed 'a subject of vast importance' - and whether it is the effect of habit, or the result of principle, I am incapable of deciding, but my *heart bids me dissipate* your ray of hope. And does Clara really hope - and am I fated to extinguish the dying spark?
>
> But why this haste in disclosing my intentions to your friends? If you particularly wish it, my *obedience* shall be immediate. But consideration whispers, the consequences will be unpleasant. And, *should that be the case*, of what avail will be the consent of your friends, whilst *you* discard me as a Dissenter? - Oh! Clara! pity me! What a misfortune is it to be deprived of the sweetest of human enjoyments by a slight difference in religious sentiment!
>
> I wish particularly to see you, and unless I hear again from you, I will be at Spratton Church on Friday night.
> Yours ever,
> Thomas Peck.[128]

---

128 T. Peck to C. Bosworth, undated, c.1816 (watermark 1813), N.C.R.O., Bos. Coll.

Clara's early disclosure to her family and friends caused Thomas
some surprise and a degree of annoyance. Perhaps he did not know
her sufficiently well to realize that, for an Evangelical, 'Religion was
a subject of vast importance', and she would not have passed it off
as a mere excuse for her refusal. Thomas had underestimated her
spiritual devotion, and even asked if it was merely habitual. Though
he judged the 'difference in religious sentiment' between them as
'slight', it was sufficient for Clara to reject his proposal, and to class
him as a 'Dissenter'. But what constituted that difference? It is not
clear why he intended to 'be at Spratton Church on Friday night'.
Did it indicate that Thomas was an Anglican, or was he hoping to
meet Clara outside after some kind of gathering there? Was he an
Orthodox Anglican and not an Evangelical? That this was sufficient
for her to consider him a Dissenter appears somewhat extreme, but
it must be remembered that, conversely, some Orthodox Anglicans
tended to consider Evangelicalism within the Established Church a
strand of Nonconformity.

The Bosworth family's antagonism towards Orthodoxy had
probably been intensified by the controversies that had arisen
between Thomas Jones and Herbert Marsh. Thomas Peck was
writing from Northampton where perhaps he belonged to a
Methodist Church. If this was the case, despite his thinking there
existed only a 'slight difference in religious sentiment' between
them, she, like most other Anglicans, would have classed all types of
Methodist sectarianism as Dissent. An even greater division existed
between them if Thomas's allegiance was to another Dissenting
strand, such as the Congregationalists, or Baptists. At Creaton the
Congregational Chapel was thriving and in Maddock's time there
had been some accession of Anglicans to it. Evidence from the
letter written to Clara by Thomas Jones some years later, when she
was staying at Bath, confirmed that he preferred her not to have too
much to do with Dissenters:

> I should feel more gratified to hear that you attend to your
> satisfaction in the Established Church than that you go
> constantly to a Dissenting Chapel however respectable.
> And I am informed that there is a very good man at one
> of the Churches in Bath. It is a Welsh name, I believe, it is
> Morgan.[129]

There is every reason to suppose that from her earliest days Clara had heard this type of antagonism voiced at Highgate House. Jones expressed his dislike of Dissent when writing many years earlier to his clergyman friend, Mr Griffin. 'They are too fond of Dissenters for me', he declared, of two clerical neighbours.[130]

Would Clara have preserved Thomas Peck's letters throughout her life if she had not wished to keep something tangible that sustained a lingering affection for him? Apart from the irreconcilability of their basic religious differences, what alternative reasons could there have been for Thomas Jones, her family, and her friends to urge Clara not to marry her lover? There may have been other detrimental aspects of Thomas Peck's life or character, but it must be remembered that Clara had been brought up at the centre of local Evangelicalism, under the guidance of the leading Evangelical clergyman in the area. A major concern surely would have been the way in which her marriage to a Dissenter would be perceived by others. Certainly, within the local community, the Bosworth girls were expected to marry men of 'vital' Christianity. The mores of Spratton and Creaton at that time were probably similar to those which, according to Everitt, existed in rural communities during the early part of the nineteenth century. He has written thus of Hayslope, the tight-knit, fictional country parish at the centre of *Adam Bede*.

> In an enclosed community like the one George Eliot described people tend to look more to the past, to custom, to early attachments and impressions, than in a more open society. The past is the principal external avenue open to them, the past of their own local world, of their own 'connexion' and its families. Over the years the early experiences of the community come to be sublimated in its moral code and ideals, and loyalty to these becomes the supreme necessity, the absorbing interest, a claim superior to every external loyalty.[131]

129 Jones to C. Bosworth, 28 January 1825, N.C.R.O., Bos. Coll. Simeon's dictates on the matter were different. Though firm in his view that Dissent was an evil, he justified 'the individual Christian's resorting to a Dissenting chapel if the established pulpit was occupied by a "light, trifling clergyman"', meaning by one who did not declare the 'Gospel truth': see G. F. A. Best, 'The Evangelicals and the Established Church in the early nineteenth century', *Journal of Theological Studies*, N.S., X, Pt.1, April 1959, p.71, citing A. Brown, *Recollections of Conversation Parties with Simeon* (1863), p.224.

130 Jones to Rev. Mr. Griffin, Shrewsbury, 6 November 1799, N.C.R.O., ZB1052/2.

131 Everitt, *Pattern of Rural Dissent*, p.66.

For Clara, primacy of Evangelical principles in personal decisions would have given an even greater awareness of her moral, as well as her spiritual, responsibilities. She must be loyal to Thomas Jones, her family and the Church. Above all, she must be guided by what she felt God wished her to do. Jones often reminded her of this in his letters. This extract is from one he wrote to Clara in June 1821:

> 'Set the Lord always before you.' 'In all things acknowledge him, and he will direct your steps'. 'Look at the ways of grace in the redemption and salvation of perishing sinners, till your heart rejoices in God your Saviour, till your soul is taught to triumph always in Christ Jesus. What are all things else compared with this felicity?'[132]

As usual, biblicism is apparent with quotation marks indicating extracts from the Bible. Here Jones had adapted Psalm 16: 8, 'I have set the Lord always before me', and Proverbs 3:6: 'In all thy ways acknowledge him, and he shall direct thy paths'. One cannot be precise about his penultimate sentence but the phrases are similar to those used in miscellaneous verses from Psalms, John and 2 Corinthians. Thomas Jones was so intimately linked with Clara's family that he would have expected, and been expected locally, to conduct her wedding ceremony at Spratton Church, as he did a few years later for her sister. A difficult situation was inevitable for them all if Clara insisted on marrying Thomas Peck. That, as his wife, she would turn to his sphere of 'Dissent' must have been of major concern.

Was Clara's other suitor regarded by her family and friends as an ideal match for her on grounds of religion? The Rev. David Owen, one of Thomas Jones's Welsh friends, had known the family at Highgate House for a long time and it was his brother John who had married Selina Bosworth, Clara's sister. Selina had died only four years before David Owen wrote to Clara proposing marriage. His offer contained nothing of the amorous fervour expressed in Thomas Peck's letters and was made before real courtship had begun. That these early nineteenth-century letters of proposal, written by two different men to the same young woman, have survived is probably unusual. They are of special value here because

132 Jones to C. Bosworth, 6 June 1821, N.C.R.O., Bos. Coll.

they provide such a striking contrast in style of approach, especially with regard to religion. There can be no better example of how Evangelicals were more pious in their correspondence than non-Evangelicals. Owen's is a substantially different letter from that of Thomas Peck and is somewhat stilted. Like the Reverend Mr Collins and his proposal to Elizabeth Bennet, 'he set about it in a very orderly manner, with all the observances which he supposed a regular part of the business'.[133] The excitable Mrs Bennet urged Elizabeth to accept the clergyman's proposal and was more than a little surprised and disappointed at her daughter's refusal of so fortunate an offer.[134] However, there is no evidence to show that Mrs Bosworth tried to influence her daughter similarly. Owen wanted Clara to see that his intentions were honourable before their 'acquaintance' became more 'intimate'. He was then forty-one and she twenty-eight. The formality of his letter can only be appreciated if it is quoted in full:

Dec. 12, 1826   Old Bodnod, Near Conway

Dear Miss Bosworth
Should the purport of this Letter be not agreeable to your mind, I hope it will not lessen our mutual regard for each other. As I am now permanently settled probably for life, I feel inclined, if that be the will of Providence, to change my condition, provided I could find a person likely to be a help meet for me; and I beg leave to say that I do not know at present of any young Lady, to whom I feel disposed to offer my hand, but yourself. It is right for me also to say, that this is not a sudden thought; for ever since the first time I had the pleasure of seeing you, which is now more than nine years ago, I have always had some faint hopes of this kind; but adverse circumstances, which I need not now particularize, prevented me from indulging them.
    From some distant hints, which I expressed to you some years ago, I should think that you are not altogether ignorant of my attachment to you, but not knowing your

133 J. Austen, *Pride and Prejudice* (1813, 1994 edn), pp.84–5. There is also a striking similarity between David Owen's proposal and that of the fictional Rev. Casaubon to Dorothea Brooke in G. Eliot, *Middlemarch* (1872, 1982 edn) pp.43–4.
134 *Ibid.*, pp.86–8.

mind upon the subject, I do not think it prudent to say much more at present, and besides, for any thing I know, you might already be engaged to another gentleman, and if this be the case, it would be useless for me to enter into any particulars. But if you have no engagement of this kind, I should be very happy to commence a more intimate acquaintance with you. When I was at your house this last time, I once thought of opening to you my mind; but upon second consideration, I preferred to do this in a Letter. I cannot however conclude without telling you openly that the decision of this subject rests entirely with yourself. May He who is the Ruler of hearts, and the wise Disposer of all events, direct your mind in this important concern. In all our undertakings, we should endeavour to know the will of God, otherwise we cannot expect His blessing upon us; and in order to obtain this knowledge, we should seek it by earnest prayer, fully determined through His grace to follow the leadings of Providence as far as we can see them, and striving 'to bring every thought to the obedience of Christ';[135] and then we may reasonably hope that He will be our Guide through life, our Support in death, and our Portion in eternity. It is not only our duty, but our highest privilege, to draw nigh to God that we may obtain the knowledge of His will, for it contains nothing but what is for our good. And moreover He expects His children to consult Him in all their transactions; and though in many things they follow the path which He has ordained for them yet when they do this rashly, without due regard to His will, they sin against Him, and bring themselves into trials and difficulties, which might be avoided by having a single eye towards the obedience to God.

I must now conclude, at the same time requesting you to favor me with an answer as soon as you conveniently can; for, notwithstanding my belief in superintending Providence, I must confess that I feel some degree of anxiety respecting the result of what I have communicated to you in this Letter. I hope your worthy Mother is getting better.

I remain, Dear Miss Bosworth
your very faithful and sincere friend,
David Owen.[136]

We shall never know Clara's inner feelings about this proposal. Yet for some reason she kept the letter, which inevitably contained a degree of sermonizing. She was urged to turn to God for her response, but how did she decide what the Almighty required of her? It can be argued that, whatever her final decision, Clara believed she had reached it through divine guidance. Her reverend suitor, too, could reconcile her rejection with the will of God and probably suffered much less heartbreak than Thomas Peck. There is certainly no impetuosity of sexual emotion about this letter; he expressed 'regard', not love. Yet his sincerity was probably genuine even though his strategy appears rather calculated. Owen wished Clara to know that his intentions were honourable before making more intimate approaches to her. We can only guess her real reasons for not marrying him. Perhaps she felt guided to stay at Highgate House to care for her mother and her late sister's little girls (also David Owen's nieces), by now aged about four and five. On the other hand, the prospect of being 'help meet' to Owen in Wales may have appealed little to her. A degree of irony might be seen in her decision. She had turned down Thomas Peck's proposal because she considered him a 'Dissenter', and then refused a serious offer of marriage from a pious Evangelical clergyman. David Owen never married but survived another forty years after proposing to Clara. 'The wise Disposer of all events' took him from this earth in 1866, at the age of eighty-three. Clara had died eighteen years earlier and was only fifty.

Selina Bosworth

For Clara's sister, Selina, circumstances were very different, and Evangelicalism in her choice of marriage partner was to assume great significance. There can be little doubt that her intended husband, the Rev. John Owen (1788-1867), received universal approval. He was two years younger than his brother David. John Owen was another Welshman who belonged to the Evangelical School in the Established Church.[137] In 1851 he wrote his *Memoir of the Rev. Thomas Jones*, of whom he was a close friend and admirer. It was probably through attending clerical meetings at Highgate House that the Owen brothers came to know the Bosworth girls.

135 From 2 Corinth., 10:5.
136 D. Owen to C. Bosworth, 12 December 1826, N.C.R.O., Bos. Coll.
137 H. Smith, *Early Associations and Recollections*, H. P. Owen Smith (ed.), (St Albans. 1886), quoting letter from Rev. E. Morgan to the author, p.2, N.C.R.O., Bos. Coll.

Selina and John were married by licence at Spratton Church on
10th May 1820, and the ceremony was conducted by Thomas
Jones.[138] At that time Owen was curate of Rothley in Leicestershire,
where he and his wife lived until her death only two years later.
This was after the birth of their second child, Selina. They already
had a daughter, Matilda, but the girls were so young when their
mother died that they could have had little or no memory of her.

Very soon after Selina's death, Owen produced 397 *Lines to the
Endearing Memory of [his] Departed Wife*, which were printed in a
grey-covered booklet. Undoubtedly, a lengthy obituary relating to
his wife's death would have been expected, especially as he was a
pious man of the cloth and practised in literary endeavours.
Descriptions of death-bed scenes were all too common, often in
verse, and their usual style made them vehicles of both warning and
hope.[139] They were also intended to console the bereaved, but the
composing of them served as a calming release of the authors' own
emotions.[140] Predominantly, Owen's *Lines* are a view into Selina's
spiritual world. Even though his commentary was biased by
clerical Evangelicalism, it should not be too harshly judged with
regard to its veracity and motive. The *Lines* opened in true
Evangelical style:

> Far gone to regions of eternal bliss
> Is my Beloved, my first of earthly things.
> She was prepar'd: O blessed be his name,
> Who doeth all things well, forever blest
> His name, forever, ever, ever blest.
>
> From youth, if not from infancy, impress'd
> Had been her mind with fear and love divine,
> Sufficient to preserve her from the ways
> Of sinful folly, and decide her choice
> In a concern of life, the first, but one,
> Her choice of Partner;[141]

Selina was 'prepar'd' for death and perhaps Owen was claiming it

138 N.C.R.O., microfiche 295p/3.
139 Tolley, *Domestic Biography*, pp.80–1.
140 *Ibid.*
141 J. Owen, *Lines to the Endearing Memory of a Departed Wife* (Leicester, 1822), pp.3 & 4.,
    N.C.R.O., Bos Coll.

partly his success. This is mentioned more fully below. His reference to her religious code having been 'sufficient' 'to decide her choice' of him, an Evangelical minister, for her husband might be seen as rather pointed in the light of objections to Clara's marriage to Thomas Peck. Owen wrote in a later footnote that, 'from a child till she was married, [Selina] lived under the care and ministry of the most [E]vangelical Preacher of the day, the Rev. T. Jones...the burden of whose preaching may be considered to be, the entire helplessness of man and the all-sufficiency of the Saviour'.[142]

Owen could not forego an opportunity to use his wife as an example of the way in which even very young children could be taught the 'divine truths'.

> When almost an infant, at least when very young, she was greatly affected, as she told her husband not long before her death, by reading 'Janeway's Token'; that she used to cry and weep much by herself, wishing she was like some of the characters described in that little book. This shews the usefulness and the necessity of giving to children such books as are likely to make a religious impression on their minds. The seed of piety may have been then sewn in her heart, which, after meeting with various checks, and hindrances, at last grew and ripened into eternal life. The human mind cannot be too soon stored with divine truths, communicated best, no doubt at first, by plain and interesting accounts of good characters, particularly those of the Bible.[143]

James Janeway (1636?-1674) was a Nonconformist minister who produced several religious works. His *A Token for Children: being an account of the conversion, holy lives and joyful deaths, of several young children, etc.*, was published in 2 parts in 1671-2. 'This extraordinary collection' went into many extended editions and was still in demand as late as 1892.[144] Early nineteenth-century literature written specially for children was 'a comparatively new genre and [E]vangelicals played a significant part in its

142 *Ibid.*, p.15n.
143 *Ibid.*, p.4n.
144 The Rev. A. Gordon, 'James Janeway (1636?-1674)' in S. Lee (ed.), *Dictionary of National Biography*, XXIX (1892), pp.246-7.

development'.[145] Vividly descriptive and emotional texts, written in a simple literary style, could affect a sensitive child deeply, which was the aim.

   Her husband has given the impression that no-one other than he witnessed Selina's death, and this was probably unusual in Evangelical families. It was customary for a group of relatives to be gathered round the deathbed posing questions carefully designed to extract 'dying testimonies'.[146] There is insufficient space here to quote all that Owen recounted of his conversation with the dying Selina, but these few lines must suffice to show that their last words were in the question and answer style:

> When ask'd, how was her mind,
> The answer was, – 'Tis comfortable –
> 'A sinner great I am, – a Saviour too I have;
> And that is all' – 'And all you want' replied
> Her overjoyous Partner. The next word
> She spoke was this – 'I'm dying;' and she died,
> Or rather slept, – slept in the Lord, until
> The resurrection; and her soul secure.
> Committed by her Husband to the hands
> Of her Redeemer, was then guarded safe
> By hosts of waiting angels to the place
> Prepared by God for his elect, a place
> Of rest, of peace, of glory ineffable. –
> And what indeed but well was all this done.[147]

   At the end of the booklet, in what he called, 'Two or three observations suggested by the foregoing case, which claim particular attention', Owen summarized those of his *Lines* that referred specifically to Selina's spiritual progress.[148]   These observations will be given here as he wrote them. Though they will be preceded by some of the distinguishing lines from the poem, it was in his footnotes that Owen made his view of Selina's internal world of belief most explicit. His booklet would have been produced for private circulation among family, friends and clergy associates, and he seized the opportunity to sermonize in it.

145 Rosman, *Evangelicals and Culture*, p.114.
146 See *Ibid.*, p.103.
147 Owen, *Lines*, pp.8-9.
148 *Ibid.*, pp.24-7.

Through such obituaries many others were able 'to hear both the comfortable words and the challenge to recommitment'.[149]   If the fears of the dying individual were revealed, the community could share and work with them. Belief in his authority as a husband and in his professional superiority probably made Owen feel he had every right to disclose the doubts Selina expressed some months before she died.

Owen's first 'observation' was:

> *That great privileges require great services. This was the deep conviction of my dear Departed.*
>   - though not vigorous,
>   Until of late, few months before she left
>   Her tabernacle of clay: her soul's concern
>   Was then her chief; too long, as she confess'd
>   Too long, too much neglected. Light divine
>   Illumin'd then the scenery within,
>   And shew'd the turns and motions of a heart,
>   Too much enslav'd to worldly things, too little
>   Devoted to its God, and too neglectful
>   Of privileges great as e'er enjoy'd.[150]
>   (b) The burden of sin, the contrite heart, was felt;
>   Fear, jealousy and hope by turns prevail'd;
>   Peace, comfort, joy but sparingly vouchsaf'd.[151]

The footnote, marked (b) is worth quoting in full:

> (b) Several months before her illness, she betrayed more than usual concern for her soul's welfare. One evening she disburdened her mind most freely to her Husband, which delighted him not a little. What distressed her mind was the little use she made of her privileges. She spoke something to this purpose:- 'No one has ever been more highly privileged than I have. Before and after I came to this place, I have enjoyed the advantage of hearing the truth; but have not profited as much as I should. I am afraid there is no mercy for me, because I have been so unfruitful.' When told that God was abundant in mercy, and ready to

149 Rosman, *Evangelicals and Culture*, p.103.
150 See Luke 12:48, 'For unto whomsoever much is given, of him shall be much required.'
151 Owen, *Lines*, pp.4–5.

receive and pardon every true penitent, 'Mine', she said 'is
no common case. I have been highly favoured, and yet
have neglected the one thing needful too much.[152] I have
not served God as I should. I have been too much taken up
with the concerns and vanities of the world'. - It was said
to her in reply, that her confessions were such as they ought
to have been, and the stronger these views were the better,
and that such a conviction alone could lead her to Christ,
for his *free* salvation. - Be it remembered, these were the
confessions of a person in conduct strictly moral, who
attended regularly to the common duties of Christianity. It
was the religion of the heart that she found herself
deficient in; what pressed so hard on her mind was the
want of devotedness to God.[153]

To his Evangelical readers, Owen's disclosure of his wife's
expressions of guilt and ideas of her own inadequacies would have
been acceptable. Today they sound rather pitiful. Almost certainly
Selina had little to reproach herself for. She had borne two children
in the same number of years and, if like many other mothers she
also assisted her husband in his work, she must have had little time
for her own quiet, religious introspection.[154] Owen was rather
judgemental and patronizing at this point, and in some other parts
of his *Lines*, in order to convey his Evangelical message.
Furthermore, he was letting the world know that he had been the
one to guide Selina aright. He had led her to confession of her
faults and to subsequent full conversion. She had died happy in
assurance that the 'promise of gratuitous pardon was all her
Salvation'[155]. The extract from the footnote carried an additional
message: to be 'strictly moral' and to attend 'regularly to the
common duties of Christianity' were not the full expression of
Evangelicalism. This was the subject of his next 'observation':

*That true religion is nothing less than the devotedness of the heart
to God.* Of this my late companion was very sensible. A
deficiency in this respect, in addition to a defective

152 See Luke, 10:42.
153 Owen, *Lines*, p.5n.
154 See Davidoff & Hall, *Family Fortunes*, p.90.
155 Owen, *Lines*, p.26n.

improvement of privileges, was the only thing that distressed her mind.[156]

Selina felt guilty that Evangelicalism had not been of supreme significance in her life. 'With no small concern did she lament that the world had too much of her heart, and God too little'.[157] In his opinion, her devotedness to God had at one time lacked that vital, spiritual centrality more fully explained by Hannah More in her notion of '*The religion of the heart*':

> *There* it subsists as the fountain of spiritual life; *thence* it sends forth, as from the central seat of its existence, supplies of life and warmth through the *whole frame...there* is the vital principle which animates the whole *being* of a Christian.[158]

Owen's *Lines* continued to follow the customary style. They contained 'hints' for those who eventually would face death themselves.[159] But surprisingly, these were addressed specifically to Selina's relatives and friends in the footnote quoted below, many of whom must have lived in the Spratton area:

> She gives not way a moment to an anxious thought,
> Most willingly resigning to God.
> The care of all she loved,(n) being occupied
> In higher things, in setting forth the praise.
> Of him who sav'd and glorified her soul.[160]

Note (n) reads:

> Her love to her friends, especially to her relations, was very great. The evening preceding the day of her departure, she spoke of them in the most touching manner, being greatly comforted with the hope of seeing them in Heaven. She mentioned many of them by name, the living as well as the dead. With respect to some of the living, she expressed

156 *Ibid.*, p.24.
157 *Ibid.*, p.25n.
158 More, *Practical Piety*, p.13.
159 See Tolley, *Domestic Biography*, p.81.
160 Owen, *Lines*, pp.16-7.

great anxiety, fearing they were not in a safe state; and more
than once requested her Husband to pray for them. 'I am
afraid', she said, 'that God's dispensations are not blessed to
them, that they are too neglectful of the one thing needful'.
The possibility of not seeing them in glory seemed too
much for her mind to bear. Let all her relatives and friends
take this to heart. Not to make the soul's concern the one
thing needful in her judgement, and according to scripture
too, will exclude us from heaven: and one of the many
mortifications and disappointments which the lost shall
experience, will be that of never seeing those whom once
they greatly loved in this world.[161]

According to her husband, Selina's wish had been for him to
pray for those she considered not to be in 'a safe state', and most
likely she would not have wanted him to disclose that she had
named names. It would be interesting to know if her relatives at
Highgate House thought it a betrayal of Selina's confidences. On
the other hand, they might have been willing to accept that
Evangelical activism predominated over verbal intimacies. But who
were the ones Selina named? The question may well have led to
accusations and searching of consciences. However, a death in the
family usually brought its members closer together in mutual grief
as they accustomed themselves to the thought that heaven was the
place where they would all be reunited.[162]

The last of Owen's 'observations' summed up the basic
Evangelical beliefs which her husband had seen finally embraced by
Selina moments before her death. Here, more than anywhere else
in the *Lines*, there must be the caveat that the words were not
written by the individual concerned and that a cleric had used an
opportunity to sermonize, as expected. Owen's 'observation' will
be given in full after those of his lines which refer most concisely
to Selina's assurance of God's reconciliation to sinners. Clearly, he
saw himself as a terrestrial instrument of her salvation.

> To strengthen more her confidence in God,
> His willingness to save was brought to view.
> That God was ready to be reconciled,
> She was assured, yea reconciled to Her,

161 *Ibid.*
162 Tolley, *Domestic Biography*, p.83.

If only she desired his peace, and wish'd
To be for ever His. God's word was read
Where t'is declared, that He in Christ his Son,
Hath reconciled unto Himself the world,
Imputing not to them their trespasses(f)
Exclaim she did, - 'That, that will do for me,
'Imputing not to them their trespasses.'
So filled with peace and comfort was she now,
So elevated 'bove all doubts and fears,
That she addressed her partner thus -
'My *dear* Husband, *dear* Husband, this you'll have,
'This consolation, this, yea this at least,
'That you have been the means of saving one,
'One sinner, and that one your wife.' [163]

(f) 2 Corinthians, v.19.

Such dramatic dialogue was typical of the contemporary Evangelical literary genre that recounted pious deaths, but it is difficult not to regard some of it as fictional.

Owen's concluding 'observation' ran thus:

That a free gospel is alone suitable to an awakened sinner. This was also most strikingly exemplified in the case of my dear Partner. Nothing suited her wants but an entire free promise of forgiveness and acceptance with God through the merits of the Redeemer: it was the only thing that removed her burden and relieved her mind. The promise of gratuitous pardon was all her Salvation. The preciousness of the gospel is never so impressively seen, as when it comforts and cheers a mind, fully sensible of its demerits, on the borders of eternity. O, who can declare the value of that, which can fill with joy and peace a Soul that is deeply conscious of its sins and unworthiness! But how little is known of its value! The truth is, that the Gospel is one of those things which can alone be really learnt and understood by *experience*. None but a truly convinced sinner can appreciate its worth, can feel and see its suitableness to the necessities of our state. When there is a clear insight into the wickedness and depravity of the heart, and a clear view of sin in its deformity and obnoxiousness to God, then nothing can bring substantial relief but a dispensation of *free* grace.[164]

In this summing up of his late wife's firm desire for God's grace John Owen reduced Evangelical doctrine to the essentials.[165] He firmly believed that Selina's response to his ministry had at the last brought her a happy death. As we already know, she was buried beside her two younger sisters near the pathway in Spratton churchyard. One of them had died only about sixteen months previously.

3.6 The Next Generation

A letter written to Matilda Bosworth (Thomas's wife) in November 1842, has provided firm evidence that George Bugg's daughter, Eliza, continued the close family association with those at Spratton. Having recovered from a serious illness, she informed Matilda:

> I have indeed been brought from the very gates of death; but I may also say I have been very near the Gates of Heaven. The joys I experienced in the midst of my bodily sufferings were at times beyond all expression. - But oh! the anguish of mind I endured on account of sin and a view of my deserving ever-lasting destruction on account of it, I think I can never forget. Oh that the remainder of my days may be spent to the Glory of Him who hath loved us and given himself for us...I am sorry to say Papa has not been well lately, he has an attack of Influenza...With kind regards to Mr. Bosworth and first love to yourself.
> Believe me, My dear Mrs Bosworth,
> very affectionately yours
> Eliza Bugg. [166]

Here again we have an insight into the internal world of another believer, albeit the daughter of an Evangelical clergyman. Crucicentrism is apparent; the doctrine of Christ's substitutionary atonement was clearly established in Eliza's spirituality. Joyous

164 Owen, *Lines*, pp.26-7.
165 Knight, *The Nineteenth-century Church*, p.50.
166 E. Bugg to M. Bosworth, 22 November 1842, N.C.R.O., Bos. Coll.

anticipation of heaven had eased her physical suffering but she still recognized need for perseverance. Such written commentaries by Evangelicals after recovery from illness were stereotypical.

Matilda and Selina Owen remained very much part of the Bosworth family. Their Aunt Clara played a significant part in the children's upbringing during the years immediately following their mother Selina's death. The evidence is that they lived at Highgate House for much of the time until their father married again, therefore Thomas Jones must have figured prominently in their early lives also. When the girls were about the ages of nine and ten, Clara became very concerned about their education and had made this the 'main subject' of a letter to her brother-in-law. Presumably she, and perhaps Jones, had been teaching them, but in this reply Owen indicated his wish for the situation to alter, though he had done little about the situation so far.

> I must first speak on the main subject of your letter... One of the reasons that induced me to change my condition, was the intention of giving my children a domestic education. Situated as I now am, having no very extensive clerical charge, I think it but proper and right that I should devote some of my time to the instruction of my children. Circumstances, arising mostly from what may be called accidental occupations have hitherto, since my marriage, hindered my intentions...And when I return, if the Lord pleases, I shall commence seriously the undertaking...Their education must be pursued regularly at home or from home. Of your kindness I am deeply sensible.
>
> You have done far more for them than I have done and I must now do my part...They must therefore be prepared to return to Quinborough about the middle of next month. If I live, and if the Lord will enable me I intend that they should finish their education at some respectable school.[167]

Clearly, Owen's second marriage had been partly one of convenience. In August 1845, the Rev. Owen became vicar of

---

167 J. Owen to C. Bosworth, written from Blackpool, 20 September 1831, N.C.R.O., Bos. Coll. He had taken three services on the previous Sunday at Preston, a town of 'immense cotton factories', in 'one of the new churches...large, well built, but difficult for preaching owing to the echo. It was well attended, especially by the poor'.

Thrussington, Leicestershire. Matilda and Selina still visited their
Aunt Matilda and Uncle Thomas at Spratton when they could, to
assist with their growing family of four children. They also gave
very active and useful support to their father in Church matters:
'The dear girls are now such helps to me in the Sunday School and
in other things, that I cannot well spare them *both* at the same time,'
he wrote. This was in answer to a request from Thomas Bosworth
in March 1843 when he and his wife needed assistance, probably
after the birth of their son, whom they named Thomas Jones
Bosworth.[168] Their firstborn had been a daughter, Helen. In her
formative years she, too, was open to influence from her relations
and the Rev. Thomas Jones, for he was still living with them. A
letter dated March 1846, from Matilda Owen to her relatives at
Spratton when she was about twenty-five, contained 'a hymn for
Helen to learn.'[169] Evangelicals realized the importance of ensuring
that their faith was carried from one generation to the next.[170]
Many Evangelicals regarded 'their excessive watchfulness' of young
relatives as part of their activism, 'regarding themselves as divinely
appointed spiritual supervisors'.[171] Something of this attitude can
be seen in another letter Matilda Owen wrote to her Aunt Clara
concerning Helen and Tom:

> I have another little hymn for Helen and Tom to learn. I
> think particular care should be taken in always making a
> distinction between them, concerning poetry and sacred.
> They should never be allowed to repeat the latter but in
> serious devout manner. They are not too young to have
> them directed at all times in a proper way. They are not too
> young to know that they are wicked and naughty by nature
> and that they need to be made good. Dear little creatures it
> is an important office and great responsibility to have them
> to train up.[172]

Here Matilda was expecting adult seriousness from very young
children, but this was not unusual.[173] Such expectations were

168 J. Owen to T. Bosworth, 29 March 1843, N.C.R.O., Bos. Coll.
169 M. Owen to M. Bosworth, March 1843 [sic], N.C.R.O., Bos. Coll.
170 Davidoff & Hall, *Family Fortunes*, pp.108-9.
171 Rosman, *Evangelicals and Culture*, p.99.
172 M. Owen to C. Bosworth, dated merely 'Tuesday night', N.C.R.O., Bos. Coll.
173 See Rosman, *Evangelicals and Culture*, p.99.

evident in Mrs Sherwood's *The History of the Fairchild Family*, a very popular fictional work for children, written in three parts and designed to convey serious Evangelical messages.[174]   Probably the book was well known in the Bosworth family. This short extract from it indicates that, like Helen and Tom, the Fairchild infants were taught hymns: 'Mr Fairchild said, "It is a fine morning, my little ones: we will take a walk to the top of the hill and sit there, under the shade of the trees: and we will sing a hymn of praise to God"'.[175]   In addition, Mrs Sherwood's narrative clearly illustrates that Mr Fairchild had no doubt concerning his children's ability to understand the doctrine of total depravity, which he taught them regularly.   Here he began in terms of endearment after they had been reading from the Bible: '"You will find by these verses, my dear children', said Mr Fairchild, 'that the heart of every man is entirely and utterly corrupt; and that there is no good in us whatever: so that we cannot, without God's help, think even one good thought"'.[176]   On another occasion this is how he introduced a time of family prayer: '"O, Lord, hear the prayers of us poor wicked children and give us clean and holy hearts"'.[177]

Communications from Matilda Owen to her aunt Clara at Spratton also indicated a continuing concern for Mr Jones.   But evidence from a letter she wrote to Matilda Bosworth in Feb. 1846, after a visit to Spratton, shows that they were all on friendly terms with his successor, the Rev. Bartlett.   Yet Evangelicalism was in danger of gradually being replaced by Higher Churchmanship under his leadership there.   Matilda Owen had been reluctant to report this to her father when she returned to Thrussington. 'Please remember me to Mr Bartlett', she wrote, 'I did not tell how ultra orthodox he was in commencing lent so early.'[178]   No precise explanation of this last statement can be offered here. It can only be suggested that either Jones or Bartlett had been following the practices of one of the early churches in which the forty days of Lent included or excluded Saturdays and Sundays and Holy

174 M. M. Sherwood, *The History of the Fairchild Family, or the Child's Manual, being a Collection of Stories calculated to show the Importance and Effects of a Religious Education,* Parts I (1818), II (1842) & III (1847).

175 Sherwood, *The Fairchild Family*, Part I, (1879 edn), p.3.

176 *Ibid.*, p.13.

177 *Ibid.*, p.16.

178 M. Owen to M. Bosworth, 20 February 1846, N.C.R.O., Bos. Coll.

Week.[179] Matilda Owen had already mentioned a few years earlier, in March 1843, that the Oxford Movement were beginning to gain ground in the Thrussington area. This is the way she viewed the change:

> Papa has gone to a clerical meeting in Rothly...about his Lent provision - they are to discuss fasting and Saints days. All the Clergy - especially the young men about here I truly believe are Puseyites. I cannot think what will become of our own poor Church but I feel sure of this if such fooleries as are now practising in this neighbourhood continue, all the truly pious people will turn Dissenters.[180]

J. Shelton Reed's *Glorious Battle* has shed light on Matilda's comments concerning the 'fooleries' she knew were gradually being introduced locally by 'Puseyites'. These could have been any of the several Anglo-Catholic innovations concerning church furnishings, forms of worship and frequency of church services, new patterns of dress for clergy and choir, described by Shelton Reed.[181] For example, a litany desk, a credence table, candles and a coloured altar cloth may have been introduced, together with chanted psalms and intoned prayers; perhaps a surpliced choir had appeared and the minister had taken to wearing an embroidered stole over his surplice.[182] Various outward marks of reverence could have been revived, like 'bowing to the altar or at the name of Jesus or the Gloria Patri, turning east for the creed, and the like'.[183] And maybe the local clergy were proposing more strict observance of fasts and feasts.

In 1849 Matilda Owen married the Evangelical Rev. Harry Smith, Vicar of Christ Church, St. Albans, who had been born into a farming family at Little Creaton. Selina did not marry and continued to help her father at Thrussington, where she was a district visitor. Her brother-in-law Harry's memoir, *Early Associations and Recollections*,[184] has given this and other information

179 See S. M. Jackson (ed.), *The New Schaff-Herzog Encyclopedia of Religious Knowledge*, vol. IV (Michigan, 1967 edn), p.282.
180 M. Owen to M. Bosworth, March 1843 [sic], N.C.R.O., Bos. Coll.
181 J. Shelton Reed, *Glorious Battle: the Cultural Politics of Victorian Anglo-Catholicism* (Nashville, Tennessee, 1996.)
182 *Ibid.*, p.30.
183 *Ibid.*, pp.30-1.
184 H. Smith, *Early Associations and Recollections*, p.61.

about Selina and Matilda in their last years:

> I must not close this chapter without some brief allusion to
> Mr Owen's two daughters. The elder – my own dear wife
> (of whose goodness I dare not venture to speak) was taken
> to her rest during the early part of her father's illness; the
> younger sister, Selina Bosworth Owen, was spared to the
> happy end of that long and painful period – faithfully and
> kindly to tend her aged parent, and for some years after
> laboured on in the parish, till it pleased God to call her also
> to rest, after a short illness, December 5th, 1878, and she
> was laid in the same tomb with her father, in the
> churchyard at Thrussington, where they had been so much
> beloved by the friends and neighbours of that village.[185]

Noticeably, Selina was not buried at Spratton near her mother.
Smith's memoir has left an enchanting picture of the local scenery
and way of life in Spratton and Creaton during the early nineteenth
century until he left home. His allusions to women who
worked for the Evangelical cause in these and other nearby
communities when he was a boy have been useful supplements to
other evidence. Their names will occur at appropriate points in the
next chapter.

Even when Thomas Jones Bosworth was in his early twenties,
his cousin Selina Owen, by now turned forty and writing from
Christ Church to him at Spratton after her sister Matilda's recent
death, was still concerned about his 'spiritual welfare', as this
extract shows:

> Sept. 29, 1863
> My dear Tom
> Though I am truly tried with trouble I must send you a few
> lines on your Birthday to assure you that I shall feel a deep
> interest both in your temporal and spiritual welfare; in the
> latter a peculiar interest. I cannot tell you dear Tom what
> *deep* waters I have held to Jesus through since last we met.
> Dear Papa is still at times very much depressed and nervous.
> Oh I do desire that God may in mercy spare him, and
> restore one *so dear*. I seem to have been deprived of my

185 *Ibid.*, p.85.

dearest ones at once, but I must be still and say 'it is the Lord'.[186] What I have to do is to pray for submission. May you never rest until you know that God in whom we *live* and *move* and *have* our *being*.[187] Think of my *precious Sister* and your dear Cousin. How suddenly was she [taken], the trial of separation is *most difficult to bear*, and what would it be if we could not think of her as in a better world. Her loss can *never be total*. Your dear Mamma is now with us. The dear children are pretty well. Mr. Smith is now just gone over to Welford, indeed he has a trial. I am now sitting by dearest Papa, his state gives me great anxiety. I can only leave all with the Almighty and pray that I may profit from my *severe trials*. I think of your *tried* cousin. I hope you do...Have you seen my dear old house lately?[188] I think of it with *painful pleasure*.
Your truly affectionate cousin,
Selina B. Owen.[189]

The tone was somewhat admonitory and warning, with much spiritual expression, and signalled Selina's fear that Evangelicalism was becoming less significant in the life of this male descendant of the family. However, what Selina saw as Tom's backsliding may not have been a declining interest in religion, but his response to changing ideology. By the 1860s Evangelical thought was turning to ideas of heavenly reward rather than hellish retribution.[190] For Evangelicals, Jesus was beginning to be seen not as 'the stern judge of humanity and the victim in the transaction of substitutionary atonement', but as a 'friendly big brother, waiting to welcome the faithful to his family in heaven'.[191] Some time later Selina wrote to Tom again enclosing 'the best of books', the Bible, with her best wishes and love, hoping that he 'may prove [himself] worthy of the name' he bore.[192] From Selina's comments, it seems he was always

186 Quoting 1 Sam, 3:18 & John, 21:7.

187 See Acts, 17:28.

188 Meaning Highgate House, which had been sold by auction on 8 October 1858 as part of a 'Valuable Freehold and Tithe Free Estate' of land, etc., including 11 cottages: see Sale Cat., N.C.R.O., D1562.

189 S. Owen to T. J. Bosworth, 29 September 1863, N.C.R.O., Bos. Coll.

190 See Knight, *The Nineteenth-century Church*, pp.57-8; also Bebbington, *Evangelicalism*, p.145.

191 Knight, *The Nineteenth-century Church*, p.60.

192 S. Owen to T. J. Bosworth, c.1864, N.C.R.O., Bos. Coll.

dilatory in writing to his relations.[193] Nevertheless, on the same ledger stone in Spratton churchyard that bears his parents' names can be discerned 'Thomas Jones Bosworth and his wife, Annie'.

193 S. Owen to T. J. Bosworth, 16 April 1878, N.C.R.O., Bos. Coll.

Chapter 4

WOMEN'S EVANGELICAL ACTIVISM
IN CREATON, SPRATTON AND DISTRICT

This chapter considers mostly the united response of women in Creaton, Spratton and neighbouring villages to calls for local Evangelical activism. Requests for female assistance came from The Church Missionary Society and The British and Foreign Bible Society, two national organizations for mission and philanthropy that held great religious significance in communities throughout England. Evangelicals, always anxious to remain in a state of grace, feared complacency. This could be partly avoided by active efforts to convert others, disciplined conduct in everyday life, hard work and lack of pride. Many women saw that these requirements could be fulfilled through sustained missionary efforts in their own parishes. However, voluntary work was impossible for countless working-class wives, mothers and daughters whose families depended for survival on their earnings outside the home, or the income they provided from their cottage industries. Wealthier female parishioners were likely to have the opportunity to exhibit Evangelical virtues through various kinds of mission among their poor neighbours. For many women, missionary work promoted their independence, widened their social contacts and was a diversion from the boredom of domestic routine.[1] However, what Anne Summers has called 'the argument from boredom', that wealthy women 'busied themselves with the poor because they had nothing else to do', should be used with care. It is 'belittling and insulting' to female visitors to suggest that they had few other ways of filling the leisure hours gained through employment of servants; they could have occupied themselves with activities of a much more self-indulgent nature.[2] Surprisingly, it was only when all-male committees running some religious philanthropic organizations recognized their inability to achieve the desired results without female help that they took official action for women to become involved. Evidence has shown that, even

1 S. Lane, *Forgotten Labours, Women's Bible Work from 1804-1895, with particular reference to the British and Foreign Bible Society*, unpublished M.A. dissertation, Bristol Univ. (1994), p.7.

2 A. Summers, 'A home from home - women's philanthropic work in the nineteenth century', in S.Burman (ed.), *Fit Work for Women* (London, 1979), p.38.

though they were vital to the operation of both the Church Missionary Society and the British and Foreign Bible Society, women accepted male supervision of their activities and worked to the rules which men formulated. It was often in their own local communities that women 'took their first, frequently timid steps in charitable institutions'.[3] Because of the numbers involved in the Northamptonshire district centred on Creaton, especially in the work of the Bible Society, united female activism on the scale that occurred was witnessed there for the first time. The commitment of local women to regular visiting was conspicuous and openly confirmed their dedication to Evangelical mission.

4.1 Creaton Branch of the Church Missionary Society

The Church Missionary Society (originally called the 'Society for Missions to Africa and the East instituted by Members of the Established Church') had been founded in 1799. From the start, members of the Clapham Sect supported the prominent Evangelical clergy involved in the Society's formation.[4] Its early years were controversial and there were also difficulties in finding men willing and able to act as missionaries.[5] However, from 1812 new enthusiasm and self-confidence led to the formation of associations in different parts of the country, and in 1816 the Society began publishing its *Quarterly Papers* with the aim of winning active interest from children and the working classes.[6] In 1817 the Creaton Branch of the organization was set up.

In addition to Creaton and Spratton, the local Branch encompassed several other villages in the area - Guilsborough, Althorpe, Pitsford, Clipstone, Cottesbrook[e], Brixworth, Scaldwell, Church Brampton with Chapel Brampton, Ravensthorpe, West Haddon, Winwick, Draughton, Old, and Hollowell. As Thomas Jones and his parish were at the hub of Evangelicalism in this part of the Midlands, it was appropriate for the Branch to bear Creaton's name. There are eight extant Annual Reports issued by the Creaton Branch, but the earliest of these relates to activities during the fifth year of its operation, from May 1822 to May 1823. The other Reports we have cover only seven of the years during the

---

3 Prochaska, *Women and Philanthropy*, p.23.
4 Elbourne, 'The foundation of the Church Missionary Society', pp.249-50; Overton, *The English Church in the Nineteenth Century*, p.258.
5 *Ibid.* pp.257-262.
6 *Ibid.*, p.263.

period 1823-4 to 1830-31; that for 1829-30 is missing.[7] With the
exception of the one delivered in 1828, when he was ill, the yearly
summaries of activities were written by the Rev. Thomas Jones,
Secretary of the Branch, and read by him at the Annual Meetings.

The Fifth Report of the Creaton Branch was 'Read at a Meeting
held at Spratton Church, Northamptonshire, on Tuesday, May 27th,
1823.'[8] There is no mention of any women being present and
possibly females were not expected or encouraged to attend,
though the printed annual reports would surely have been made
available to them. As indicated below, this *Report* bore testimony to
the subordinate role played by women in their work for the
organization at local level and has provided evidence that within
the Creaton Branch, as generally in Anglican Evangelical circles at
this time, females were thought of as 'the weaker vessels'. Such
attitudes were reinforced by the Bible. 'Ye wives, be in subjection
to your own husbands;' can be found in 1 Peter, 3:1; and 'Ye
husbands, dwell with them according to knowledge, giving honour
unto the wife, as unto the weaker vessel,' follows soon after, at verse
7. Typically, all three officers and twelve committee members
elected at the Meeting were men. The *Report* admitted that the
total amount raised during the year had not been so large as 'on
previous occasions', and it was regretted that the 'diminution' had
been produced by 'unavoidable circumstances'.[9] Thomas Jones was
careful not to blame the women for this in his report.   He
continued:

> We must not despond at any discouragement that may
> meet us. We are not to expect that such work as the
> Missionary cause shall go forward without opposition...[10]
> Shall we then be discouraged by the weakness of the
> *Instruments* that carry on the work, for it is chiefly carried
> on by the weaker vessels. No, they are in many respects the
> fittest instruments for such work. They often excel in

7   All in N.C.R.O., Bos. Coll., and printed in Northampton.

8   *The Fifth Report of the Creaton Branch in aid of the Church Missionary Society for Africa and
      the East* (Northampton, 1823).

9   Probably reflecting that 1822-23 had been a period of particular agricultural distress.

10   There may have been local 'opposition', as Thomas Sikes (1767-1834), vicar of
      Guilsborough, was a strong member of the High Church Party and 'known locally as
      "the Pope"': see Reardon, *Coleridge to Gore*, p.35-7; also Moorman, *History of the Church*,
      pp.309-10.

fidelity, skill, zeal and diligence: Let them say what can poor feeble instruments like us do in such a great work? Recollect, that it was a woman that saved Moses, and Moses saved the lives of all Israel, and Israel saved the world; for out of Israel came the great deliverers of mankind. Let faithful females then go forward, they know not yet, of what great blessing they may be made to this world.[11]

Though the female supporters were given credit for their excellent qualities, nevertheless there was a patronizing element in Jones's reference to them, almost as if he found it necessary to justify women's involvement and had to pander to the social attitudes of his male colleagues. But did the women consider themselves weaker vessels? Certainly, the female 'Penny Collectors' should not have been classed as such. Their vital work for the Society was probably at times quite arduous both physically and emotionally, for it involved going from door to door raising penny contributions from those who, in some cases, may well have been almost destitute. Though Mrs Bosworth was an annual subscriber but not a penny collector herself, Clara was, and it must be questioned whether they and others were really happy for such stalwarts of their own sex to be classified as 'poor' and 'feeble'. It is likely that several of the female annual subscribers and collectors were local personalities in their own rights, of fairly substantial, independent means, and could claim to be more educated than some of the men attending the Annual Meeting.

The Penny Collectors named in the *Fifth Report* totalled twenty-six; there were nineteen women and seven men. Between them they collected in the sixteen adjacent parishes. Probably many of the women collectors were relatives of local farmers. Extant sources for nominal linkage are few therefore it has been difficult to tie up female collectors from Creaton and Spratton with men of the same surname. An early nineteenth-century tithe list for Creaton, and an 1837 valuation showing owners of land and other property in Spratton have provided a small number of surnames.[12] Three of these can be tied to Creaton Branch

---

11   *Fifth Report* (1823), p.10.
12   See *Valuation of the Lands, Buildings and Property within the parish of Spratton in the County of Northampton made 30 Nov. 1837*, N.C.R.O., 295p/71, and *Payment of Tithes, Creaton, 1800-50*, N.C.R.O, 90p/38.

Committee members and they, in turn, to three women collectors. Three other women's surnames can be linked with male signatures on a letter (1830) to Sir James Langham of Cottesbrooke Hall from his farming tenants in the area.[13] The 1819 Constable's (Militia) List for Creaton, already mentioned, has given the names and occupations of seventy men in the parish, but none of them had the same surname as any of the female collectors. Most likely several of their households were among the poor donating their pennies.

The Penny Collectors for Little Creaton were Miss Bosworth (Clara), and Mr Smith; they had raised £2.7s.8d. Miss Cook had collected £3.10s.0d. in Spratton itself. When added to the contributions gathered by three other females, and a man who was probably the husband of one of them, the total for Spratton parish was £17.11s.4d. If we assume that they had collected a penny a week from each house visited, this total had come from about 81 households. In a parish containing almost 200 dwellings, this represented approximately 40 per cent. It cannot be judged how much pressure was applied locally to urge people to contribute, but both rich and poor could have been subject to forceful persuasion from collectors, the pulpit, printed tracts, or from their families and friends.[14] It must be remembered that this was an Anglican organization and that local Dissenters may have been contributing to their own missionary societies. Furthermore, a certain proportion of the local population were likely to have been unattached to any denomination.

In Creaton parish there were only two Penny Collectors for the Church Missionary Society during the year ending May 1823. A Mrs Clayson had collected £6.8s.1d., and a Mr Orland £2.12s.0d.in the twelve months, making a total of £9.0s.1d. This averaged 41 pennies per week, and, again assuming this was a maximum of a penny per house visited, it had come from about 45 per cent of the 110 households estimated to be in the parish at this time. From the odd halfpenny that has cropped up in the figures, it might be assumed that occasionally a contributor was unable to afford a penny out of a very meagre income, and the possibility of additional small change being emptied from pocket or purse is a less likely explanation. If the former was the case, then a larger number of families may have contributed but, in any event, the

13 *Letter.* 18 male tenants to Sir James Langham, 6 December 1830, N.C.R.O., L(C)1181.
14 Prochaska, *Women and Philanthropy*, p.39.

Creaton and Spratton inhabitants had been generous in such hard times. As the collectors almost certainly knew the personal circumstances of most people they visited, an intimate and sympathetic relationship was more likely to have been fostered here than in towns and cities. Several generations of the same families had lived in villages like Creaton and Spratton; the Bosworths immediately come to mind. Collectors and penny subscribers alike were familiar with the vagaries of country life. Though some collecting rounds in these parishes were perhaps not extensive, a number of the houses were quite scattered and the 'feeble instruments' were expected to collect weekly in all winds and weathers.

The Missionary Society's funds were also swelled considerably by annual subscriptions from those more affluent members of local communities who probably did not wish, or would not have been able to act as collectors. Significantly, of the twenty-four annual subscribers named in the 1823 list for the Creaton Branch, seventeen were men,[15] and only seven were women. Prochaska has made reference to the difficulty usually found in determining the social class of women subscribers to philanthropic societies from the limited information included in subscription lists, but it has been facilitated to a little extent here by investigations already carried out for this study. It is likely that most female subscribers were 'middle class, using the term in its widest sense to include all those who came between manual workers earning wages on the one hand and the landed gentry on the other.'[16] Of course, it could never be proved that a married woman always made charitable contributions from her own purse. A comment by the distinguished preacher Rowland Hill in 1812 indicated that '"the ladies [did] not generally carry the larger purse" and their contributions to philanthropy were little more than "pin-money" vouchsafed by their good husbands'.[17] Women were often willing for their donations to be attributed to their marriage partners.[18] However, the following are cases in which donations from husbands and wives were shown separately.

The first-named female on the Creaton Annual Subscribers' list

---

15   Ten were either officers, or committee members.

16   Prochaska, *Women and Philanthropy*, p.41.

17   *Ibid.*, p.23, quoting *Report of the Proceedings...when an Auxiliary Bible Society was established, for Southwark and its Vicinity* (Southwark, 1812, p.31)

18   Lane, *Forgotten Labours*, p.49.

for 1822-23 was Mrs Bishopp, the wife of Dr. Bishopp, of Thornby
Hall, situated about four miles from Spratton. Dr. Bishopp was a
medical man, and his name headed both this list and that of the
Committee members. He and his wife had contributed £1.1s.0d.
(a guinea) each; an expression of equal status might be seen in this,
and later evidence will indicate that Mrs Bishopp was a lady of
means in her own right. The President, Mr. Robert Ramsden and
his wife were two of the other 'Annual Subscribers'. They were
probably the wealthiest people in Spratton for, as will be shown in
more detail later, Mr. Ramsden had married one of the daughters
of the landowning Plumptre family of Nonington, Kent, featured
in my second chapter. Mr. Ramsden's subscription was £3.3s.0d.
(three guineas) and his wife's the lesser amount of £2.2.0d. (two
guineas). This smaller sum might be judged as upholding the
general notion of female subordination. Nevertheless, the above
examples of marriage partners' donations being shown separately
may be taken as indication of the individual status granted to wives
in wealthier families. Many middle- and upper-class women were
financially independent and their economic influence has often
been underestimated.[19]   Among the other five female annual
subscribers was 'Mrs Bosworth, Highgate House'. She had
contributed £1.1s.0d., the same amount as the remaining four
women, one of whom was the wife of a committee member. This
was a worthwhile amount for a woman to donate in a lump sum,
relative to early nineteenth-century monetary values, and giving an
annual subscription could be seen as a status symbol.

Donations in missionary boxes at 'Highgate House', the 'Girls'
School', and the 'Boys' School', had raised 14s.0d, £1.1s.6d., and
3s.6d., respectively, to add to the Spratton total. From what
Prochaska has indicated, it was not unusual for women and children
to place collecting boxes in 'homes, servants' quarters, churches,
chapels, schools, hotels, railways stations, and other public places'.[20]
It can be imagined that Mrs Bosworth placed the box at Highgate
House in a strategic place to attract the attention of travellers who
stopped off at her premises. The list of those, whose 'Donations'
totalled £1.18s.6d., was given separately from that of the 'Annual
Subscribers'. It named only one woman, but eight men, seven of
whom were from Ravensthorpe. The men gave amounts of 10s.0d.

19 *Ibid.*
20 Prochaska, *Women and Philanthropy*, p.86, quoting *Children's Missionary Magazine*, III (Jan.
    1850), pp.19-25.

or less. This could have been their own choice of charitable giving from family funds, or possibly it was their way of showing support for female relatives engaged as collectors. Alternatively, perhaps they were instances of wives being willing for their contributions to be attributed to their husbands.

In the following year, 1824, the same twelve male representatives remained on the Committee of the Creaton Branch, but they were joined by another man. The balance sheet for 1823-24 showed that the number of female 'Annual Subscribers' had increased by two, making a total of 9 against the 21 men named. Just one more woman had been recruited to the band of 'Penny Collectors', so there were now 20 females, and 7 males on the list. The majority of the names were those given for 1823, thus the desired continuity of relationship between visitor and household was probably largely achieved. However, the total sum collected was £3.17s.3d. less than for the previous year. In his *Sixth Report*, Jones reiterated words of encouragement which the 'weaker vessels' could hold on to as they traversed their rounds, extracting pennies from their less fortunate neighbours: 'Even the *poor* that subscribe their penny a week, are among the *Instruments* in God's hand, to save the world: to destroy the reign of sin, and to establish the reign of grace over the whole earth'.[21] Whether the poor really gave willingly from their meagre earnings is open to question. However, official reports of the various philanthropic societies gave the impression that 'the labouring classes contributed without hesitation and without harm to their standard of living', while some critics argued that 'indiscriminate canvassing compromised and impoverished the working classes.'[22]

The *Seventh Report*, dated May 1825, is incomplete and the missing pages are those with the names of penny collectors, annual subscribers and amounts. However, we do have the list of officers and committee members elected. It is plain from this and subsequent Reports, that male dominance perpetuated in the management of the Branch. Jones's 1825 address held a more than usual masculine appeal and contained no reference to the women's work. The tone of this sentence is typical of his whole message:

21 *Sixth Report* (1824), p.11.
22 Prochaska, *Women and Philanthropy*, pp.43-4.

We have abundant *cause to thank God for what we do see.* We
see hosts of men of all ranks in society, coming forward
voluntarily, of their own accord, to promote the
Missionary cause, and to send men of God to publish the
everlasting Gospel to our perishing brethren in heathen
lands.[23]

Jones's *Eighth Report* (May 1826) voiced his disagreement with
'the strong and widely spread opposition' to the Church Missionary
Society, but, in furtherance of his arguments, he turned to similes
reflecting the unifying qualities of feminine love and benevolence.
He viewed the Society as 'so closely united' with the Church of
England, 'that their mutual interest and relation [were] inseparable,
as that of a mother and her daughter'.[24] Then he went on to say, 'It
is quite unfair to view the Old[25] and New Missionary Societies as
rivals. Nay, rather let them be considered as two amiable sisters, born
of the same parents, and engaged in the same work of charity and
benevolence'[26] In his *Tenth Report* (1828), Jones gave this
encouragement to those who had committed themselves to the
Church missionary cause, the majority of whom were 'weaker
vessels':

Let our faithful Collectors know, that in going from house
to house to receive the pence of the poor, and the poor in
contributing their mite, that these small things are
connected with the most glorious of all the works of God;
they are like drops of dew that blend with the great ocean
of love and mercy.[27]

Successive years saw fluctuations in the money raised for the
Creaton Branch. The *Thirteenth Report* (1831) showed that men
were still in charge, but rather significantly, the number of female
Annual Subscribers had increased to 12, against 21 males.[28] The

23 *Seventh Report* (1825), p.6.
24 *Eighth Report* (1826), p.10.
25 Meaning The Society for Promoting Christian Knowledge, founded in 1699 for home
    mission and philanthropy; and The Society for the Propagation of the Gospel in Foreign
    Parts (essentially a High Church society), established in 1701 for missionary activities
    overseas.
26 *Eighth Report*, pp.10-11.
27 *Tenth Report* (1828), p.9.
28 *Thirteenth Report* (1831).

Penny Collectors had reduced considerably in numbers; there were now only 13 women and 3 men, and the money collected was £41.4s.7d. This did not compare well with total given in 1822-23 (£79.6s.4d.) Contributions from other sources were also down, as illustrated below. The total sent to the Parent Association had decreased considerably over the years, from £352.4s.10d. in 1826 to £177.6s.9d. in 1831. However, it was declared in the Report that, although the diminution was regretted, the officers and committee were bound to rejoice that the Association, since its establishment twelve years earlier 'had remitted nearly £3,000 to the Parent Society'. It can be recognized that only the dedicated response of the 'weaker vessels' had made it possible to raise such a considerable sum. There can be little doubt that the formation of the Creaton Branch of the British and Foreign Bible Society in 1826 was responsible for the decrease in contributions, and that some of the female collectors now worked for this new cause. Competition for funds was inevitable in a rural area where incomes were affected by fluctuations in agricultural market forces and unemployment, at times making family budgets very limited and unpredictable. All but the sternest of 'female instruments' must have found it difficult to ask for pennies towards more than one Evangelical organization, and labours were doubled if the women had to collect on two different days in a week. Arguably, most of the poverty stricken had insufficient funds to allow for two contributions every week, and local people in general may have felt that mission and charity 'should begin at home'. For those of the poor still destitute of the word of God, the opportunity of obtaining Bibles for themselves, which could be looked at in their own homes with their families, must have held far greater appeal than giving their pennies solely towards spreading the Gospel to heathens in foreign lands, about whom they knew virtually nothing.

This investigation of the fortunes of the Creaton Branch of the Church Missionary Society should not be concluded without reference to the dedication of local children in helping to raise funds. Philanthropic selflessness was a virtue to be learned at the mother's knee, and from her example. In Evangelical families, 'often the first lesson a mother drummed into her children was on good works, for active charity was thought to be a hopeful sign that progress towards conversion was being made'.[29] The list of 'Donations' to the Creaton Missionary Society during 1822-23 included two items connected with children. The first, 'A small gold seal by a school boy' sold for 14s.0d., was probably a sacrificed treasured possession. The second, a 'Thank offering [£1.1s.0d.] for the education of a child', may have been a mother's way of showing appreciation for the teaching of her son or daughter at Sunday School, or in the village School. No doubt it was partly a token of thankfulness that her own child had learned about Jesus, when there were so many wicked little heathens in foreign lands who had not been so blessed. But it was by their own hard work, too, that the 'little vessels' (as Prochaska has called children of Evangelical parents)[30] contributed to the local missionary cause. In the 1824 Creaton Report it can be seen that another £59.10s.1d. was raised for the Association from a 'Missionary Sale' at Spratton, which was an innovation for the Branch. This was held at Spratton Hall, the home of Mr and Mrs Ramsden. The success of this first Sale illustrated what could be achieved by wholehearted commitment, and the results must have stimulated everyone to even greater efforts. Within two years the sale was contributing as much as £103.2s.1d. Actual figures of what was raised at charity bazaars are not often to be found.[31] Perhaps such records for rural communities are particularly difficult to trace. Certainly a good deal of effort and dedication went into raising such large sums.

The following extract from *The Eleventh Report* (May 1829) itemized gifts brought by children to the Spratton Sale:

'The people bring much more than enough'[32], yet it has been truly gratifying to observe the large accumulation of articles for sale, from the circumstances of *all* giving a *little according* to their ability. The favourite toy, or pincushion has been cheerfully sacrificed; the egg, the little parcel of sugar, the rabbit, the plant, the basket, and many other small offerings of children, and of those in humble life, seem to bear the inscription 'They have done what they could'.[33]

29   Prochaska, *Women and Philanthropy*, p.73, quoting C. Anderson, *The Domestic Constitution; or, the Family Circle the source and test of national stability*, (Edinburgh, 1847) p.417.

30   *Ibid.*, pp.73-94.

31   *Ibid.*, p.53.

32   Exodus 16:5; 'The people bring much more than enough for the service of the work, which the Lord commanded to make.'

33   *Eleventh Report* (1829), pp. 15-16.

It was not unusual for a child to 'consecrate' a small animal 'to the cause'.[34] Very likely children had made some of the items for the Spratton Sale. Inculcating habits of labour, self-discipline and sacrifice in the young enhanced a woman's own prospects of remaining in a state of grace. She was working for Christ in guiding the children aright. Whether the 'little vessels' whose mothers supported the Creaton Branch Auxiliary were ever engaged in house-to-house collections is not stated.

The list of 'Donations' for 1825-6 shows that 'Produce of the lace-pillow at Spratton Girls' School' had raised 13s.0d. The following year the amount from the same source totalled 7s.6d. The sums varied until 1828-9 when 15s.6d. was raised from the 'Lace Pillow and Work', but this time no specific institution was mentioned. However, there is evidence that a sewing and lace school for 20 girls existed at Creaton in 1818,[35] which might still have been in operation. In November 1828 a Juvenile Association within the Creaton Branch was established. The Rev. J. F. Cobb, Jones's curate at Creaton and joint secretary of the Branch, was able to say in the *Eleventh Report* that it promised

> to prove a powerful auxiliary, not only to the funds of this society but to that interest in Missionary labours which every lover of Zion would wish to see growing with his children's growth and strengthening with their strength.[36]

Thereafter, the produce of the lace pillow was not shown as a separate item. It was probably taken into the sum raised by 'Spratton Juvenile Mission', which was £18.3.0¼d. that year. The Juvenile Mission could not have operated without parental support and practical assistance, in which the mothers surely played the major part. The charitable pursuits of children 'reflected those of their parents, especially their mothers, who, quite naturally, wanted their sons and daughters to be like themselves'.[37] A developing practice within missionary societies at this time was the local organization of regular working parties at which women and

---

34 Prochaska, *Women and Philanthropy*, p.86.

35 Select Committee on Education of the Poor &c., Parliamentary Papers IX (2): *Digest of Education Returns, County of Northampton, 1818* (1819), Creaton (signed 'Thomas Jones') p.647, N.C.R.O. open shelves.

36 *Eleventh Report*, p.6,

37 Prochaska, *Women and Philanthropy*, p.94.

children made items for bazaars. Juvenile working parties resembled those run by women, and a mother was usually in charge to ensure good behaviour.[38] Confirmation that such gatherings were held at Creaton or Spratton is not given. In 1831, the contribution from Spratton Juvenile Mission fell to £9.12s.3½d. Most likely, by then, the Bible Society had gained priority interest and effort.

There was no mention of a Missionary Sale in the *Thirteenth Report* and, as has been said, no detailed reports beyond 1831 have been located. However, evidence suggests that funds were raised by holding a special Church service each year. A poster headed 'The Church Missionary Society' advertised that 'The Sixteenth Anniversary of the Creaton Association' would 'with Divine permission, take place at Spratton Church on Wednesday, 14th May, 1834, at 6 o'clock in the evening', when a representative from 'the Parent Society', and a 'late Missionary in India', along with several 'other Clergymen' were to be present.[39] It can be expected that there was much female representation in the congregation and again at the 'Sermon' preached at Spratton on the following evening by the Vicar of Raunds, in aid of funds for the Church Missionary Society.

4.2 Creaton Branch (Auxiliary) of the British and Foreign Bible Society

Female involvement in the work of the Creaton Branch of the British and Foreign Bible Society is dealt with second here because its establishment in the area came after that of the local Branch of the Church Missionary Society. For pious women, what could illustrate the significance of Evangelicalism in their lives more than distribution of the Scriptures, and dissemination of their personal beliefs among others in their own communities? The *First Annual Report of the Creaton Branch of the British and Foreign Bible Society* was delivered to the Annual Meeting on Thursday, 12 October 1826. It is the only extant record for the Branch, but it is especially important because it recorded the instigation and setting up of the six Ladies' Bible Associations that were to function within it. Before entering into a discussion of the *First Report*, something should be said about the establishment of this national Evangelical

38   *Ibid.*, p.87.
39   The Church Missionary Society, *Poster* (1834), N.C.R.O., Bos. Coll.

organization that claimed the dedicated allegiance of thousands of women representing different religious denominations.

Amid considerable controversy between Evangelicals in the Anglican Church and their Orthodox opponents, the British and Foreign Bible Society was formed in March 1804, with the specific aim of supplying Bibles and New Testaments ('Scriptures'), without note or comment, on a world-wide basis.[40] The Society was founded in a collaborative spirit between Anglicans and Dissenters and its emphasis was clearly Evangelical.[41] Only the Authorised version of the Bible was allowed to be distributed but members could add their own choice of prayer book or tract.

In its early days, Bishop Marsh of Peterborough was counted among the Society's strongest antagonists. He argued that the Book of Common Prayer should be distributed with the Bible as it 'was the Church's practical guide to the Holy Scripture', and he was concerned that its messages might be interpreted falsely 'by the ignorant'.[42] It is more than likely that educated Evangelical women in his diocese, particularly those such as Clara Bosworth who were closely associated with Thomas Jones, knew full well of their bishop's hostile views. Much published material on the matter emanated from Marsh's own pen and some of his opponents were only too ready to argue against him in print. For example, a letter written by one of them to the editor of the *Gentleman's Magazine* explained the grounds on which Marsh based his opposition. They were that, 'The Bible Society [was] a British Institution, that tend[ed] to the domestic distribution of the Bible without the Prayer Book; therefore the Bible Society [was] detrimental to the Church of England'.[43] However, as the letter-writer stated, no canons or articles of the Church 'express[ed] any necessity for distributing it' and, furthermore, the Prayer Book had never featured in the 'true Protestantism' of Dissenters. It was the prospect of co-operating with Dissenters that led many Anglican clergy to continue their opposition, even though many of them could find no real objection to unity of missionary purpose.[44] In

40 Jones had planned two schemes for mass-production of Bibles in Welsh (1791 and 1802), both of which failed: see Martin, *Evangelicals United*, p.83.
41 Lane, *Forgotten Labours*, p.68.
42 Nockles, *The Oxford Movement in Context*, p.108.
43 Scrutator Oxoniensis, 'Letter on The Bible Society', *Gentleman's Magazine*, LXXXII, Pt 1 (1812), pp.219-20.
44 Members of the Established Church, 'Review of "A Defence of the Bible Society"', *Christian Observer*, XVII (1818), pp.604-5.

1813 Marsh submitted to the overwhelming resistance he faced
from advocates of the Bible Society. He acknowledged that trying
to oppose 'the fervour of religious enthusiasm' with which the
Society was supported was like attempting to stay 'a torrent of
burning lava' flowing from 'Etna or Vesuvius'.[45]

The British and Foreign Bible Society was administered by an
all-male body of officials, so women could distance themselves
from such public controversies. Until 1817 the work of the
Auxiliary Associations operating at local level was carried out
exclusively by men. However, by that time internal tensions had
become acute and, because of serious financial problems, the
Society needed to exploit all its resources and was glad to avail itself
of willing female support.[46] The Bible Society's agent was a
Quaker, Charles Stokes Dudley (later to become Anglican) and to
him fell the responsibility of setting up a system of Ladies'
Auxiliaries throughout Britain. It was his wish that these would be
formed wherever there was no Gentlemen's Auxiliary, or 'where
those already in existence appeared to have become languid and
inactive'.[47] Women were confident that, if their associations were
given the chance to expand, they could be instrumental in saving
the Society from financial disaster.[48] The local collectors, or 'Bible
Ladies', as they became known, were to prove themselves the
financial mainstays of the organization and, for them, there must
have been a sense of achievement in a sphere where men had not
been so successful. In Charles Dudley the Bible Ladies had a strong
ally, for clearly he was an advocate of women's work and had
confidence in their abilities. He believed it was 'becoming in
women as well as men to aid so valuable a purpose'.[49] It was to him
that the Ladies' Auxiliary Associations owed, 'if not their absolute
origin, yet that regular and systematic incorporation which drew
forth their active exertions, and qualified them for undertaking a
separate and...a very efficient department of service'.[50]

Women felt drawn to Christ's work because he had respected

45 R. H. Martin, *Evangelicals United, Ecumenical stirrings in Pre-Victorian Britain, 1795-1830*
    (Matuchen, N.J., 1983), p.104, citing H. Marsh, *A Reply to the Strictures of the Rev. Dr.*
    Isaac Milner (1813), p.141.

46 Martin, *Evangelicals United*, p.114.

47 J. Owen, *The History of the Origin and First Ten Years of the British and Foreign Bible Society*,
    V (1820), p.356.

48 Martin, *Evangelicals United*, p.114.

49 C. S. Dudley, *An Analysis of the System of the Bible Society* (1821), p.359.

50 Owen, *History of the Origin of the B.F.B.S.*, V, p.355.

mothers, wives and daughters, and had needed their help and compassion. There were plenty of women in the Scriptures with whom they could identify themselves in their benevolent undertakings.[51] The Bible Ladies' work among the poor, sick and disabled lay, not only in making them aware of God's comforting words in the Bible and collecting their thankful pennies, but also in showing understanding of their distress and perhaps providing some relief by way of food, clothing and medicines. As many saw it, Christ had been a faith healer who had mixed with the common people. Women were already proving themselves able and dedicated workers in domestic visiting and mission among the poor in expanding urban areas. The work of the Bible Society reflected the same general objectives as those for other early nineteenth-century visiting organizations. These were,

> to carry the Church to the homes of the uncommitted; to offer discriminating charity based on an accurate knowledge of personal circumstances; better still, to attack poverty at its assumed roots by recreating a capacity for self-help in the poor; and to improve social relationships and reduce class-tension.[52]

From the beginning, this philanthropic aspect was envisaged as an integral part of the women's labours for the Bible Society. Charles Dudley argued that Bible work should be viewed as a suitable occupation for ladies, 'in the same way that other forms of philanthropy were well-established outlets for female talents'.[53] But there were complaints about the over-enthusiasm demonstrated by some Bible Women who entered parishes uninvited, and no security was given that female visitors would refrain from using their activities for political ends.[54] The worries reflected wider concerns about the position and employment of women in society at large. Not the least of these was that the lady visitors would neglect their own domestic responsibilities in a zeal for philanthropic work. In villages such as those in the Creaton Branch, the women probably felt under closer scrutiny from

---

51 Prochaska, *Women and Philanthropy*, pp.16-17.
52 H. D. Rack, 'Domestic visitation: a chapter in early nineteenth century evangelism', *Journal of Ecclesiastical History*, vol. 24, no. 4 (Cambridge, 1973), p.357.
53 Lane, *Forgotten Labours*, p.10.
54 See Martin, *Evangelicals United*, p. 115.

neighbours than in larger settlements and tried to avoid criticism.
It was realized that many of the Bible Ladies were unlikely to
have had experience in dealing directly with the poor, but Charles
Dudley was careful to give them clear, practical guidelines in his
*Hints Relative to The Duties that Devolve on the Officers and Collectors
of Bible Associations*.[55] 'Let all things be done decently and in
order',[56] was the Biblical message carried on its title page. The term
'Hints' was probably chosen judiciously; Dudley knew that he was
directing them to 'Ladies' and might have thought they would be
offended if he classified his suggestions as 'rules', although some of
them obviously were. Certainly in guidelines such as the following,
he did his best to echo middle- and upper-class social attitudes
towards their less fortunate neighbours. Collectors were advised
not to change their districts once they had been chosen, because
'the poor, grateful for those visits of mercy, gradually become
attached to the Collectors', and 'frequent change of districts
impairs, if it do not destroy, this effect, with all its collateral
advantages'.[57] Requests to be allocated to a different round were
probably less likely in a rural community than in a town. There
must have been few Bible Ladies resident in the villages within the
Creaton Auxiliary who were unfamiliar with the layout of their
own communities and, if in any doubt, they could easily gather
information about the households they were offering to visit. It
can be safely assumed that families such as the Bosworths, who had
lived in Spratton for at least three generations, knew the family
histories and present circumstances of most of their village
contemporaries. Dudley was sure that there was no need to tell the
'benevolent Ladies who [were] in the habit of visiting the humble
abodes of poverty and industry...that the slightest marks of
attention and respect [were] peculiarly grateful to the poor'.[58] He
knew that some upper- and middle-class women living in urban or
country areas already had contact with the poor. Perhaps they
had given assistance through their own private philanthropic
initiatives, had distributed religious tracts, attended Methodist
class-meetings,[59] or had collected for one of the denominational

---

55 C. S. Dudley, *Hints Relative to The Duties that Devolve on the Officers and Collectors of Bible
    Associations Extracted from the Analysis of the System of the Bible Society* (1823), N.C.R.O.,
    Bos.Coll.
56 1 Corinthians, 14:40.
57 Dudley, *Hints*, p.13.
58 *Ibid.*, p.15.

missionary organizations. However, in Dudley's view, those who had 'not yet acquired an intimate knowledge of this numerous class of their fellow-creatures', would soon find 'that the surest passport to the heart of the cottager [was] the evidence of interest and kindness'.[60]   Clearly, he thought it necessary to include such statements. In both town and country the social gap between rich and poor had widened considerably during the late eighteenth and early nineteenth centuries. Probably many of the prospective Bible Ladies had contact with the poor only through employing them as domestic servants and were used to dealing with them from a position of authority. However, a dictatorial approach in the homes of city slum-dwellers or rural cottagers was unlikely to achieve the desired results for the Bible Society.

Although the local Auxiliary of the British and Foreign Bible Society was to encompass several other parishes, it adopted the name of 'Creaton Branch', as the Church Missionary Society in the area had done. The Minute Secretary reported at the first Annual Meeting that there had been objections to the foundation of the Creaton Auxiliary, but these were 'aimed almost exclusively against the *expediency* of the measure'.[61] The Church Missionary Society was already supported in the area and most likely collections for other Evangelical charitable causes were also made from time to time. Expectation of raising additional regular subscriptions might have appeared unrealistic in some people's eyes. Difficulty in finding a sufficient number of women to work for yet another organization, and rivalry in recruiting collectors could have been envisaged as additional problems. A matter of specific debate was that other Societies might already be working locally in the 'immediate sphere' of that proposed by the Bible Society; this probably meant the distribution of Bibles by older organizations such as the S.P.C.K. However, 'an accurate investigation into the state of the neighbourhood' showed that this was not the case.[62]

Such pragmatic concerns having been aired, the Creaton Branch of the British and Foreign Bible Society was established in 1826, under a conspicuously all-male administration. Mr Robert Ramsden was elected President and Treasurer, Thomas Jones and

59 For examples see Prochaska, *Women and Philanthropy*, pp.118-22.

60 *Ibid*.

61 *First Annual Report of the Creaton Branch of the British and Foreign Bible Society* (Northampton, 1826), p.8.

62 *First Report*, p.8.

Dr Thomas Bishopp Vice Presidents, and the Rev. James Clark of
Guilsborough, a Nonconformist, one of three Secretaries. The
Committee comprised twenty-nine laymen. Clearly, Jones had put
aside his dislike of Dissenting ministers. Several of those who
attended the Annual Branch Meeting and eight annual subscribers
were reverend gentlemen, some of them Dissenters. Probably they
all wished to show support of the Ladies' Bible Associations in these
ways, but whichever Church or Chapel they represented, it was
sensible to ally themselves to the local Auxiliary. Thereby they
would be in a position to exert a measure of control over the Bible
Ladies who were being given approval to enter their traditional
sphere of pastoral work.   It was impossible to regulate the
interaction between individuals and, as females were not permitted
to 'preach from the pulpit', those who might have wished to do so
were given an opportunity to sermonize in their own way to their
poorer neighbours as they collected subscriptions for Bibles.[63]

The 'extensive district' covered by Creaton Branch as a whole
comprised 'about 36 villages, with an estimated population of
14,000', and the 'sphere of...operations' was divided 'into Six
Districts'.[64] It is clear that the Creaton Auxiliary, from the very
beginning, had an understood administrative structure and *modus
operandi*. Correct procedures were dictated by the Parent
Association, to whom the male Committee members of the
Auxiliary were accountable. As letters in the Bible Society Archives
show, a representative from headquarters was always invited to
attend the Creaton Branch Annual Meeting.[65]   Each of the six
Districts in this Auxiliary, namely Spratton, Welford, Guilsborough,
Ravensthorpe, Moulton, Scaldwell, had a Ladies' Bible Association,
which appointed its own female Committee. The Districts were
divided into villages contained within them and these were then
sub-divided into smaller districts (or visiting rounds). It was only
in their Association Committees, at the lowest level of the Bible
Society management, that women were permitted to take up an
administrative role. It was made patently clear that they were
responsible to their male Branch Committee and they were seldom
allowed   direct   contact   with   the   Parent   Society.   Any
correspondence to the latter must first be approved by the Branch

63 Lane, *Forgotten Labours*, p.28.
64 *First Report*, p.9.
65 The British and Foreign Bible Society Archives are housed in Cambridge University
    Library.

Committee, who would direct it to headquarters if they considered it appropriate.[66] The Bible Ladies usually visited in pairs. For many of these women it was probably a first taste of communal Evangelical activism, but for all of them it was a new experience in that Anglicans and Dissenters found themselves working together for the common Christian purpose of disseminating the word of God. At the same time they presented a public image of unity in their endeavour to relieve distress among the poor.

We do not know if females were present at the first Creaton Branch Meeting, but women were forced to wait until 1831 before being allowed to attend the Annual Meeting of the British and Foreign Bible Society at national level.[67] The male administrators elected for the Creaton Auxiliary in 1826 came from fourteen different parishes within a radius of something between five and ten miles, and no doubt some of their own womenfolk were among the Bible Ladies. Examination of the list of forty-one Annual Subscribers has shown that only four were women, and, as might have been expected, two of these were Mrs Ramsden and Mrs Bosworth. All who gave 'free' contributions 'of half-a-guinea and upwards per annum' were entitled to receive a copy of the Annual Reports of their particular Association, and of the Auxiliary to which it was connected.[68] Unfortunately, there is no official record of those ladies who served on the Committees for each of their Associations, neither is there full indication of who the female visitors were. Nevertheless, though the women remained unidentified in the Report, it is clear that they had made an auspicious beginning, for the Minute Secretary recorded at the Annual Meeting on Thursday, 12th October 1826:[69]

On the Motion of the Rev. Thomas Jones,
Seconded by the Rev. Benjamin Hobson,
Resolved unanimously,
'That this Meeting, rejoicing in the encouraging fact, that

---

66 Lane, *Forgotten Labours*, p.8.
67 *Ibid.*, p.20.
68 Dudley, *Hints*, p.17.
69 Three secretaries were in office, Rev. J. Cobb, Rev. J. Clark, Mr W. Smith; none was designated 'Minute Secretary' in *First Annual Report*, p.1.

more than *one hundred and fifty Ladies* are now engaged in
conducting the Six Associations connected with the
Society desires to express its cordial acknowledgments to
those estimable individuals; and commends them to God,
and to the word of His grace, as the spring and motive of
Christian exertion.'[70]

There was no mention of 'feeble instruments' here, but such a
description would surely have been thought a misnomer in this
particular context. Furthermore, utmost tact was probably exercised
as Charles Dudley, the champion of female involvement, was named
present at this Meeting.

The first four of the six Creaton Associations of Bible Ladies
had been formed early in 1826, at Spratton, Welford, Guilsborough,
and Ravensthorpe, the other two more recently at Moulton, and
Scaldwell. The 'many favourable circumstances attendant on the
[later] formation of the [last] two, afford[ed] the most sanguine
expectations of their future usefulness and prosperity.'[71]   Male
adminstrative superiority in the Auxiliary was confirmed. It 'had
been the happy lot and privilege of [the] Committee to watch over
the rise and progress of [the] various operations' of their Ladies'
Associations.[72] The following much longer extract from the *First
Report* is worth quoting as evidence of the subordinate role the
Bible Ladies were estimated to have played at local level. Yet in
fairness to whoever wrote the Report, possibly Thomas Jones, he
endeavoured to give credit where he saw credit was due, first to
God and then to the women's Associations, though he did refer to
their 'feeble beginnings':

> In the review of a multitude of practical proofs of the
> advantages and success which have attended the progress of
> the Associations during the past year, your Committee see
> abundant cause for cherishing the liveliest gratitude to God
> who has given the increase, and at the same time, derive
> ample encouragement for the active prosecution of the
> noble and delightful work in which they are engaged. 'The
> blessing of the Lord which makest rich,'[73] has rested on

70   *First Annual Report*, p.6.
71   *Ibid.*, p.10.
72   *Ibid.*
73   Proverbs 10:22.

their feeble beginnings, and this they hope still to enjoy, whilst 'in simplicity and godly sincerity'[74] they 'do good and communicate'.[75]

Of the particular concerns of your own Society, the Committee have but little to state. Viewing itself chiefly in the capacity of a Guardian and Superintendent of your Associations, and as the channel of your resources, the duties which have devolved upon it as such, your Committee have discharged with ease and delight.[76]

The female visitors had shown themselves more than capable of responsible organization at local level. Nevertheless, there was no suggestion anywhere that women might, after all, have the qualities to be effective at the higher echelons of the Society. Mary Wollstonecraft's claim in the 1790s that the mental capacities and organizational skills of women had been stifled by their upbringing and the conventional role allocated to them, was proving increasingly difficult to refute.[77] The Ladies of the Spratton Association Committee met regularly on the '2nd Tuesday of every month at two o'clock precisely, at the Infants School, Spratton'.[78] Had the Bible Ladies' success and exemplary commitment urged the men of the Creaton Branch Committee to reconsider their own contribution to the effort, and to meet monthly as the women were doing? The Branch Report continued:

In the prospect, however, of the extension of their [the Committee's] sphere of action, they feel the great importance and necessity of charging themselves with motives to increased diligence and regularity in prosecution of their work; they propose henceforward to hold their Meetings every Month, instead of every other Month, as heretofore, this would excite one another to do whatsoever they do with all their might, and to engage in the business of the Society 'with good-will as to the Lord,

---

74   2 Cor.1:12.
75   Hebrews 13:16.
76   *First Report*, pp.17-18.
77   Wollstonecraft, *Vindication of the Rights of Woman*, pp.73-7.
78   *Collecting Book 42* (printed), copy for use by Spratton Ladies' Association, not fully completed, but with meeting and collecting dates, N.C.R.O., Bos. Coll.

and not to men.'[79]

The table below was contained in the Creaton Annual Report and recorded quantitative evidence of the Bible Ladies' success in the four earliest Branch Associations.[80] It would have been compiled from the meticulous weekly records they were obliged to keep.

Summary view of the state of all the Associations

	Spratton	Welford	Guilsborough	Ravensthorpe	Moulton	Scaldwell	Grand Total
Districts	21	12	15	11	13	9	81
Collectors	47	20	23	23	25	15	153
Subscribers							
Free	198	93	106	71	...	...	468
Bibles	419	256	204	178	...	...	1057
Total	617	349	310	249	...	...	1525
Distributed							
Bibles	78	73	47	17	...	...	215
Testaments	57	65	19	37	...	...	178
Total	135	138	66	54	...	...	393
Collected	£. s. d.	£. s. d.	£. s. d.	£. s. d.			£. s. d.
	135 10 9	93 7 1	89 1 7	59 17 3	...	...	377 16 8
Voted free	66 0 0	28 0 0	22 0 9	20 0 0	...	...	136 0 9

The total number of people who had 'subscribed for copies of the Holy Scriptures in the first four Associations' was 1,057, and 393 copies had been distributed, so there were still 664 subscribers to whom Bibles had not yet been issued. Moulton and Scaldwell Associations contained 22 extra districts and 40 collectors had been recruited to work in them but, as they had been formed only recently, they had not been operating long enough to produce statistical data for the Annual Report. The number of Bible Ladies in the six Associations was now 153 but none of them was named. One can only suggest that some were related to the ten ministers identified on the list of subscribers. Perhaps others were relatives of

79 Ephesians 6:7; *First Report*, p.18.
80 Appendix A, *First Report*, p.10.

the farmers whose names were also included, who have already been dealt with as Committee members of the local Church Missionary Society Branch, or subscribers to it. In the first four Associations, 113 Ladies had visited 'between 15 and 16 hundred families; and...as nearly as [could] be ascertained, 46 only remain[ed] destitute of the Word of God'. If the women worked in pairs and the total of homes first visited is counted as being 1,550, the approximate number of families approached by each pair was 27. The total number of subscribers was 1,525, so their success rate was little short of one hundred per cent, calculated on the basis of one contribution from each family. However, what the percentage rate was in relation to the total number of families living in all the villages constituting the first four associations cannot be ascertained, because most of the villages have not been identified. Also, an accurate comparison between the success rate of the local Branch of the Church Missionary Society and the Bible Society, in terms of penetration of the total community of potential families, cannot be made. As stated above, the Branch is reported to have consisted of 'about 36 villages with an estimated population of 14,000'. These numbers are uncertain and they may or may not have included the Moulton and Scaldwell associations, for which no figures relating to subscribers were given.

Dudley's *Hints* expected Bible Ladies' visits to be of sufficient duration to allow some conversation with the poor upon whom they called, in order to assess their spiritual and physical needs. Collectors were urged to discover intimate details about their subscribers, which could have proved embarrassing for both parties, but such questioning was to apply 'exclusively to the poor'. One important assessment to be made was the number in each household who were literate and utmost tact must be exercised when asking questions on this subject. The *Hints* suggested that an answer would be 'best attained by requesting to know how many [could] read', as few would wish to acknowledge that they could not.[81]   Illiterate parents of literate children should be tactfully encouraged to ask their offspring to read the Bible to the whole family.[82]   In a village, it is likely that the Bible Ladies did have an idea of literacy levels in the families they visited. For some of them their rounds surely required a good deal of time, physical energy and emotional stamina. Even if they already had superficial

81   Dudley, *Hints*, p.15.
82   *Ibid.*

knowledge of the domestic circumstances of their poorest
neighbours, to witness poverty, sickness and inadequate housing
conditions, perhaps for the first time at close quarters, would be
upsetting for women of a sensitive nature or delicate constitution.
Merely hearing about destitution was very different from coming
face-to-face with it on a doorstep.

In his reasons for setting up the Clothing Club, Thomas Jones
left the following evidence of poverty he encountered at Creaton
and Spratton when he had the curacies of both parishes.[83] The
degree of destitution he found was probably representative of the
other villages covered by the local Bible Ladies' Associations. Jones
was 'much concerned to see so many of the poor so much in want
of clothing, and that their beds had nothing on but dirty rags'. He
considered it far better to act on his old principle, 'help the poor to
help themselves', than to proffer 'gifts'; the poor valued 'the produce
of their own labour much more than alms'. Jones devised a self-
help scheme that entailed weekly savings, 'from one penny to
twelve', which he collected 'in the Vestry every Monday morning,
at half-past eleven'. Proportionate bonuses were added at the end
of the year 'according to their subscriptions,' whereupon 'blankets,
sheets, rugs, ticks, shirting, calico, flannel, baize, cord, canvass, jersey,
aprons, & c.' were distributed.

It is possible that, in a country area such as this, a Bible Lady's
round included households containing one or more members
employed by her own relatives. Whether such a link made things
easier, or more difficult, is hard to assess. Domestic servants were to
be asked to subscribe only after permission had been sought of
their Mistresses.[84] Propinquity would have given opportunity for
the village poor to observe the more fortunate lifestyles of most of
their visitors and there must always have been the chance of an
unpleasant rebuff on other than religious grounds. Nevertheless, as
already shown, the Bible Ladies had met with a high degree of
success in their sphere of operation. The men attending the Annual
Meeting were told:

> Your Committee cannot pass over a circumstance so
> replete with proof of the beneficial results attendant on the
> establishment of the Society, without recording their lively

83 Owen, *Memoir*, p.129.
84 'Suggestion, 3', *Collecting Book*.

sense of gratitude to Almighty God for having employed them as agents in circulating so many Copies of His Word, fully persuaded that herein their labour will not be in vain in the Lord. Whilst they would rejoice in Him being called upon to view their connected Associations as so many channels for conveying the Words of Eternal Life to their destitute neighbours ever mindful of the ulterior object for which their Society has been formed, they hail with unmingled delight the receipt of £136, as a free remittance to the Parent Society in London.[85]

The women deserved this approbation for raising so large a sum in an agricultural area where household incomes were low and uncertain.

The Bible Ladies of the Associations attached to the Creaton Branch had found much satisfaction in their first year's work. They had done more than merely uphold 'the great and only object of the Bible Associations', which was to encourage 'the Labouring Classes' to buy Bibles firstly for themselves, and then to subscribe towards supplying them 'for the WHOLE WORLD'.[86] 'A spirit of industry, of economy, and of self-denial, ha[d] not unfrequently been manifested through the instrumentality of the same means'.[87] In their reply to the Bible Society's call, the local female visitors had achieved much.

4.2.i The Bible Ladies of the Spratton Association
This part will be devoted to the work of the Bible Ladies in the Districts covered by the Spratton Association, and the guidelines which suggested the parameters within which they should operate. As Sarah Lane has said, most of the scholarly analysis of the British and Foreign Bible Society has been at 'the national, and therefore male-dominated level', and very little investigation has been made into 'women's Bible work, although Frank Prochaska examines it in the context of women's philanthropic work'.[88] It must be admitted that Sarah Lane has gone a long way in making up the deficiency, but her general study has not provided comprehensive details of any specific Auxiliary and its Ladies' Bible Associations. *The First*

85 *First Annual Report*, pp.11-12.
86 *Collecting Book*, inside front cover.
87 *First Creaton Branch Report*, p.13.
88 Lane, *Forgotten Labours*, p.9.

Annual Report of the Spratton Ladies's Bible Association, affiliated to
the Creaton Auxiliary, can give insight into the response of
local women to the challenge of group activity in this
sphere of Evangelical mission and philanthropy.[89] Charles Dudley
acknowledged that the community was the place in which the real
work of the Bible Society was done:

> Collectors are the life-blood of every Society...It is not a
> compliment earned by appearing once a year, with a look
> of interest, at a public meeting, or even once a month at a
> Committee-meeting: it is the reward of retired,
> monotonous, persevering exertion; of many a weary step,
> and patient word; receiving little excitement from the eye
> of man, and able to endure with meekness his ridicule and
> censure.[90]

The Bible Ladies functioned at an individual level of
communication and for many of them such participation must have
been a completely new and enlightening experience. The *Spratton
Report* has revealed something of the social attitudes of local
middle-class women towards the poor, whom they visited in a spirit
of Evangelical commitment. As far as can be ascertained, that
Report is the only extant record of its kind relating to any part of
the Creaton Auxiliary. It has provided both qualitative and
quantitative evidence of the Bible Ladies' work in the Spratton
Association and contains valuable information about the way in
which the Society worked at local level. The competent *First
Report* was presented on 4 October 1826, probably at a Committee
Meeting arranged to take place just before the Branch Annual
Meeting. It reflected the general high standard of the records kept
by the Ladies' Bible Associations.

The Spratton Ladies' Association was the largest of the six that
made up the Creaton Branch. It covered the villages of Spratton,
Creaton, Brampton, Brixworth, Cottesbrooke, and Harlestone.
Dudley had warned the Bible Ladies 'against the temptation of *too
extensive* usefulness', and thought a reasonable limit for one round
was 'about forty or forty-five families'.[91] Even so, in a scattered,

89 *First Annual Report of the Spratton Ladies' Association* (1826, manuscript), pages not
    numbered, N.C.R.O., Bos. Coll.
90 Dudley, *An Analysis of the System of the Bible Society*, p.537
91 Dudley, *Hints*, p.13.

rural community, this could have entailed an extensive distance to traverse. It is fortunate that there is a separate handwritten *Paper setting out the Districts and the rounds of the collectors*, which specified the routes to be covered within each village of the Spratton Association.[92] Though the printed table in the Branch's Annual Report indicated that the Association comprised 21 districts, the handwritten paper showed 19, but this was likely to have been compiled in the early days of the Creaton Branch when that number of rounds was thought adequate. Perhaps further division was later considered necessary because some collectors were calling at more houses, or walking longer distances, than others. Each round was clearly delineated on the list and, if the Bible Ladies kept to the prescribed routes, there was no encroachment on each other's territory. Though the collectors were not named, some of the inhabitants were. Unfortunately, the occupations of only a few of the latter were given, but one or two bear familiar names that have already been connected with farming. Even so, the scant occupational details and the sitings of named public houses, schools, tollgates, brick-kilns, etc., transfer a sense of intimacy with the locality, giving today's readers an albeit limited picture of the social mix and layout of the villages in which the Bible Ladies went from door to door.

Spratton village appeared first on the paper, and these extracts will serve as a few examples of how its six districts (or rounds) were specified. 'District No.1' was defined thus: 'From Mr. Smith's round by Baker's Alley to Mr. Eaton's including the three houses to the East and thence by the Blacksmith's Shop to the Boys' School'. 'District 3' covered the route 'From the Boys' School inclusive down to the Brick Kiln house and up to Mr. Walton's'. 'District No.5' was 'From Mr. Wright's Shoemaker, round by Mrs. Bigg's to Mr. Thos. Wright's and thence to John White's and back to the Penfold'. These are examples of rounds in some of the other villages in the Spratton Association: Creaton, 'District No.8...From Mr. Bosworth's to the Church with the houses on the Turnpike Road', which has a particularly familiar ring about it. Further on, at Brampton, there was 'District No.12: Chapel Brampton, including the Tollgate, two Lodges and the Fish Inn'. 'District No.13' was located in Brixworth, 'From the Lord Nelson to the Coach and Horses taking in both sides of the way: down High

---

92 *Paper setting out the Districts and the rounds of the collectors*, N.C.R.O., Bos.Coll.

Street, and up Silver Street to the Turnpike and including Mr. &
Mrs Innes'. 'No. 16' in Brixworth was 'From George Haines's
taking a circle on the south to the Cross, round by Mr Foster's up
to the Peacock Inn including all the houses in the Cross Circle.'
'District 17' covered 'Part of Cottesbrooke, from Mr Garners'
taking the Street on both sides as far as the Brewhouse, and up to
the Boys' School including the Alms Houses.' Even today, many of
the named landmarks in these villages are discernible.

When the rural Bible Ladies ventured on their rounds for the
first time, they probably had a far better knowledge of the
demographic details of their village communities than many of
their counterparts in towns and cities. The women's approaches to
deprived neighbours surely varied as much as their personalities,
from the unbearably aggressive talker to the unconfident persuader.
The *Hints* recommended that collectors would best receive co-
operation if they were seen as wise and prudent 'Christian Females,
animated by Christian zeal, but governed by Christian principles',
and the most valuable and attractive collector would be '"the
ornament of a meek and quiet spirit, which is in the sight of God
of great price"'.[93]

There were forty-seven collectors for the twenty-one districts
covered by the Spratton Association, which might indicate that
some ladies visited in threes. Perhaps this number provided for
reserves to operate temporarily in the event of illness, severe winter
weather, or absence from home of a regular collector. It was
important that the system of visiting each week should be
maintained. The Report from Spratton Ladies' Association
recorded that there were forty-seven Ladies on its Committee, so
the collectors perhaps made up the whole body of this tier of local
organization. Dudley's *Hints* on forming Association Committees
gave instruction that, 'where a Lady appear[ed] suitable for the
appointment, and [was] interested in the object, the Collectors
should propose her admission on the Committee, in their Monthly
Report'. The Spratton Committee Meetings were sizeable
gatherings if all forty-seven of its members attended. As they
represented several different villages, it can be safely assumed that in
the early days many of the women did not know each other. The
rules of the Bible Society prescribed that Associations were to
appoint their own President, Treasurer, and Secretary.

93 Dudley, *Hints*, p.26, citing 1 Peter 3:4.

Unfortunately, the individuals who undertook these offices in the Spratton Association were not named.

A new Evangelical milieu of inter-denominational tolerance and religious social experience was presented to this group of women. The following extract from the *Spratton Association First Report* has given their view of this new integration, which they considered one of the 'collateral benefits' gained from setting up the local Branch of the Society 'in this place and neighbourhood':

> ...they wd. not overlook that wh., while it is to some an object of terror or derision is in their eyes one great glory of the Church of Christ: a glory wh. is peculiarly heightened by means of the Bible Socy., viz. the delightful union of heart & hand, of mind & energy among all classes & denominations: the practical realization that we have one LORD - one work - one hope - one home.

> Here the rich man's Guinea, and the poor man's penny meet together; &, if given from the same motive have equal weight in the balance of the Sanctuary. Here the churchman & the dissenter each looking to the same Captain of their Salvation, each listening to the same imperative command, forget that they are in different companies in his regiment, & press forward to fight the common enemy.

However, there is no intimation that women from different denominations visited together on any of the rounds. The eight 'suggestions' printed in the Collecting Book can be recognized as shortened versions of some of Dudley's *Hints*. They were instructions rather than 'suggestions', and these posed a further challenge to the Bible Ladies. The strict guidelines must be followed and accurate monetary records kept, but it gave women opportunity to display their capabilities for interpreting rules correctly and keeping detailed accounts of money collected and Bibles distributed.

Dudley's expected procedure for lending Bibles has served as an example of the way in which a precise course of action was usually specified and has indicated the meticulous nature of the records that the Bible Ladies had to keep.[94] It was permissible for a Bible

94 Dudley, *Hints*, p.21.

or [New] Testament to be lent to a poor person before the purchase price had been fully paid. The *Hints* gave clear instructions to be followed if a loan was made.[95] 'The Collectors who recommend[ed] individuals for Loan Bibles, or Testaments, [were] responsible to the Bible Secretary for their safe return.' The Ladies were warned that some 'persons' might hide the fact that they already had a Bible or Testament, in the expectation that they would then receive them as gifts. 'The idea of being gratuitously supplied should never be suggested', but anyone in 'absolute distress' should be told that a recommendation for a loan copy would be made to the Committee. In such an event, this procedure was to be followed:

> When Collectors recommended an individual for a loan in their "Monthly Report" (Appendix No. VIII) and it [had] been voted by the Committee, a ticket (Appendix No. V) [was] delivered at the table, which [was] subsequently signed by the Collectors, and given to the poor person. The party [was] to be distinctly informed that the Bible or Testament [was] lent for a month; and that the Committee expect[ed] it [would] be diligently read, and carefully preserved from injury.

The Bible Ladies should then call regularly to see the loan copies; once a week was desirable, but the inspection should certainly be carried out monthly. 'Temporary possession of this inestimable treasure' had often 'induced the receivers to become subscribers for Bibles, and to relinquish those vicious and extravagant habits which had previously, led them to believe they were unable to spare a penny a week.'

The Spratton Association's *First Report* indicated that nine Loan Bibles and Testaments had been handed over during the year. The paragraph on these 'few cases' has provided unwitting (or perhaps witting) testimony to the Bible Ladies' success in inculcating the middle-class attitude that the result of saving money was the pleasure of personal ownership. For the poor who had been allowed loan copies, the disciplined, regular investment of their pennies had given its reward:

---

95 *Ibid.*, pp. 21-2 (Dudley's appendices numbers).

The Loan Stock has been a source of great satisfaction to your Committee, for tho' the cases are few where a family is wholly destitute of the scriptures, yet in those few cases the value set upon the Loan has been truly gratifying; and the possession of it far from leading the individual to be indifferent as to procuring a Bible has induced them to become steady subscribers with a growing desire to be able to attach to the valued Treasure those endearing words 'My Own'.

It must have been difficult at times for some of the more sensitive Bible Ladies to adhere to all the rules, especially to take back a Bible after the prescribed period if contributions could not be paid. They were never to offer to pay a poor person's subscription themselves to save such a situation. According to the *Spratton First Report*, no Bibles had been distributed 'gratuitously' in their Association and none had been sold under cost price.

To prepare the way for new religious attitudes and commitment in the homes of all the destitute was an impossible task. In some areas of the country, the poor had sometimes been known to pawn their Bibles, but how many of the ladies in the Spratton Association would have wished to ask pawnbrokers in the district 'not to receive Bibles in pledge; and solicit their co-operation', as suggested in the Collecting Book? Part of the visitors' task was to inculcate middle-class moral values as well as religious ideas into the poor. Thrift, personal responsibility and morality could be taught along with Biblical messages. It was in the home, however humble, that transforming standards could be set by women. What is striking about the Bible Society's middle-class opinion of the poor is that they were all categorized as having low domestic and moral standards, along with lack of ambition. Dudley's *Hints* specified habits which the Bible Ladies were to foster in their unfortunate neighbours. They should suggest:

the advantages of cleanliness, sobriety and economy - the duty of loyalty, and subordination to their superiors - the importance of having their children educated, and of learning to read themselves - and the blessing attending a state of independence, and freedom from pauperism.[96]

96 Dudley, *Hints*, pp.27-28.

Here we can see the clear political message the Bible Ladies were also expected to carry from door to door. They were to be useful instruments in supporting the social attitudes of leading Evangelicals, such as Wilberforce and Hannah More. Though they should better themselves to a certain extent, the poor were to be dutifully loyal to their social superiors, resigned to their lot, and any aspirations of an equal society must be quashed. Edmund Burke, politician and philosopher, had made the definitive statement on proletarian life:

> To be enabled to acquire, the people, without being servile, must be tractable and obedient...They must labour to obtain what by labour can be obtained; and when they find, as they commonly do, the success disproportioned to the endeavour, they must be taught their consolation in the final proportions of eternal justice.[97]

The collectors in the Spratton Ladies' Association were able to report some instances of responsible attitudes that had been developed among their poor subscribers, who had suffered exceptionally hard times:

> In the midst of peculiar sickness & poverty the poor have manifested a forwardness to subscribe for a Bible, & an earnestness to possess the treasure wh. have greatly encouraged yr. Committee. Far from seeking for any idle excuses for not paying the usual subscription, they have frequently left their card & penny at a neighbour's house, if obliged to be absent themselves, or if they thought that the infectious nature of the fever in the family might deter the collector from calling: & a little school girl knowing that she cd. not be spared the ensuing week to come to the school where the collector called for her subscription begged to be allowed to give a double contribution on the preceding Monday. Thus where the want of a will could easily have framed excuses, a willing mind has, as easily, removed apparent difficulties & hindrances.

---

97 E. Burke, *Reflections on the Revolution in France* (1790, 4th edn), p.359, cited in Hammonds, *The Village Labourer*, p.208.

One method by which the Bible Ladies were to inculcate self-reliance, and responsibility in the poor can be detected in those of Dudley's *Hints* which gave comprehensive directions to be followed before, and after, Bibles were handed over. The collectors had to record the dates subscriptions were paid, the names of the subscribers, the numbers who subscribed 'free', that is, those who continued to donate their pennies after they had purchased their Bibles, and those who were still paying towards the cost of their copies.

The Spratton *First Annual Report* numbered 284 people as 'Bible Subscribers not yet supplied'. Dudley tried to cover all eventualities. 'When evident poverty and discouragement, on the part of the subscriber, render it expedient to deliver the copy before the cost price has been paid, it should be done with a clear understanding that the subscription is to be renewed when ability admits'.[98] However, the poor deserved respect, and were to be allowed 'the most perfect liberty of judgment' in deciding whether or not to continue subscribing once their Bibles had been paid for. The influence that a collector may have supposed her station in life gave her was never to be used in 'soliciting free contributions from the labouring classes', because this went against the 'principle of Bible Associations', which was to excite and encourage 'a spirit of proper independence among the poor'.[99] They were to make up their own minds. This seems contrary to the other instruction that the Bible Ladies should encourage a subordinate attitude in the poor. Apparently their unfortunate neighbours were to be taught monetary self-reliance, but ambitions of material and socio-political equality were to be subdued. However, this kind of ambiguity was common at that time. Agricultural wages were very low but if a family had a few savings and a little property, thus appearing able to survive without recourse to the parish, even though at times needing to do so, they might be punished for their independent spirit.[100] To save local Poor Law payments, the more indolent and profligate labourers living on parish assistance would often be employed instead of those practising hard work and self-help, thereby destroying incentives to improve their lot.[101] In a rural area, such as that covered by Creaton Branch, the Bible Ladies' message of 'the blessing attending a state of independence and freedom from

98 Dudley, *Hints*, p.15.
99 *Ibid.*, p.17.
100 See Hammonds, *The Village Labourer*, pp.225-7.

pauperism' may well have fallen on many deaf ears.

Free contributions for Bibles were never to be accepted from those receiving parochial relief.[102] For the Spratton Ladies this instruction was sometimes difficult to adhere to, as the following extract from their Report shows:

> Yr. Committee are fully convinced that, far from being guilty of any unkindness in calling upon the poor for free contributions, they have been the honoured instruments of gratifying one of the most earnest desires of the pious cottager, and of increasing his joys for time & for eternity. Their only trouble on this subject has been to restrain the actings of the heart in those, who while under the painful necessity of receiving parochial relief wd. fain spare a part of their scanty allowance to minister to the spiritual wants of their fellow creatures.

One Bible Lady had been 'overcome by the earnest entreaties' of a man, 'who after a long life of honest industry, had been compelled to throw himself upon the parish for relief', but wished to continue subscribing his penny a week because he longed 'to see all [his] fellow creatures flocking into Zion'. In anxiety to obey instructions, 'the poor man's penny was returned to him'. Written in colourful and sentimental language, such heartening accounts in the Spratton *First Report* left no doubt concerning the local Bible Ladies' delight in what they had achieved, but these anecdotes of success were bound to be subjective. It was probably thought unwise to mention any rejections. Stories of failures were not recorded. We might question whether some local subscribers handed over their pennies for pragmatic reasons. Would their chances of continuing employment be hindered if they did not, or would they be among the last to be hired for seasonal labour if they defaulted? It can be argued that some merely wished to belong to a group distinguished by contributing to the Bible Society.

101 *Ibid*. See also Snell, *Annals of the Labouring Poor*, p.101: With the decline of yearly hiring of farm servants, moral responsibility of employer towards servant had virtually come to an end. 'Faced with "morally" unjustified authority, no longer economically supportive in the old manner, the "labourer" developed a peculiarly contradictory position. On the one hand he was dependent... On the other, he moved hesitantly towards principles of self-help, class isolation and "independence" – the ambivalent but legitimating cliche of the period.'

102 Dudley, *Hints*, p.16.

The way in which a Loan Bible had altered the simple life of a
'labouring Man' added pathos to the Spratton Association's *Report*,
yet at the same time the writer has conveyed the superior class
attitude of sympathetic complacency towards the hard life of the
agricultural labourer. There is a somewhat Biblical ring about the
extract. This particular man not only read his Bible at home with
his family;

> but took it with him to the field, to cheer him in the
> appointed intervals of labour, & when he seated himself
> beneath a hedge to rest & feed his weary body, he refreshed
> his precious soul also from these wells of salvation.

When the full subscription had been paid and the Testament had
been received, he is said to have remarked to his wife, 'I consider
this money the best laid out of any you have ever paid since we
have been married'. Interestingly, this might indicate that the
responsibility of women cottagers included management of
domestic finances, and that they were usually the ones who handed
over the pennies every week. Dudley had suggested that Monday
morning was the best time for visiting as it was when the poor were
most likely to have money available. The Evangelical idea of the
Scriptures providing metaphorical nourishment for the spirit was
used again in this account of 'a poor Woman' and her Loan Bible.
Asked if she read it daily, she replied, 'Oh, Yes. I cannot do without
it; I want it to feed upon; and besides I can meditate when I awake
in the night upon what I have read in the day'. Apparently, 'in some
cases much [was] committed to memory, probably from the very
feeling that the Bible [was] only a Loan'. Yet the collectors could
learn a wise lesson from their 'poor neighbours'. They should
remember that their own Bibles must soon be handled by others,
and 'other eyes must soon dwell upon the sacred pages...when the
summons of death shall inform them that the period of the Loan
of this, and every other talent is expired'.

The Bible Ladies of the Spratton Association were also
indebted to the poor for other things they had learned in their
'cottage lessons'. They no longer took their own good fortune for
granted and had been forced to revalue the 'too-often squandered
or disregarded penny' when they saw the store laid upon it in the
cottage economy. The following anecdotal evidence was given. An
old woman, described as 'a very poor subscriber', had confided to

a Bible Lady that on one occasion she had no penny for her subscription the day before the collectors were due to call, 'nor did she know what to do for one'. Her little girl was given a penny at Sunday School, which she willingly gave to her mother towards 'procuring a Bible'. These other children must have come from better-off homes. There was the story of the small boy who, as well as subscribing for his own Testament, was asked to contribute 'something for the poor heathen'. He presented a shilling to the Collectors 'to get a Testament for a little black boy'. He was advised by his parents that 'he had better give a penny a week for the black boy, or his charity purse wd. soon be empty'. However, he insisted on donating his shilling, which was received 'with great pleasure'. Another little girl had 'enquired whether GOD made the heathens'. When told that he had created everyone, she gave a shilling to buy them a Bible so that they would learn about him. A third had asked for a Bible in large print so that she could read it when she was old. Such copies were available for those with poor sight. Though the women's stories may have been embellished a little by their own language, they were probably fair representations of their encounters. The *Branch Report* also included this item which had come from another of its Associations, but there is no mention of which one. 'A few young Ladies at your Cash Secretary's School have felt the impetus, and by weekly contributions have augmented our funds'. A collecting box 'kept for this purpose' had produced 14s.0d., and the girls wished to continue subscribing.

The Bible Ladies of the Spratton Association were able to report:

> The Association has also been the means of forming an increasingly strong bond of union between the poor and their more affluent neighbours. The former have found with gratitude that there are hearts ready to lighten their burdens by all the kindness of sympathy, & the latter have been convinced that the heart of the poor is susceptible of the power of persevering kindness & affectionate interest. The card & the penny placed in readiness on the Monday, & the hearty welcome of the poor cottager whose manner & lips have said, We quite count upon our Monday visits, thus have contributed to cheer the Collectors in their

weekly rounds; while the sickness, poverty, & affliction with wh. their visits have made them acquainted have been calculated to enforce the too-often forgotten value of health, peace & sufficiency.

Here, there are no evident feelings of guilt about the state of the poor in the neighbourhood and clearly the Bible Ladies upheld the prevailing class system. Like many others working in such fields of endeavour, they believed the social divisions God-given.[103] However, the women had offered sympathy and kindness. Nowhere in the Report is there reference to practical assistance being given to the sick, the poor and the afflicted. Possibly the Bible Women considered the local philanthropic aspect was already covered by Jones's Clothing Club, the Sick Club, and another of his schemes through which, in hard winters, he bought quantities of bread, meat and flour from local suppliers at reduced prices and sold them cheaply to the needy.[104] In addition, he himself paid for a woman at Creaton to teach poor girls to sew and the time came when at least one person in every house in the parish 'could make a shirt'.[105]

The *First Report of the Spratton Ladies' Bible Association* has confirmed the degree of poverty which existed in this part of rural Northamptonshire as the second quarter of the nineteenth century began, and has qualified the *laissez faire* attitudes that the Bible Ladies perpetuated on behalf of middle- and upper-class society. There is no suggestion here, or in the *Creaton Branch Report*, that radical social changes should be made to transform the lives of the poor. Only through self-help and serious religion were the lower orders to improve their lot. However, some of the nation's poor who had learnt to read in Sunday Schools and had been urged to study the Bible, not least by Bible Women, began extracting their own messages from it. For example, as Thompson has indicated, lay preachers turned Chartist leaders 'were willing to speak to the text, "He that hath no sword let him sell his garment and buy one."'[106]

103 See Prochaska, *Women and Philanthropy*, p.125.
104 Owen, *Memoir*, p.126.
105 *Ibid.*
106 Thompson, *The Making of the English Working Class* (1963, 1980 edn), p.440, quoting Luke, 22:36.

4.3   Local Women's other Evangelical work and involvement

It can be argued that often in a small community the same women involved themselves in several different aspects of Evangelical parish work. We know from the memoir of her brother, the Rev. Henry Smith, who married Matilda Owen, that Miss Maria Smith was a Bible Lady. She also collected for the Society for Promoting Christianity among the Jews. Maria was, 'with [their] dear mother, usefully engaged in various ways in the village of Creaton, doing good service in the Sunday School, and to the Church choir, playing the harmonium in Church, visiting the poor of the parish, and distributing tracts'.[107] Her religious life had been one of gradual growth, 'under the associations' of Thomas Jones and John Cobb, and the Smith's home had been 'a seed plot of piety' under the influence of their 'dear father and mother's Christian example'.[108] Maria's social status was probably typical of many of the Bible Ladies who inhabited this predominantly agricultural area. The Smith children inherited a 'modest patrimony consisting of a house and land' at little Creaton, where their father and they had been born, and which lay in the 'peaceful valley' of Spratton parish.[109] Maria Smith never married.

In Thomas Jones's own manuscript (found after his death) there is evidence of women's other responses to Evangelicalism in the locality. His reference to Mrs Ramsden of Spratton Hall and her sister, Miss Helen Plumptre, who lived with the family, bears witness to their role in assisting Mr Ramsden in his parochial endeavours:

> In the year 1818, it pleased God to bring into that Parish [Spratton] a family which has been a great help and comfort to me, and an immense benefit to the parish, and to the whole neighbourhood to a considerable extent. I allude to Robert Ramsden, Esquire; who continued to reside there for thirteen years. Schools and religious institutions were established and conducted by him; and he derived no small assistance from his invaluable sister-in-law, Miss Plumptre, and from Mrs Ramsden. Such a family, I

---

107 Smith, *Early Associations and Recollections*, p.23.
108 *Ibid.*, p.22.
109 *Ibid.*, pp. 5 & 8.

never expect to see again, whose only and constant aim was to do good, to serve God, and their generation.[110]

Why the family came to Spratton has never been discovered. That Anglican Evangelicalism was being practised locally may well have been a deciding factor. Miss Plumptre's name appeared before Mrs Ramsden's in the above abstract and John Owen mentioned her several times in footnotes in his *Memoir of Thomas Jones*.[111] The Evangelical activities of the Plumptre daughters living at Fredville, Nonington, Kent, have been mentioned in my Chapters 2 and 3. The eldest daughter, Frances Matilda, had married Robert Ramsden on 29 July 1816.[112] It was her first sister, Annabella Helen, who was living with them at Spratton Hall. Thus, the Plumptres and Ramsdens were two families of the landed gentry united not only by marriage but also by their strict Evangelicalism. It would be interesting to know if their status hindered the two sisters from being teachers at the Sunday School which Mr Ramsden had set up and financed, or members of its committee. Most likely a committee had been formed to manage the School's affairs.[113] Whether or not they were Bible Ladies is also open to question, but evidence already given has shown that they were used to dealing with poor cottagers when at Nonington.

In 1818, out of a Creaton parish population of '345'...'all the children of the poor (about 80 in number)' were being taught in the Sunday School,[114] but there was no such institution in Spratton parish at that time.[115] Perhaps they joined the one at Creaton. Christian instruction of the young was an obligation commanded by God in Proverbs 22:6: 'Train up a child in the way that he should

110 Quoted in Owen, *Memoir*, p.92.

111 John Owen, author of *The History of the Origin and First Ten Years of the British and Foreign Bible Society*, should not be confused with John Owen of Thrussington.

112 *Parish Register*, Church of St Mary, Nonington, Canterbury Cathedral Archives, U3/118/1/5 (microfilm). See Burke, *Landed Gentry*. Both families were originally from Nottinghamshire.

113 See K. D. M. Snell, 'The Sunday-School movement in England and Wales: child labour, denominational control and working-class culture', *Past & Present*, no. 164 (August 1999), pp.164-5.

114 Parliamentary Papers (1819) IX/2, *Digest of Education Returns, County of Northampton* (1818), p.647.

115 See *Ibid.*, p.660: 'An estate of 70 *l.* per annum was left for the use of the poor, but from which they derive no benefit, as it is not expressly stated which way the poor are to enjoy it, and the farmers apply the whole to help the levies. The curate [T. Jones] expresses a wish that it was possible to remedy this evil, without putting it in chancery.'

go, and when he is old he will not depart from it'. William Wilberforce had declared that the female sex were better fitted than men for the 'important task which devolves on it, of the education of our earliest youth'.[116] An extant manuscript list of *Resolutions* was compiled for the conduct of Creaton Sunday School and the handwriting is very like that of Clara Bosworth.[117] Though undated, there can be little doubt that these rules were in operation during the period under discussion here.

The village children were probably very young when they started at this Evangelical Sunday School, and the Resolutions indicate the strictness of what was expected from them 'in the first four Classes'. It can be imagined that occasionally the female teachers had some difficult cases to deal with, but their instructions were very clear. Because Sunday School rules of the time may not often be located, it is worth quoting the Creaton ones in full:

> Resolved that a Character Card be provided for each Child in the first four Classes in place of Tickets. Such card with the name and number affixed to it to be given to the Child upon his or her producing a bag or case proper to contain the Card, till which time the Card to be carefully kept by the Teacher. The Teacher to dwell upon the value and importance of the Card in order to ensure its being kept safe and clean. To remind the Child that it is all it has to shew for his or her conduct in the school and that in losing this record he or she would lose all title to reward up to that period and will be required to pay one penny for a new Card. The different marks for good, indifferent and bad to be neatly entered by the Teacher with ink in the respective columns. A Hymn, Collect or portion of Scripture shall have an indifferent mark if three decided mistakes be made and a bad mark in case of more. A bad mark under *Conduct* is to be considered a severe punishment, as annulling every good mark for the day. (This mark to be considered). This mark to be incurred by ill behaviour during divine service or wilfull absence from it, as well as by ill-conduct in the school. And when a Child is obstinately idle, saucey or ill-behaved it shall be

116 Wilberforce, *Practical View*, p.259.
117 *Resolutions: Creaton Sunday School*, undated manuscript, N.C.R.O., Bos.Coll.

formally expelled the School. The Children in the respective classes to have precisely the same portion assigned them in reading and repeating whether it be verses, hymns, catechism, Collect. And in the case of any Child proving incompetent to read or repeat equally with the others after full trial such Child to be removed to a lower class.

Evangelicals laid particular stress on catechizing. This is borne out in an article in the *Evangelical Magazine* urging adults to catechize children 'with diligence' and to explain what they learnt 'with familiarity'; there should be no delay in teaching the young about the love and admonition of God for 'Satan beg[an] early to enlist them into his service'.[118] Perhaps the Creaton Sunday School card could serve as a reference when a child applied for employment. However, nowhere was there mention of teaching the children to write, but predominating Sabbatarian views may have disallowed the activity.[119]

Miss Helen Plumptre played an important role in Thomas Jones's life and ministry. Her support was capable and wholehearted, as Owen has reported, and her notes on some of Jones's sermons were published under the title *Baskets of Fragments*.[120] Domestic commitments were likely to have been fewer for Miss Plumptre than for Mrs Ramsden, and Evangelical activism gave unmarried women a sphere in which to express their own personalities and talents. In 1831 the Ramsdens moved back to the family seat, Carlton Hall, Nottinghamshire, and Miss Plumptre went with them. Owen has evidenced that she sustained her interest in the poor of Creaton and Spratton long after she left and that Jones wrote to her often. This comment in one of his letters has confirmed that Helen Plumptre's new community were also benefitting from her devotion to the Evangelical cause: 'Right principle alone can truly reform a nation; and you contribute at Carlton far more towards saving the country from ruin than all the political unions in the Empire. Whatever goes to demoralize a

---

118 'M.' (Probably H. Mends, one of the stated contributors), 'Thoughts on the importance of catechising youth', *Evangelical Magazine* VIII (1800), pp.234-5.
119 See Bebbington, *Evangelicalism*, p.123; Laqueur, *Religion and Respectability*, pp.124-5; Snell, 'The Sunday-School Movement in England and Wales', p.129.
120 Author given as Thomas Jones, *Baskets of Fragments: or notes from sermons*, 2 vols (1832-33).

country can never lessen its sufferings, but must hasten its ruin.'[121]

Mrs Bishopp was probably more involved at parish level in Thornby, but there is evidence of her considerable support of Evangelical clergy, locally and further afield. John Owen addressed his *Memoir of Thomas Jones* to 'Mrs M. J. Welton Bishopp, Thornby Hall, Northamptonshire', in this manner:

> Dear Madam,
> I dedicate this Volume to you for several reasons: you knew Mr Jones intimately from childhood; you entertain the highest respect for his memory; you materially promoted his comfort in his old age; you have supplied me with important materials, and it has been through your encouragement and solicitation that I have undertaken the work. There is another reason which is personal: it is to you that I am indebted for my present position in the Church; and I wish to leave to posterity a memorandum of your great kindness and liberality...
>
> I am, dear Madam, yours
> With high esteem and gratitude,
> John Owen.
>
> Thrussington,
> April 1851.[122]

Clearly, Evangelical religion was a significant element in Mrs Bishopp's life. She had known Thomas Jones from her earliest years and it can be assumed that her introduction to John Owen was through him. 'Mrs Mary Jane Weltden Bishop' [sic] had presented Owen to the Thrussington living on 27 August 1845.[123] The presentation deed dated 7 August 1845 designated her 'Mary Jane Weltden Bishopp of Thornby, widow'.[124] There can be little doubt that her forebears had lived at Thornby. The indications are that 'Welton' was an Anglicized spelling of 'Weltden' and that the latter was her maiden name. In official documents dated after her husband's death her surname was continually written as 'Weltden

121 Undated letter, see Owen, *Memoir*, p.278.
122 Owen, *Memoir*, p.v.
123 Peterborough Diocese, *Institutions Book* (1839-1862), p.54, N.C.R.O., ML734.
124 Leicestershire C.R.O., presentation deed 7D55/1008/1, 7 August 1845.

Bishopp'.[125] This was probably because she wished to hold on to her own family name when she was widowed; her husband was always referred to as 'Dr. Bishopp'. Weltdens had lived in Thornby at least since the seventeenth century,[126] and Bridges stated that one of the 'possessors of estates' at Thurnby [sic] in 1791 was 'Mr Weltden', who laid 'claim to the Manor'.[127] Obviously, Mrs Bishopp was a dedicated lady of some means, who wished to do all within her power to see Evangelical clergy installed. Further evidence is to be found in one of Jones's letters to Clara: 'Mrs Bishopp is about buying the next presentation to the Living of Naseby for Jones the Curate. The terms are settled'.[128] In 1841 'James Jones, aged 20, Clergyman' was a member of Mrs Bishopp's household at Thornby Hall.[129] However, on 30 March 1847 James Jones was 'instituted to the Vicarage of the Parish Church of Naseby', on the presentation of 'George Ashby Maddock of Greenfield near Shrewsbury, Salop.'[130] Mrs Bishopp was then aged 69 and she lived until 26 October 1863. Perhaps she did acquire the advowson and then passed it on to Maddock, whose surname is familiar because of the Rev. Abraham Maddock's curacy at Creaton before that of Thomas Jones.

This chapter has highlighted that female activities in spheres of Evangelical religion were largely governed by their social status and men's attitudes towards women. As we have seen, some women helped to perpetuate the system. They were unable or unwilling to change a situation clearly defined by masculine rules and social inequalities. The Bible Ladies were at the forefront of new ecumenical co-operation for mission at parish level and, as well as accepting their own restricted roles, they supported organizational methods that clearly defined the parameters of local female activism for those poorer than themselves. Evidence given in this close investigation has shown that a limited rural area of Northamptonshire can well illustrate how women's diverse

125 See N.C.R.O., Indenture (Conveyance), 18 June 1864, ZB1158/51; Indenture (Lease), 3 January 1867, B/G79.
126 See Anne Weltden born 1678, Thornby Register of Baptisms, N.C.R.O., microfiche 318p/1.
127 J. Bridges, *The Histories and Antiquities of Northamptonshire* (Oxford, 1791), p.584.
128 Jones to C. Bosworth, undated, c. 1840, N.C.R.O., Bos. Coll. Creaton is 3 miles from Thornby, Naseby 2 miles from Thornby.
129 Thornby, *Census Enumerators' Returns*, N.C.R.O., microfilm M345.
130 *Institutions Book*, N.C.R.O., ML734, p.54. His predecessor had been presented to the living by Hannah M. Maddock, of the same address, in June 1819, ML733, p.306.

responses to Evangelicalism usually accorded to their places in society. Female landed gentry at Spratton Hall were prominent in Church life and gave private assistance to Thomas Jones. The wealthy Mrs Bishopp was particularly significant in her practical help during a long association with Thomas Jones, and as patron of John Owen. Organized groups of middle-class 'ladies' collected subscriptions for home and overseas mission, and distributed Bibles to their less fortunate neighbours. Numerous local poor women contributed their pennies to these missionary endeavours, most likely promising to encourage Evangelical piety and morality in their own homes, went to church or chapel themselves, and sent their children to Sunday School.

Illustrations

Extract from letter, Mrs A.M. Lukyn to Mrs M. Strong, 25th March 1813.

Anthony Lukyn, a Celebrity of Canterbury, photograph, 1959,
of portrait by John Wollaston, 1742.

Fredville, the Seat of John Pemberton Plumptre, Esq., M.P., reproduced from lithograph by R. Martin in The Epitome of the History of Kent, 1838.

St Andrew's Church, Spratton, drawing about 1820, unsigned.

Highgate House, Spratton, drawing about 1820, unsigned.

Highgate House, Spratton.

A room in Highgate House, Spratton.

Cellar in Highgate House, Spratton.

Church of St Michael and All Angels, Creaton, drawing, about 1830, unsigned.

Rev. Thomas Jones (of Creaton), drawing unsigned.

The Cross Circle, Brixworth, Northamptonshire.

William Carey.

Carey's Pulpit, Hackleton Baptist Church, Northamptonshire.

BAPTIST LEADERS OF THE EARLY NINETEENTH CENTURY

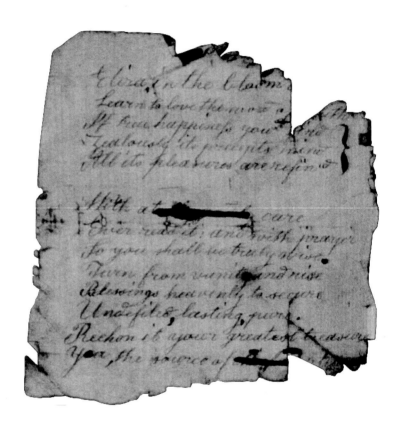

Eliza Westbury's poem in William Knowles' diary.

Chapter 5

ELIZA WESTBURY (1808 - 1828) AND THE PARTICULAR BAPTISTS AT HACKLETON, NORTHAMPTONSHIRE

5.1 Introduction to Eliza Westbury

'If ye continue in my word,
then are ye my disciples indeed.'
John 8:31.
Text preached at the baptism of
Eliza Westbury, Sunday, 7 May 1826.

'Whereas ye know not what shall be on
the morrow. For what is your life?
It is even a vapour, that appeareth
for a time, and then vanisheth away.'
James 4:14.
Text preached at the burial of
Eliza Westbury, Sunday, 20 April 1828.[1]

It can be seen that an interval of just under two years separated the baptism and burial of Eliza Westbury. Both of these rites were administered by the Reverend William Knowles who was then pastor of the Particular Baptist Church at Hackleton, Northamptonshire, the Evangelical community to which she belonged. Aged twenty when she died, Eliza had earned her living from lace-making and spent the whole of her short life in Hackleton, a hamlet in the rural parish of Piddington which included an area of Salcey Forest. The parish was situated just over five miles from the county town and about four from the Buckinghamshire border.

---

1   Rev. W. Knowles, Diary 1811-1833 (manuscript, pages unnumbered), N.C.R.O., HBC8. John 8:31 tells how Jesus was disclosing to those Jews in Jerusalem who had some faith in Him, 'that in order to be His disciples they must accept His word, and find in it the freedom He proclaimed': see M. Dods, 'The Gospel of St. John', vol. I, p.206, in Robertson Nicoll (ed.), *The Expositor's Bible* (1910). In James 4:14, the Apostle was 'addressing godless persons' and reminding everyone, not only non-believers, of the instability and transitoriness of life: see A. Plummer, 'The General Epistles of St Jude and St James', p.267, *The Expositor's Bible* (1907).

On 23 April 1826, Eliza and a Mary Willett[2] 'spoke their experience' at a Hackleton 'Church Meeting' and 'were unanimously received'.[3] By this it can be understood that they had given a responsible and credible account of their conversion to Evangelicalism. They had turned 'away from their sins in repentance and to Christ in faith'.[4] Thereby they had satisfied the prerequisite for acceptance into full membership of their Church and for baptism as believers. A fortnight later, on 7th May, they were both baptized by immersion.[5] Eliza had already been christened in the Parish Church of St. John the Baptist at Piddington on 22 May 1808 soon after her birth.[6] On that occasion, through the promises made on her behalf by her godparents, she was pronounced 'regenerate', 'grafted into the body of Christ's Church' and 'an inheritor of [His] everlasting Kingdom', according to Anglican Church liturgy for the 'Publick Baptism of Infants'.[7] However, most Evangelicals recognized conversion, not baptism, as the moment of regeneration.[8]

2   Probably Mary, daughter of Hugh and Dorothy Willitt [sic], christened at Piddington, 5 March 1797, *Piddington Parish Register*, N.C.R.O., microfiche 266p/3.

3   *Hackleton Baptist Church Book*, 1781-1869, (manuscript, pages unnumbered, most items, dated), N.C.R.O., HBC16.

4   Bebbington, *Evangelicalism*, p.5.

5   Knowles, *Diary*, N.C.R.O., HBC8.

6   Her parents, William Westbury and Elizabeth York had both been christened at Piddington, on 16 August 1789 and 27 March 1785 respectively, *Piddington Parish Register*, N.C.R.O., microfiche 266p/3.

7   In *The Book of Common Prayer and Administration of the Sacraments and other Rites and Ceremonies of the Church according to the use of The Church of England*. However, all Baptists found paedobaptism unacceptable. They read passages such as Mark 1; verse 5: John baptized 'all the land of Judaea, and they of Jerusalem' in the River Jordan, 'confessing their sins'. See also E. A. Payne, *The Baptist Union; A Short History* (1958), p.273, citing The Baptist Union's 'reply to a letter from the Archbishop of Canterbury' (1889): 'Our churches hold and teach that the New Testament law of Baptism requires a profession of faith in the Lord Jesus Christ as a prerequisite to the administration of the rite; or, as it is well expressed in the Catechism of the Church of England, in answer to the question, "What is required of persons to be baptized"? - "Repentance, whereby they forsake sin, and Faith, whereby they steadfastly believe the promises of God"; and that the administration of baptism to infants, "when by reason of their tender age" they cannot satisfy these conditions, is contrary to the practice of the Primitive and Apostolic Church.'
Yet only an Anglican baptism certificate was recognized as proof of identity for legal purposes, see Knight, *The Nineteenth-century Church*, p.25.

8   The issue has posed a perennial problem for Evangelicals in the Anglican Church: see Bebbington, *Evangelicalism*, pp.9-10.

Though a young working woman of few educational opportunities, during her limited period of survival after being baptized, Eliza managed to write the words of around one-hundred-and-fifty congregational hymns and some poems. Through verse she was able to share her Evangelical beliefs with others. In Eliza's writings can be seen the four main characteristics of Evangelicalism described by Bebbington - activism is evident in her production of the poems and hymns, conversionism can be recognized in her own conversion and, as biblical references given here will demonstrate, biblicism and crucicentrism have been manifested in many of her verses. Eliza no doubt rejoiced in her literacy and perhaps felt it her duty to thank God by applying her artistic talents to activism of this kind. Furthermore, an artist could find fulfilment in the high emotion and imagination that were central to Evangelicalism.[9] We can argue that the wider opportunities for learning and self-expression brought by being able to read and write were distinctly evident for this intelligent girl living in a community where illiteracy was all too common, especially among the older female generation. Eliza's own parents had been unable to sign their names when they were married in Piddington Parish Church on 18 November 1807.[10] It is likely that her two unmarried aunts, who in 1828 were sharing the Westbury household, also could not write. Nevertheless, even those who made a mark might well have been able to read, and not to count them among the '"literate" would be to fundamentally misunderstand the cultural context of nineteenth-century England, where, for the labouring population, reading was literacy'.[11]

A few months after her death, a selection of Eliza's compositions were published in a small book entitled *Hymns by a Northamptonshire Village Female; To which is added, A short Account of her Life.*[12] The 'short Account' was printed at the beginning and, though certainly not very long, it is a most useful miniature

9 See D. Cecil, *The Stricken Deer: the Life of William Cowper* (1929, 1943 edn), p.83.

10 *Piddington Parish Register*, N.C.R.O., microfiche 266p/4: William Westbury to Elizabeth York. They each signed with a cross. No doubt Elizabeth was already pregnant, for Eliza was baptized only six months after the wedding. Pre-marital pregnancy was common among the poorer classes during the early nineteenth century: see Snell, *Annals of the Labouring Poor*, p.354.

11 B. Reay, 'The context of meaning of popular literacy: some evidence from nineteenth-century rural England', *Past and Present*, No. 131 (1991), p.129.

12 *Hymns: by A Northamptonshire Village Female. To which is added, A short Account of her Life.* (Northampton, 1828), N.C.R.O., HBC71/1.

biography on which to build:

> Eliza Westbury was the daughter of William and Elizabeth
> Westbury of Hackleton, Northamptonshire. She was born
> in the year 1808. Her father died in the faith of the gospel,
> in the year 1811. At an early age she was sent to a Sabbath
> School, and made pleasing progress in learning. She, at
> times, felt conviction of sin; but remained a stranger to
> religion until the beginning of the year 1825, when it
> pleased God to seal upon her heart a few words which
> were spoken to her after she had been hearing a Sermon
> to young people. In May, 1826, she joined the Baptist
> Church at Hackleton, of which she was an honourable
> member till her death. During the last two years of her life
> she composed about one hundred and fifty Hymns, besides
> other poetry from which the following are selected and
> published, under the impression that they will be
> acceptable to her Christian friends. Most of them where
> [sic] composed while she was earning her living at lace-
> making, and which she used to write at her leisure. Her
> own experience will be seen in the piece of poetry at the
> end of the hymns, which was found after her death. She
> was frequently deeply impressed with the evil of sin, and
> was fearful lest she should deceive herself: but her death
> was attended with peace and with the hope of a blessed
> immortality.

This sad account then followed:

> The providences with which the family to which she
> belonged was visited were very affecting; within sixteen
> weeks out of five persons who resided in the same house,
> four were removed by death.

> On the fourth of January, 1828, her mother died; on the
> 20th, one of her mother's sisters; on the 11th of April,
> death visited her, and on the 18th of the same month
> another of her mother's sisters; but unto them all there is
> ground for hope that death was gain, and that though they
> are absent from the body, they are present with the Lord.
> Reader! prepare to meet thy God![13]

Evangelicals were constantly exhorted to preparedness for a sudden meeting with their Maker and Hackleton Particular Baptists at that time must surely have seen how urgent their response should be.

Though Eliza's father, William Westbury, was mentioned only briefly in the 'short Account' it has confirmed that he was an Evangelical. We do not know how he earned a living but his father, also William, had been a cordwainer,[14] and perhaps the two men had followed the same trade. Further mention of William junior can be found in the two-page *History of Hackleton Sabbath School*, from which the following details will be taken.[15] William Westbury had been 'the strictest of the strict Churchmen' but seceded from Piddington Parish Church after his conversion in 'the old Meeting House' at Hackleton in 1809. He had struggled with his conscience about wishing to attend the Baptist Chapel to hear 'a very good preacher' at the suggestion of a friend. He 'prayed about it', felt he should go and was converted at the meeting. Soon afterwards he was baptized and the event will be described here a little later. He 'became a good man, a faithful man who found God above many'. Thus Eliza's father had decided to leave the established church and 'commit [himself] to an alternative community, the gathered church of the believers',[16] a significant move for any young man. The consequent loss of personal liberty was a payment required by full commitment to Evangelical Nonconformity.[17] It usually meant a disciplined life with regular attendance at religious gatherings, an abandonment of frivolity and cruel sporting practices, soberness in all aspects of living, perhaps breaking of friendships. As Doreen Rosman has shown, not all Evangelicals conformed to this strict code of behaviour. For instance, Fowell Buxton, a committed Evangelical clergyman, did not give up shooting. However, examples of those who continued their cruel sports were perhaps more common within the Church of England, where so many members of the leisured classes could be found, than within dissent.[18] William Westbury was one of three men who established the Baptist Sabbath School at Hackleton

13 *Hymns by a Northamptonshire Village Female*, pp.i-ii.
14 See *Constable's (Militia) List* (1786), Hackleton, *sub* Wymersley Hundred, N.C.R.O. 984/9.
15 Anon., *History of Hackleton Sabbath School* (c.1881), N.C.R.O., HBC43.
16 Davidoff & Hall, *Family Fortunes*, p.130.
17 Gilbert, *Religion and Society*, p.87.
18 Rosman, *Evangelicals and Culture*, p.122.

some time between his conversion and death. It was their contribution to activism within their own Evangelical community.[19] Even though very young when her father was involved in this work, Eliza may have accompanied him to the Sabbath School on occasions. He died on 11 September 1811 at the age of twenty-two and was buried in Hackleton Baptists' graveyard by Eustace Carey, the nephew of Dr. William Carey. More will be written about William Carey further on in this chapter. Eliza was three years and four months at the time of her father's death, therefore old enough to miss him.

The 'short Account' gave no indication of where Eliza and her female relatives were interred and most of the epitaphs on the few memorial stones still standing in the small graveyard at Hackleton have been eroded. However, an extant enumeration of 'Persons buried in the burial ground belonging to the Baptist Meeting at Hackleton' in each of the years 1813 to 1828 has proved particularly useful in remedying the deficiency.[20] This has shown that three males and four females were buried there during 1828, the year of the greatest number of deaths recorded in the list. Though the enumeration named no individuals, the numbers for each year can be tied up with Knowles's conscientious entries in his diary naming those who died and the dates of their funerals. Thus it can be deduced that Elizabeth Westbury, Eliza Westbury, and her unmarried aunts, Charlotte and Harriett York, were the four women laid to rest in the Hackleton Baptists' graveyard in 1828. However, why so many deaths in one household occurred within such a short time cannot be ascertained, but a poor living environment, conducive of rapid spread of infection, was probably the cause. It can be assumed that the fifth person sharing Eliza's household in 1828 was her brother, George. Christened in Piddington Parish Church on 9 July 1809, he was about fourteen months younger than his sister, therefore only nineteen when he lost these four close, female relatives.[21]

19 See Laqueur, *Religion and Respectability*: Within Dissent the 'new activist, lay dominated, largely poor, religious community provided a large proportion of early Sunday school workers'. For some, the primary function of Sunday School teachers was to spread 'the Word of God, an end valuable for its own sake', pp.3-4. This was possible even if a teacher was illiterate. See also Bebbington, *Evangelicalism*, p.129: Sunday School teachers were 'overwhelmingly male' at that time.

20 Paper inserted at front of Knowles, *Diary*, N.C.R.O., HBC8..

21 *Piddington Parish Register*, N.C.R.O., microfiche 266p/3. A George Westbury was baptized by Knowles on 27 May 1851, but this may not have been Eliza's brother.

Madeleine Marshall and Janet Todd have recognized hymns as religious poetry and noted their important place in the study of literary tradition, explaining that hymns were often read in private as well as sung in public.[22] It was not unusual for a writer's hymns and poems of a religious nature to appear in the same publication. The penultimate item in Eliza's book was given the title, 'On the Death of the Author's Mother' and was numbered '72', seemingly appearing as the last of the hymns. Though its eight verses had Evangelical connotations, they cannot be judged suitable for singing. This will be evident when the poem is discussed below. The final item in the book was unnumbered and entitled, 'Verses, containing an account of the writer's experience'. Comprising fifty-four stanzas of rhyming couplets, they were clearly meant to be read. The reference to them in the 'short Account' gives anticipation of a valuable source for discussing the significance of Evangelicalism in Eliza's life. This poem must have been written some time after her conversion in 1826 and, as it was discovered only after her demise, probably no-one else had seen it other than perhaps those within her own household. The analysis given later will confirm that these 'Verses' have recorded a young woman's difficult spiritual journey towards a change of heart. The evidence is that, in the light of spiritual conversion, Eliza's recognition of her waywardness and periods of Christian unbelief during her misspent teenage years proved an almost unbearable burden at times. In addition, the poem has given a little insight into how Evangelicalism affected the day-to-day existence and relationships of this 'Northamptonshire village female' from childhood to early womanhood.

Eliza's Evangelical religion pervaded her working life inasmuch as most of her hymns 'were composed while she was earning her living at lace-making, and which she used to write at her leisure'.[23] Seemingly, she was so proficient in her skill that she could safely divert her concentration from working at her pillow to composing. Probably she had attended one of the nearby lace schools like many other local children, some of whom might have been as young as four.[24] Family circumstances without a father's income may well

---

22 M. F. Marshall & J. Todd, *English Congregational Hymns in the Eighteen Century*, (Kentucky, 1982), pp.1-27.

23 *Hymns by a Northamptonshire Village Female*, p.i.

24 R. M. Serjeantson & W. R. D. Adkins (eds), *The Victoria History of the County of Northampton*, II (1906), p.338.

have made it vital for her to earn money from her craft at a very early age. 'Essentially lace-making was a cottage industry, chiefly undertaken by women and girls...All along the Buckinghamshire border [with Northamptonshire] it was prominent.'[25] The craft tended to carry on from one generation to the next so it is likely that Eliza's mother and her aunts all contributed to the family income by selling lace they had made.[26] Lace-makers often worked in groups and in fine, warm weather they usually sat outside. There is no indication that Eliza openly tried to convert others, but perhaps in the first instance she repeated her newly-composed verses to her companions as they sat together at their pillows. Maybe they even practised them to well-known hymn tunes for it was not unusual for lace-makers to sing as they worked.[27] The Rev. John Newton, Evangelical Anglican minister of nearby Olney, about whom much more will be written here, had realized 'how useful hymns might be in cottages where the simple folk sang Lace Tellings at their work'.[28] Through regular singing together in groups, many hymns were committed to memory, thus helping to unite the literate and the illiterate.[29] Eliza wrote mostly in common, short or long metre which would have made selection of a tune not too difficult. These metres were and still are the standard rhythmic patterns most frequently used and familiar to hymn singers of all denominations.[30] Examination of some of Eliza's hymns further on in this chapter will reveal their Evangelical content.

---

25 Everitt, *Pattern of Rural Dissent*, p.35. In 1811, out of the 497 families living in Olney, 377 were engaged in Trade, Manufacture and Handicraft; in 1821 the figures were 557 and 283 respectively: see *Abstracts of Answers and Returns*, 1811, p.78; 1821, p.16.

26 See Sergeantson & Adkins (eds), *V.C.H., Northampton*, II, pp.336-339, for 'Lacemaking' in Northamptonshire.

27 The proficiency of children working in lace schools was judged by the number of pins stuck in their cushions in an hour and they often chanted traditional lines 'to assist themselves in counting the amount of work to be got over...These and the more elaborate songs sung at the pillow were called "Lace tellings"' [or 'tells']: see T. Wright, *The Town of Cowper* (1893), p.12.

28 B. Martin, *John Newton: a Biography* (1950), p.235.

29 Ditchfield, *The Evangelical Revival*, p.101.

30 For application of these metres see J. R. Watson, *The English Hymn; a Critical and Historical Study* (Oxford, 1997), pp.32-36. Marshall & Todd, *English Congregational Hymns*, p.13.

5.2 The historical development of Evangelicalism at Hackleton

An understanding of the Evangelical principles and practices that had been established among the Particular Baptists at Hackleton by Eliza Westbury's time, and which thus affected her own religious life and thought, can be gained only by giving an insight into developments there during the last two decades of the eighteenth century and the early nineteenth century. The Hackleton Particular Baptist community was probably unusual in that it had evolved through very close contact with a number of eminent Nonconformist personalities, about whom much has been written in historiographies of Protestant Dissent.

> Several of the most influential figures in Baptist and Congregationalist circles during the [eighteenth] century had been Northamptonshire pastors, in particular Philip Doddridge, the two John Rylands, and William Carey. Carey's tenure of office in the county had been brief, but as a son of Northamptonshire and founder of the Baptist Missionary Society, he became something of a local hero. The influence of the John Rylands, father and son, had been fundamental in the Evangelical Awakening among Baptists, and their reign had been based for more than thirty years (1759-93) upon College Street Chapel in Northampton. Equally important, at an earlier stage in the Awakening, was the influence of the Congregationalist Philip Doddridge, not only through his chapel and academy in Northampton itself but also by means of his preaching-tours and above all his writings and hymns.[31]

Though this must be a limited discussion of events and personalities connected with Hackleton, it will still form a long section here because of the significant contributions these well-known Dissenters made to the Evangelical Movement both locally and nationally.

One of the aids to Nonconformist encroachment in a parish was the breakdown of squire-parson relationships.[32] No incumbent had been appointed to the living at Piddington Parish Church since

---

31 Everitt, *Pattern of Rural Dissent*, pp.51-2.
32 Gilbert, *Religion and Society*, pp.98.

1641 and from that time its ministry had been in the hands of successive curates.[33] Extant letters written between 1780 and 1810 have highlighted the following anomalies and ambiguities existing at Piddington which did not bode well for an ideal Anglican ministry. The presentation was a royal donative that went with the ownership of nearby Horton Hall, and the appointed curate was responsible for both Horton and Piddington Churches. In 1780 the curacy was in the hands of a Fellow of Lincoln College, Oxford, who resided in the College. Perhaps this was because 'the squire had long appropriated the living of £300 a year, the parsonage, the glebe, and all tithes, sending his house minister "at times" to do duty'.[34] A less than adequate ministry at Piddington was being performed on a voluntary basis by the vicar of Roade, six miles distant.[35] Such a situation could only have played into the hands of local itinerant Evangelical Nonconformists.

As Bebbington has commented, 'the impact of Evangelicalism on orthodox Dissent in England and Wales did not become general until the last years of the eighteenth century'.[36] Conversionist zeal, 'insistence on high standards of piety and personal morality' were as characteristic among Evangelical Baptists and Congregationalists of the period as they were within Methodist ranks.[37] Itinerancy, local preaching and the voluntary activities of lay people were an integral part of Evangelical Nonconformity. Doddridge had forged strong links with the rural communities around Northampton. Carey at one time attended some Congregational prayer

33 *Bishop's Visitations*, Entry 12th July 1792: 'The Stewd of Sir Robt Gunning Bart pays 40 [pounds] per annum to the Curate. N.B. Has not been any Institution since 1641 when the Crown presented', N.C.R.O., ML582. See 19th-century copy of 1641 tract in parish register, N.C.R.O., microfiche 266p/11; also gives 'Land in lieu of Tithes under the New Enclosure (340+ acres] and money payment under Tithe Commutation (£34)'.

34 G. Smith, *Life of William Carey, Shoemaker and Missionary* (1909, 1922 edn), p.12.

35 Letter, Sir Robert Gunning to the Bishop of Peterborough, 21 Feb. 1780, N.C.R.O., G(H)734. By the early nineteenth century Sir George Gunning had inherited Horton Estate from his father, Robert, and was seemingly unaware of his duty to nominate someone for the living. No presentation had been made so the Bishop had stepped in and appointed through powers of sequestration. Extant correspondence has evidenced Gunning's absence from Horton for considerable periods, his apathy towards ecclesiastical matters, and the subsequent appointment of a curate dissatisfied with his stipend of £40 p.a.: see letters, Spencer Perceval (Northampton M.P.) to George Gunning, 1804: 21 August, 1 October, 4 December, N.C.R.O., G(H)756, 758, 759.

36 Bebbington, *Evangelicalism*, p.32.

37 Gilbert, *Religion and Society*, pp.51-2, citing Bogue and Bennett, *Dissenters*, iv, p.341.

meetings.[38] The Particular Baptist, John Ryland Jnr, also had zealously engaged in proclaiming the Gospel in the villages round Northampton in addition to assisting his father at College Street Chapel.[39] Thus he, too, came to know the young William Carey (1761-1831), who had been born at Paulerspury near Towcester and had moved to Hackleton for his shoemaking apprenticeship. Because of his Evangelical notoriety in the realms of mission and his direct historical connection with Hackleton Particular Baptists, Carey is worthy of special consideration later on in this section.

Mention must be made of another prominent Evangelical whose occasional presence among the Particular Baptists at Hackleton during Eliza Westbury's own lifetime was recorded in minutes of their meetings. This was the Rev. Andrew Fuller (1754-1815), minister at Kettering, Northamptonshire, from 1782 until his death. Fuller was perhaps the outstanding Baptist figure of the period, a theologian, whose book *The Gospel Worthy of all Acceptation* (1785), initiated a modified form of Calvinism, 'a reaction against the hyper-Calvinism of his time'.[40] He argued that, if only the elect 'could embrace the Gospel', it was pointless and wrong 'to invite the unconverted to put their trust in Christ'.[41] Bebbington has described Fuller's book as 'the classic statement of eighteenth-century Evangelical Calvinism'.[42] The 'Modern Question', as this debate was called,[43] revolved around the principle of duty faith, that is, whether all those who had knowledge of the Gospel should repent and believe in Christ.[44] Practicalities of the issue were: 'If believing was an obligation, preachers could press it on whole congregations. If it was not, they could merely describe it in the hope that God would rouse certain predetermined hearers to faith'.[45] As will be shown here, Fuller itinerated widely to preach and evangelize. However, there was severe contention between

38 Smith, *Life of William Carey*, p.11.
39 'Memoir of the late Rev. John Ryland, D.D.', *Baptist Magazine*, XVIII (1826), p.3. See also T. S. H. Elwyn, *The Northamptonshire Baptist Association: a Short History of the Association, 1764-1964* (1964), p.31.
40 Elwyn, *Northamptonshire Baptist Association*, p.32. See also, Payne, *The Baptist Union*, pp.37-8.
41 A. G. Fuller, *Andrew Fuller* (1882), p.96.
42 Bebbington, *Evangelicalism*, pp.64-5.
43 *Ibid.*, p.64: 'The controversy first arose among Northamptonshire Independents in the late 1730s'.
44 Fuller, *Andrew Fuller*, p.95.
45 Bebbington, *Evangelicalism*, p.64.

those accepting his Evangelical Calvinism and the Strict and
Particular Baptists, followers of William Gadsby (1773-1844), who
led a reaction within the Baptist Church against what became
known as 'Fullerism'. Gadsby, a minister of working-class
background, was a powerful hyper-Calvinist preacher.[46] Firmly
upholding the doctrine of predestination but repudiating
Antinomianism, Gadsby can be recognized as 'the patriarch' of
present-day Strict and Particular Baptists.[47] The Particular Baptist
churches left the body of Old Dissent to become a strand of the
New Dissent that embraced Evangelical values and methods.[48]
Fuller's special significance in this present writing on the Particular
Baptists at Hackleton is that he inspired Carey's eagerness for
mission overseas.[49] For Carey, duty faith inferred an obligation to
evangelize throughout the world.[50] In 1792 he wrote his *An
Enquiry into the Obligations of Christians to Use Means for the
Conversion of the Heathen*. However, it can be seen from Eliza
Westbury's 'Verses' that the notion of being duty-bound to believe
posed a real dilemma for her. She often found conviction
impossible, yet she never ceased questioning.

Everitt might be thought to have underestimated admiration
for William Carey locally so far as the people of Piddington and
Hackleton were concerned. Certainly, to the Particular Baptists in
the area he was more than 'something of a local hero'. Carey was
domiciled in Hackleton for ten years, from the age of fourteen in
1775 to 1785. This was the formative period of his religious
development and the most significant events in his progress towards
Evangelicalism had occurred during that time. Carey had been an
Anglican and at first seceded to Congregationalism, but two years
later he joined the Baptists.[51] Having found in the Bible his answer
to the paedobaptism question that had posed a fundamental
problem for him, according to his own account, he 'somewhat
suddenly became a Baptist'.[52] He was converted at a Hackleton
Meeting and was baptized in the River Nene at Northampton on

46 Payne, *The Baptist Union*, p.41.
47 A. C. Underwood, *A History of the English Baptists* (1947), p.185.
48 Gilbert, *Religion and Society*, pp.36-7.
49 Elwyn, *Northamptonshire Baptist Association*, p.32.
50 Underwood, *A History of the English Baptists*, p.165.
51 M. R. Watts, *The Dissenters, from the Reformation to the French Revolution*, II (Oxford, 1995), p.9.
52 Smith, *Life of William Carey*, p.12.

5 October 1783 by the younger John Ryland of College Street Chapel.[53] In view of the large number of biographies of William Carey and the prominence given him in historiographies of Protestant missionary societies, no excuse need be proferred here for assigning so much importance to his early connection with Hackleton Particular Baptists.

Boldly written on the first page of *Hackleton Baptist Church Book* was,[54] 'The Name of the Chapel in which the Church to which this Book belongs is The Baptist Chapel, Hackleton' and underneath this, in a more decorative script, the Covenant which had been 'borrowed' from College Street, Northampton.[55] This was 'Read and Assented to at the Admission of MEMBERS', therefore Eliza Westbury, like her renowned Hackleton predecessor and her own relatives, would have subscribed to its promissory words:

> We the Members of this Church of God whose Names are all inserted in this Book, do solemnly promise in the Presence of God, and of our Lord Jesus Christ the crowned King of Zion, and in the Presence of his holy Angels, and also in the Presence of each other To give up ourselves to the Lord and to one another by the will of GOD to walk together in the Profession of all Gospel Doctrines; and in an Attendance on all Gospel Ordinances; and in the Practise [sic] and Discharge of all Relative Duties, as the Lord shall enable us, endeavouring to keep the Unity of the Spirit in the Bond of Peace, as God shall enable us.
>
> AMEN[56]

The first nominal roll in *Hackleton Baptist Church Book* was dated 1781 and 'Wm Carey' was entered third on this list that contained the names of eight other men.[57] Thirteen women were named on the next page during the same year. The predominance of women at this early stage is noticeable.[58] At that time the

---

53 'Memoir of the Late Rev. John Ryland, D.D.', *Baptist Magazine* (1826), p.3.
54 *Hackleton Baptist Church Book*, N.C.R.O., HBC16.
55 *Hackleton Baptist Church Choirmaster's Notebook* (undated), N.C.R.O., HBC64.
56 *Hackleton Baptist Church Book*, N.C.R.O., HBC16.
57 *Ibid.*
58 Though probably all working-class, this may have been partly because women of all classes had fewer places for integration outside the home than men. With reference to this and the middle classes, see Davidoff & Hall, *Family Fortunes*, p.110.

twenty-year-old Carey was a young journeyman shoemaker working as well as living in Hackleton.[59] On 10 June 1781 he had married 'Dorithy Plackett', a fellow parishioner, in Piddington Anglican Church.[60] Eliza Westbury's grandfather must have known Carey and his wife, at least as neighbours, and her father could hardly have escaped growing up in the knowledge of the great missionary's work and his former life in the parish. Carey had begun his unofficial ministry by teaching the Biblical message to boys in his workshop at Hackleton.[61] In March 1785 he moved to Moulton (about nine miles from Hackleton) on becoming that Meeting's probationary minister, still eking out a living by his shoemaking. However, he wished to be 'sent out from some reputable church of Christ into the work of the ministry' and in June 1785 applied to Olney for membership, though still 'in connection with a society of people at Hackleton'.[62] The Baptist reputation at Olney was enhanced by the pastoral presence of Andrew Fuller's close friend, John Sutcliff, who ran an academy for ministers in what are now Nos 21\23 in the town's High Street. Carey was accepted by Olney Church, preaching for them and elsewhere until 1787 when he was dismissed to Moulton 'with a view to his Ordination'.[63] This duly took place. In 1789 he accepted the call to the Church at Harvey Lane, Leicester.[64] It was John Sutcliff who encouraged Carey to study Latin, through which the former shoemaker discovered his linguistic abilities.[65] In time, Carey mastered Greek, Dutch, Hebrew and Bengali, and eventually became a Doctor of Divinity.

In his *An Enquiry into the Obligation of Christians to Use Means*

59 Carey was born at Paulerspury, Northamptonshire, where he lived until he moved to Hackleton for his apprenticeship.

60 *Piddington Parish Register*, N.C.R.O., microfiche 266p/4. Dorithy [sic] marked the register with a cross. Her father became a deacon of Hackleton Baptist Church, N.C.R.O., HBC16. Eliza may have been related to the Placketts through a family marriage. See entry of marriage 22 September 1785: 'Daniel Plackett to Eliz. Westbery' [variation of spelling], both of Piddington, *Ibid*. These two surnames occur often in the contemporary parish records.

61 See photograph of the dilapidated building, *Album of illustrations and photographs*, c.mid-1900s, N.C.R.O., HBC11.

62 Smith, *Life*, p. 18, quoting entry, 17 June 1785, in *Olney Baptist Church Book* c.1752-1854, held at Sutcliff Baptist Church, Olney.

63 Elwyn, *Northamptonshire Baptist Association*, p.33.

64 *Ibid*.

65 R. H. Martin, 'Anglicans and Baptists in conflict: the Bible Society, Bengal and the Baptizo controversy', *Journal of Ecclesiastical Studies*, XLIX (1998), p.295.

for the Conversion of the Heathen, published in 1792, Carey's duty faith gave vision of wider Evangelical activism, picturing no boundaries of continent or race. It was in response to Carey's pleadings that the Particular Baptist Society for Propagating the Gospel among the Heathen was formed in that same year at a minsters' meeting at Kettering, Northamptonshire.[66] Four of the five committee members were Fuller, Ryland, Sutcliff and Carey himself, who offered to be its pioneering missionary.[67] Fuller was appointed the Society's first secretary, thus putting 'his convictions into practice'.[68] Carey returned to Hackleton very briefly just before he set out for India around 23 May 1793 to begin his work there.[69] The reports which came back from his missionary establishment at Serampore were cause for immense pride among the Baptists in Hackleton.

Carey died three years after Eliza Westbury. That he was one of her idols and an inspiration for her writing endeavours can be expected, for he demonstrated how much even a local shoemaker of little early education could achieve by applying his acquired learning to furthering the Evangelical cause. The copy of a portrait of 'Dr Carey and his Pundit' sent as a gift to Hackleton by the Baptist Missionary Society (as it was by now called) in November 1815,[70] was probably on constant display in the Meeting House. Carey's work in setting up the first English Christian Mission overseas was to inspire leaders within other denominations to adopt their own firm measures for converting heathens beyond Britain's shores.[71]

The present-day Carey Memorial Baptist Church at Hackleton was erected in 1887 as one of the Baptist Union's tributes to the

---

66 Smith, *Life of Carey*, pp.36-39; Payne, *The Baptist Union*, p.37. For more detailed account see B. Stanley, *The History of the Baptist Missionary Society, 1792-1992* (Edinburgh, 1992), pp. 9-15.

67 Smith, *Life of William Carey*, p.38.

68 Bebbington, *Evangelicalism*, p.64.

69 Noted among various items in album, N.C.R.O., HBC11.

70 *Hackleton Baptist Church Book*, N.C.R.O., HBC16.

71 See report of speech by William Wilberforce to Bath Missionary Association: '(I allude to Dr Carey). We see him rising from that poverty and that ignorance to a degree of knowledge, and then a degree of usefulness, which was scarcely ever before attained amongst the sons of men...from his knowledge and skill in the Asiatic languages, affording the greatest and most valuable assistance to the cause of Christianity.' *Baptist Magazine*, XIII, 2nd series (1821), p.133.

life and work of their great missionary.[72] A large dedication stone
on the outside wall bears the inscription:

> This
> place of worship
> was erected to the glory
> of God in memory of
> Dr Carey, the father of modern
> missions to the heathen, and one
> of the founders, and the first
> missionary of The Baptist Missionary
> Society: he toiled as a shoemaker,
> was converted to God
> and preached his first sermon in this village.

The original pulpit[73] from which Carey's preaching career
began, was removed from the former Meeting House at
Hackleton[74] to the larger one built in 1809 to accommodate the
greatly increased congregation.[75] A restoration of this wooden
preaching platform can be seen in today's building. For both young
and old worshipping at Hackleton during and after his lifetime,
Carey's pulpit has been a symbol of Evangelical conversionist zeal.

5.3 Hackleton's early nineteenth-century Evangelicals

We come now to the period covering Eliza Westbury's own life
among the Particular Baptists at Hackleton and the socio-
economic milieu in which she grew up. Piddington's geographical
situation near Northampton and its rural landscape were key
elements in shaping its employment patterns, in themselves
recognizable as factors enhancing the cause of New Dissent at
Hackleton. Undulating agricultural land and forest predominated.

---

72 The new building was erected on the same site as the previous one. See *Hackleton Baptist
Church Book*, N.C.R.O., HBC16: 'July 3 1887 was the last Sunday we worshipped in the
old chapel which had been erected in 1809' and, meantime, services took place in the
Hackleton 'Board School Room'.

73 Photograph in *Souvenir Programme* of 'Meetings to be held in connection with the
Autumn Rally', September 1945, N.C.R.O., HBC11.

74 Built by public subscription. See copy of Meeting House Certificate issued 31 March
1788, *Bishop's Visitations*, p.88, N.C.R.O., ML582.

75 See 'copy of certificate of licence of Chapel, granted 7 June 1810', inserted Rev. W.
Knowles, *Diary of texts preached, 1833-1856*, N.C.R.O., HBC10.

It was an 'open' parish and, even in the early decades of the nineteenth century, a residual antagonism towards the Established Church, overseers of the poor, and local landowners dating from the time of enclosure in 1782, may have contributed to the growth of the Baptist community.[76] It is difficult to assess what the real local socio-economic consequences of enclosure had been. However, commoners' rights for grazing and collection of fuel for their ovens and fires still prevailed in Salcey Forest as it was not enclosed until after 1826.[77] Labourers in heavily wooded areas, like Salcey, were at an advantage for there they could find employment making such things as poles, hurdles, fencing posts and charcoal.[78] It cannot be claimed that deprivations from forest enclosure contributed to Hackleton's Evangelical expansion during the earliest decades of the nineteenth century.

Gilbert has given evidence of the class and occupational structures of Evangelical Nonconformity in the early nineteenth century and shown how Evangelicalism had brought in a wider mix of society.[79] Recruitment from among artisans and unskilled labourers was particularly successful. Tradesmen and manufacturers also joined the movement, but in fewer numbers. These

---

76 *Inclosure Award, Piddington and Hackleton* (22 Geo. III, 27 Private, 1782), N.C.R.O.,
   Piddington: 0710. That dwellers were deprived of an important traditional source of
   maintenance from livestock, can be deduced from the fact that 'after the award,
   Sir Rbt Gunning' was to be exempted 'from keeping a Bull and Boar for the Use of the
   Inhabitants and Land Holders of Piddington and Hackleton'. In most rural areas,
   cottagers and other poor 'lost more than their livestock through enclosure': see Snell,
   Annals of the Labouring Poor, p.179. At Hackleton rights to collect fuel or furze were also
   affected. The Commissioners allotted '13 acres, 1 rood and 28 perches of Hackleton
   Furzes' from which 'as much as the Trustees [thought] fit' of 'the bushes, furzes and
   thorns' was to be cut each year and distributed 'unto and amongst such poor Inhabitants
   of Hackleton' as they thought 'proper Objects of Charity'. Gunning was one of the nine
   Trustees.
77 *Inclosure Award* and map (1826), Act 22, Geo.III, N.C.R.O., Stack 71,c3. Commoners
   suffered then. In Salcey (1,847 acres) the King and the Duke of Grafton already held
   254 extra-parochial acres not subject to any common or other rights. They made
   considerable gains at enclosure. After amendment of the Act, 7 distinct allotments to
   commoners of the interested parishes, Hartwell, Ashton, Quinton, Piddington,
   Hackleton and Hanslope, totalled approx. 434 acres of open plains and ridings, plus 23
   acres for collection of sere and broken wood. Though 7 allotted areas for each right
   were given, parishes were not named. From figures shown, it can be taken that 99 acres
   of open plains and ridings went to Piddington, as this ties up with the 4 acres for sere
   and broken wood quoted in Saltzman (ed.), *V.C.H.*, IV, p.279.
78 See G. E. Mingay, *A Social History of the English Countryside* (1990), p.92.
79 Gilbert, *Religion and Society*, pp.59-68.

observations are especially pertinent here for, according to Government Returns for 1811, of the 78 families (containing 157 males and 186 females) in Hackleton, 40 were employed in agriculture, 37 in trade, manufacture or handicraft, leaving only one not included in either of these. Also, of the total 91 families (196 males and 217 females) living in Piddington, 53 were in agriculture, 38 in trade, manufacture or handicraft.[80] Everitt's investigation of nearby villages of the time has indicated similar patterns.[81] The comparatively high numbers employed in cottage industries, such as shoemaking, lace-making, framework-knitting, and other village crafts in the area produced a socio-economic structure of independency conducive to the proliferation of Dissent. The Particular Baptists were the only Dissenters with a Meeting House in Piddington parish.

So far the Rev. John Sutcliff (1752-1814) has been mentioned only in passing here.[82]   However, this friend and Evangelical associate of Andrew Fuller became involved in a personal way at Hackleton during the early nineteenth century. His 'one and only pastorate' was at Olney, from 1775 until he died,[83], and his tomb stands in the burial ground of the now named Sutcliff Chapel.[84] Elwyn has written of him as 'a man of integrity, benevolence and prudence' and 'Fuller so relied upon his judgement that he often rode over to Olney to discuss things with Sutcliffe (sic)'.[85] After the death of their pastor John Luck in 1797, Hackleton Meeting was supplied by various local preachers and then, as the following undated record in the *Church Book* shows, an arrangement was made with the two nearby, highly-esteemed Particular Baptist centres:

80   *Abstract of Answers and Returns, 1811*, p.229.
81   Everitt, *Pattern of Rural Dissent*, pp.36-7. Like nearby Hardingstone, the proximity of Piddington to Northampton no doubt influenced its economy. See also Gilbert, *Religion and Society*, pp.107-9.
82   Sometimes spelt 'Sutcliffe', but 'Sutcliff' is the name on his tomb and his Chapel at Olney.
83   Elwyn, *Northamptonshire Baptist Association*, p.32. The stone shell of the present Sutcliff Church is that of the old Meeting House, c.1669, built on the site of a former barn.
84   As wording on it shows, Fuller conducted the funeral service.
85   Elwyn, *Northamptonshire Baptist Association*, pp.32-3.

We apply'd to the Rev. Mr. Sutcliff of Olney for him to supply us with his young Men and he kindly engaged to supply us evry other Lords day with a younge Man. And the other Lords day we applyd to the Brethren (that was sent out to Preach to Destitute Churches) that was sent by the Church of Christ at Northampton Meeting at Colledge Lane and they were kind to come to our assistance and at this time we are supplyd one Lords day from Olney and the other day by Mr. Abbott of Kingsthorp, Northampton'Shire.[86]

The success of these preachers and the laymen of Hackleton Church is confirmed by the increase in membership.

John Sutcliff himself was invited to baptize eight females and nine males in Hackleton brook on 17 April 1809. The stream, which eventually joins other tributaries of Northampton's River Nene, runs about four hundred yards from where the Church was sited and its waters were probably then, as now, fast-running in a wet season. The scene can be imagined from this account of the day's event:

On Monday April 17 1809 eighteen of our friends as Candidates met at Wm Shrewsburys at half past 2 (o)clock in the afternoon in the Dress that they where to be baptized in. A quarter before three (o)clock Mr. Sutcliff met the candidates and after addressing them a short time upon this Solom Occasion he gave out A Hymn which the Candidates joined by a number of friends sung with Great Solemnity. After this Mr. Sutcliff accompanied by the Candidates and friends left our Friend Shrewsburys and went down to the water which was a little distance. After he arived at the water-side he address'd a number of spectators for a short time then gave out a Hymn suited to the occasion then took up a little time in Prayer after which he proceeded to attend to the Ordinance which was done with the Greatest Solemnity and Deliberation; After the Candidates had shifted there clothes Mr. Sutcliff met them with a Number of Friends in the meeting-house there they sung another Hymn and Mr. Sutcliff prayed for

86 *Hackleton Baptist Church Book*, N.C.R.O., HBC16.

a Blessing upon what he had attended to. Then he gave
them the Right-Hand of Fellowship all that had been
Baptized, and dismissed them.[87]

There is a Biblical ring at times in this description but its style
is not that of a highly educated writer. The spectacle may well have
drawn onlookers other than Baptists, yet the seriousness of the
occasion is undoubted. The dire need for larger premises was
recorded (undated) in the Church Book:

> Our place of Worship is so overcrowded it is with great
> difficulty the people can crowd into it. This being the case
> we think it our duty to try for a New place in which we
> may meet to Worship God in a more convenient way.

A piece of ground nearby was purchased and in June 1809, in what
must have been a spirit of confidence, work was begun on building
the larger Meeting House, 24 ft by 36 ft, alongside the main road.[88]

Sutcliff performed seven more baptisms by immersion in
Hackleton's miniature River Jordan on the afternoon of Monday,
31 July 1809.[89] Five 'candidates' were female and two were male.
They included Eliza's father, William Westbury, and one of her
aunts, Charlotte York. The following record of that summer's day
baptismal event is especially interesting because it confirms that
hymn singing was characteristic of such occasions. Eliza was about
one year old at the time and may well have been carried by her
mother to watch from the brookside.

---

87   *Ibid.*

88   The first Meeting House was a thatched building in the style of a large, stone, domestic
     house, see pen drawing, N.C.R.O., HBC11. It was converted into the Pastor's Manse
     around 1810 and demolished in 1953, under the Town and Country Planning Act, for
     improvements to the site so that the present Church could be seen from the main road,
     Hackleton Baptist Church Book, N.C.R.O., HBC16; and oral evidence from one of today's
     older Hackleton residents.

89   That the baptisms occurred on Mondays, points to the continuance of Saints', or
     Cobblers' Monday, the traditional weekly day off for shoemakers. 'Saints' was normal
     usage in Northamptonshire; Thompson used both terms with reference to shoemakers,
     weavers and hurlers, see *Making of the English Working Class*, pp.338,444,448. Many
     cobblers and weavers were Evangelicals. Sporting and other events were held on
     Mondays.

A number of friends met the candidates (which were seven in number). At our Friend Shrewsbury's house; at half past 2 o'clock in the Afternoon. At 3 o'clock Mr. Sutcliff of Olney met them and after conversing with them on the nature of the Ordinance they sung a Hymn, Engaged in prayer. Then left our Friend's House; and went down to the water; and attended to the Ordinance in the same way as on April 17th.[90]

The report continued, on 'sabbath-day, Augst. 13th' the seven were 'received into full communion' and the Sacrament was administered to them. A total of twenty-four believers were baptized in 1809 and the increasing number of female members is notable.

Work on the new Meeting House was rapid and completed before the end of 1809. The great satisfaction in writing the following in *Hackleton Church Book* can be imagined: 'Wednesday, Nov. 8th is the day appointed when the Meeting-house is to be opened. Mr. Sutcliff and Mr. Fuller are fixed to preach in it'. The account of the opening ceremony on that day was short but it was an auspicious occasion for Hackleton Particular Baptists:

Public services commenced at quarter past 10 o'clock. Mr. Heighton of Road[e] prayed and Mr. Sutcliff of Olney preached from Matthew VI,10. Mr. Fuller from Kettering from I Peter II.1.2.

Other local ministers performed their appropriate functions. Eliza's father and her Aunt Charlotte, as baptized members, would surely have attended the opening if at all possible. In due course, this Church was to become Eliza's own place of worship. Thursday, 16 August 1810 saw another four female and three male baptisms in the brook, but numbers began to decrease. On 30 September 1811 two more women and one man were baptized and then just one woman and one man on 22 April 1812, all by Sutcliff.

What was in the end to prove a permanent ministerial arrangement at Hackleton began with the arrival of the Reverend William Knowles in 1812 to serve for a probationary year. Knowles had been a member of the Church at Kettering during

90 *Hackleton Baptist Church Book*, N.C.R.O., HBC16.

the Rev. Andrew Fuller's time and was trained for the ministry at Sutcliff's academy at Olney. He had already visited occasionally to preach for Hackleton Particular Baptists. Subsequently, at their monthly meeting in August 1812 the 'question was asked whether Mr. Kno[w]les then residing at Mr. Sutcliff's would not be a suitable person for Hackleton provided it was the wish of the Church in general'.[91] All but two of those present were in favour but, as some members had been unable to attend, another meeting was held on Thursday evening, 1 October. The women may have had equal rights with the men in this voting procedure.[92] Attendance at the next meeting was better and, after singing what appear to have been two favourite hymns, Watts's 'How did my heart rejoice to hear'[93] and Rippon's 'May our blest eyes a shepherd see',[94] every member was asked individually if 'they' agreed to the appointment of Knowles. The result was that 'All but four wished that it might be so if it were the will of God' and accordingly Knowles was asked to come for a probationary year.[95] He began his ministry at Hackleton on Sunday, 21 November 1812.

The numbers of new converts had been decreasing but, in February 1813, the report of the monthly meeting acclaimed, 'the Lord has appeared in a Revival amongst our younge Freinds and we think it our Duty and Privilege to have an Experience Meeting which we had for some time neglected but we now meet once a fortnight'.[96] These can be classed as 'meetings designed for anxious

---

91 *Hackleton Baptist Church Book*, N.C.R.O., HBC16.

92 This was not always the case in Dissenting chapels: see Davidoff & Hall, *Family Fortunes*, pp.133-136. Among the Baptists at Olney a woman could vote and was allowed 'to speak in the church, yet not in such sort as carrie[d] in it direction, instruction, government and authority, for she must be in subjection under obedience, not to teach nor to usurp authority over the man but to be and learn in silence (Cor. 14, 34-35; 1 Tim 2, 11.12)': see *Olney Baptist Church Book, 1752-1854*, Covenant, Article XII, revised 1767. Probably it was the same at Hackleton.

93 I. Watts, D.D., 'Psalm CXXII: Going to Church', *The Psalms of David Imitated in the Language of the New Testament And apply'd to the Christian State and Worship* (1719, 1734 edn), p.266.

94 Possibly from edition of J. Rippon, *A Selection of Hymns from the Best Authors, intended to be an Appendix to Dr. Watts's Psalms and Hymns* (1787), though not in 13th edn (1802): see Watson, *The English Hymn*, p.266.

95 In some Dissenting congregations, ministers 'held their position at the sufferance of the membership', Laqueur, *Religion and Respectability*, p.78; also Davidoff & Hall, *Family Fortunes*, p.130.

96 *Hackleton Baptist Church Book*, N.C.R.O., HBC16.

enquirers [that] could encourage the desire to believe'.[97] At the Church Meeting in early April 1813 it was agreed that 'some young friends' who appeared 'thoughtful' should be encouraged to join and two representatives were appointed to speak to them. Action and response were rapid. On Monday, April 19th 'Alin Smith, Joseph Westley and Thomas Cross gave in their experience at a Church Meeting held for that purpose' and were baptized by Sutcliff on Thursday, April 22nd.[98]

At twelve-monthly invervals William Knowles received renewed invitations to continue preaching at Hackleton and his probationary period extended into something under three years.[99] Finally, on 12 July 1815 he was 'ordained to the Pastorate Office'. The service was held at Hackleton in the presence of Robert Hall who 'delivered the introductory discourse and asked the questions'.[100] Hall was an eminent Baptist then ministering at Harvey Lane, Leicester, whom Bebbington has called 'the ablest preacher of his day'.[101] Knowles was the first ordained minister to be appointed at Hackleton.

The first three baptisms by William Knowles took place on Sunday, 14 August 1814 and, though there is no account of such, they would have been by immersion in the brook.[102] The candidates were female converts who had 'wanted encouraging in the path of duty' and had been visited with success by 'proper messengers' nominated at the monthly meeting in the previous April.[103] It was not until Sunday, 26 October 1817 that the first

97   Bebbington, *Evangelicalism*, p.8.

98   *Hackleton Baptist Church Book*, N.C.R.O., HBC16.

99   In early July 1815, 'Mr and Mrs Knowles were formally dismissed from the Baptist Church of Christ, Kettering', N.C.R.O., HBC16.

100 *Hackleton Baptist Church Book*, N.C.R.O., HBC16.

101 Bebbington, *Evangelicalism*, p.16.

102 Baptisms were now mostly on Sundays, perhaps indicating a more regulated working week. Changing employment patterns of waged labour seem apparent. *Abstract of Answers and Returns, 1821* showed a substantial local increase in agricultural employment (1811: Hackleton 40 families, Piddington 53; 1821: Hackleton 63 families, Piddington 93). Demands for military footwear during the Napoleonic Wars and industrialisation had expanded the boot and shoe industry in Northampton. The town's population was increasing rapidly (8,427 in 1811, 10,793 in 1821, 15,351 in 1831) implying a growing market for local farming products of all kinds. After the 1867 Factories Act introduced Saturday as a half-holiday for women and juveniles, Monday as a day off was gradually becoming unacceptable.

103 *Hackleton Baptist Church Book*, N.C.R.O., HBC16. 'Experience meetings' were now being held monthly on a Thursday evening.

person was baptized in a new baptistry inside the Church.[104] By this time Eliza was nine years old and it is likely that she had been taken along to witness some of the former outdoor events. Favourable weather conditions on her own baptismal day were not so important a factor as for her relatives earlier in the century. Yet some people of the parish may have regretted no longer being able to watch the more spectacular baptisms in Hackleton brook, which had been established as part of their community's religious culture. I would argue that this does not suggest a lessening of enthusiasm to follow biblical practices of baptisms in a natural watercourse, or a desire to avoid appearing fanatical in a small community. The larger chapel was a symbol of local success and it was able to accommodate a baptistry that could be used in any season of the year. As indicated below, Eliza Westbury's aunt was baptized in November.

Reports of the monthly meetings have shown that members at Hackleton continued to be assigned the task of visiting likely proselytes, who were already attending services but were not yet fully-committed Evangelicals. In most cases the personal approach brought a positive response. That persistent efforts were made to win just one extra convert locally is clear from the following records, which also confirm that Evangelicalism could cause domestic friction for a female Particular Baptist as much as for a married woman from any other denomination.[105] A report of the monthly meeting held on 30 December 1814 contained this item:

> It was agreed that two of our female friends should visit Jane Savage to enquire into the state of her mind and to converse with her on the duty and privilege of uniting with the church of Christ.[106]

That women were chosen as representatives to carry the message of duty faith to someone who presumably had been the subject of earlier discussion, is indication that it was thought a suitable task for females at a time when women's ministering role was still

---

104 *Ibid.*, noted that date.
105 For a Primitive Methodist example, see L. Wilson, '"She succeeds with cloudless brow..." How active was the spirituality of Nonconformist women in the home during the period 1825–75?', in R. N. Swanson (ed.), *Studies in Church History, 34: Gender and Christian Religion* (1998), p.351.
106 *Hackleton Baptist Church Book*, N.C.R.O., HBC16.

somewhat restricted. The answer they brought back on 3 February 1815 was: Jane Savage on the ground of her own unworthiness objected to unite with us. It was agreed that our friends should visit her again.[107]

Although Jane might have thought this spiritual explanation would satisfy her Evangelical visitors, they probably knew that she was covering up a difficult, male-dominated domestic situation. In March they were asked to see her again. More than four years had passed before Jane Savage was next mentioned. Over that period she had integrated with Hackleton Baptists to some extent and had reached the decision to be baptized. However, she had been prevented from attending the monthly meeting on 8 June 1819 'through the most violent opposition from her husband', Joseph, but still opposed him as much as she dared. He had

> several times hindered his wife from being baptized. On the 18th June 1819 she came to the church meeting related her experience and it was unanimously [agreed] to receive her as a member. Her husband finding her resolved to be baptized threw her out of doors with three of the children and would not let her enter again until she promised not to be baptized. On the day when she was to have been baptized with two other persons her husband was at work near the meeting and hearing the singing he began to reflect upon his guilt in preventing his wife from obeying the law of Christ. From this time he began to seek for mercy as a poor sinner, and has given good evidence of a real change of heart. The husband and wife were both baptized together on 16th Feb. [1820].[108]

It is likely that Eliza's aunt, Charlotte York, had attended one or more of these meetings and knew of Jane Savage's situation. As already shown, Charlotte had been a committed Evangelical since 1809 but her sister, Harriett, was not baptized until 20 November 1822, by which time the Church baptistry was in use.[109] Although the funeral of Eliza's mother, Elizabeth, is noted by Knowles,[110] there is no record of her ever relating her experience and being

107 *Ibid.*
108 *Ibid.*
109 *Ibid.*
110 Knowles, *Diary,* 13 January 1828, text preached John 7:37. N.C.R.O., HBC8.

baptized as a believer. Perhaps, like many members of Evangelical congregations, she was a 'hearer' rather than a professed convert.

When Eliza died in 1828, there were sixty-seven full members of Hackleton Baptist Church. Though he retired in 1861, William Knowles continued to preach there occasionally until he died in July 1866. His name and that of his wife, Mary, can still be read on their gravestones which stand alongside each other in the small burial ground beside today's building. It is fairly certain that Eliza Westbury had been buried not far from the spot where her mentor was laid to rest thirty-eight years later. His role in Eliza's Evangelical development was clearly the most influential and he was probably the greatest encourager in her writing. As Thompson has said, 'we should beware of giving too bleak and too unqualified a picture of the [E]vangelical churches' from the dogma taught to the young in their Sunday schools.[111] It can be imagined that Knowles became something of a father-figure to Eliza and he clearly was willing to acknowledge her talent. There are regular entries in his diary of 'Sermons to young people' given on some Sundays and, as explained in the 'short Account', it was 'a few words spoken to her after she had been hearing' one of these early in 1825 that brought her positive response and she was 'no longer a stranger to religion'.

Knowles's interest in Eliza's progress can be detected from what appears to have been an early attempt at her writing religious poetry. A scrap of paper containing the following short poem was pasted on one of the first pages of his diary.[112] That Knowles kept it, must surely be indication of some affection for her. The lines are written in ink and are probably the only extant sample of Eliza's handwriting; three minor corrections to her script can be recognized as Knowles's pen strokes:

> Eliza in the bloom of youth
> Learn to love the more a truth;
> If true happiness you'd find
> Zealously its precepts mind
> All its pleasures are refin'd.
> With a truly Godly care
> Ever read it: and with prayer

---

111 Thompson, *The Making of the English Working Class*, p.415.
112 Knowles, *Diary*, N.C.R.O., HBC8.

So you shall be truly wise,
Turn from vanity and rise,
Blessings, heavenly to secure,
Undefiled, lasting, pure;
Reckon it your greatest treasure
Yea the source of highest pleasure.

One may reasonably suggest that the poem was written very soon after Eliza's conversion, in the emotional excitement of her new-found Evangelical confidence in the all-sufficiency and truth of the Bible.

Her poem, 'On the death of the Author's Mother', can be recognized as Eliza's sorrowful response to that event and must have been written soon after Elizabeth Westbury died. Without doubt we have here a reworking of William Cowper's poem, 'To Mary'. This was written in 1793 after Cowper moved from his house in Olney to live in Weston Underwood with the Throckmortons (at what is now called 'Cowper's Lodge') when Mary Unwin, his friend and companion, suffered a paralytic stroke.[113] Cowper had also written lines in remembrance of his mother who had died when he was only about six years of age.[114] The English poet, Robert Southey (1774-1843), is quoted as naming Cowper '"the most popular poet of his time and the best of English letter-writers", and when it is taken into account that Cowper was really the Evangelical poet of the great Evangelical movement with which Southey did not altogether sympathize' the judgement can be valued all the more.[115] Cowper's lines 'To Mary' began:

113 From copy of original manuscript in Cowper and Newton Museum, Olney. For a
   similar reworking see, 'My Mary', by Northamptonshire poet John Clare (1793-1864),
   in E. Robinson & D. Powell (eds), *The Oxford Authors, John Clare* (Oxford, 1984), fn.59,
   p.489: Clare's poem makes 'an interesting contrast with Cowper's sad lament' to Mary
   Unwin but is identical to it 'in stanza-form, rhythm, and refrain'. It is one of the several
   imitations of older poets by Clare published in *Poems Descriptive of Rural Life and Scenery*
   (1820). As a contemporary of Clare, Eliza Westbury may have known of this imitation
   and felt she could use the same technique. Clare also wrote 'Lines on "Cowper"'.
114 See: *Cowper: Poetical Works (1782-99)*, H. S. Milford (ed.) (1934, 1967 edn), 'On the
   receipt of my mother's picture out of Norfolk' (1790), pp.394-96.
115 M. Seeley, *The Later Evangelical Fathers* (1879), p.81.

> The twentieth year is well-nigh past,
> Since first our sky was overcast;
> Ah, would that this might be the last!
>   My Mary!
>
> Thy spirits have a fainter flow,
> I see thee daily weaker grow;
> 'Twas my distress that brought thee low,
>   My Mary!

However, there were no religious allusions in any of the thirteen verses that make up the work,[116] probably because by this time Cowper's Evangelical optimism was being shattered by melancholic depression.[117]

Although Eliza's eight stanzas were similar to Cowper's poem in verse form, metre and repetition of a two-word last phrase, they cannot be regarded as secular. Indeed, Evangelicalism is reflected throughout her poem. In the first five verses Eliza imaged her mother as a strong, but loving Evangelical parent, her 'counsellor and guide', admonishing her for choosing a 'giddy throng' of friends. In this fifth stanza she is depicted as a gentle carer directing Eliza along the road to a more righteous way of life:

> Who lov'd to see me walk the way
> That leads to everlasting day,
> And check'd me when about to stray?
>   My Mother!

In the phrase, 'everlasting day', we can detect a lifting of imagery from the Bible, particularly Psalm 139, 'even the night shall be light about me' (v.11) and 'the night shineth as the day' (v.12). Evangelicals pictured life on earth as full of shadows, heaven as the brighter home and often exhibited this in their hymns.[118] For them, though he was writing about Methodists, Thompson has

---

116 For one analysis of the poem see W. Cowper, *The Poetry of William Cowper*, B. Hutchings (ed.), (Beckenham, 1983), pp.5-7.

117 *The Letters and Prose Writings of William Cowper*, IV, (1979), pp.xvii-xviii.

118 Tamke, *Make a Joyful Noise*, pp.42-4. John Clare used 'The joys of everlasting day' in his hymn 'The Stranger': see *Hymns Ancient & Modern* (Norwich, 1983 edn), hymn 335, v.4, l.2; variations employed by others were 'endless day', 'everlasting light', 'never-ending day'.

gone so far as to say 'Death was the only goal which might be desired without guilt, the reward of peace after a lifetime of suffering and labour'.[119] It was the greatest blessing for it was the final exit from the trials and tribulations of this life. Eliza focussed the last two verses of her poem on this Evangelical escapist view:

> It has pleas'd God her soul to take
> To heaven, where no alarms can shake;
> There may I meet, for Jesu's sake,
> > My Mother!

> Then with my Saviour I shall be,
> And I shall from all sin be free,
> And there in glory I shall see
> > My Mother!

Her last three lines may have been an adaptation of Romans 6, verses 7 and 8: 'For he that is dead is freed from sin.\Now if we be dead with Christ, we believe that we shall also live with him'.

5.4 'Verses, containing an account of the writer's experience'

The words 'writer's experience' in the title given to Eliza's 'Verses' suggest their Evangelical context. The willingness to print and distribute locally can been seen to support their verisimilitude. James Gordon has claimed that 'Evangelicalism has little that is new to offer' in the way of written historical primary sources and it 'owns few classics of spiritual autobiography'.[120] I cannot say that Eliza's poem is unique or a classic, but it is a new autobiographical source for study of Evangelical spirituality in women of the early nineteenth-century. Furthermore, I believe it to be a rarity in that it is a versified account of the spiritual difficulties encountered by a teenage, working-class 'village female' in her search for Evangelical conviction and assurance. An innate ability and a love of rhyme may have made poetry an easier, more enjoyable medium for Eliza than prose. Her familiarity with long measure and rhyming couplets in hymns probably influenced her choice of that same uncomplicated form for her poem. The 'Verses' can be seen

119 Thompson, *The Making of the English Working Class*, p.410.
120 Gordon, *Evangelical Spirituality*, pp.319-20.

as a confession of stubborn lack of will and wavering belief that made the conversion process so prolonged and unhappy for her. Yet in the end she experienced the relief of God's forgiveness and acceptance. The fifty-four stanzas are too many for reference to each one here, therefore a choice of the most relevant lines must be made. Several of the 'Verses' were taken up with Eliza's spiritual indecisiveness yet they do confirm that conversion was not always sudden and could be gradual.[121] We know that the alteration in her attitude towards religion occurred early in 1825, but it was more than a year later that she 'spoke her experience'.

Eliza's borrowing from William Cowper has already been mentioned. If she was familiar with one of his works, it is likely that she knew some of his other poems and prose. However, Eliza was probably unable to afford books of her own. We know that she attended a Sabbath School and this may have had a lending library. It is evidenced below that by 1833 Hackleton Baptist Sunday School had such a facility, the basis of which could have existed before Eliza died in 1828. If not, then possibly Knowles lent her books from his personal collection. The similarity between the versified account of Eliza's own bewildering spiritual journey and what she may have read of Cowper's tortuous seeking after assurance cannot be disregarded. Though they cannot be substantiated, there are good reasons for believing that Eliza felt a particular affinity with Cowper. First, it is likely that she had seen his autobiography, 'Adelphi', published in 1816, in which he described the mental torment of his early life and the harrowing manner of his conversion.[122] Second, in his poem 'Truth' (1782), Cowper had shown a sensitive observation of the working life of a cottage lace-maker and the consolation she found in her Bible:

> Yon cottager, who weaves at her own door,
> Pillow and bobbins all her little store;
> Content, though mean; and cheerful, if not gay;
> Shuffling her thread about the live-long day,
> Just earns a scanty pittance; and at night

---

121 See *Ibid.*, p.312; also Bebbington, *Evangelicalism*, pp.7-8.
122 Cowper, *Letters and Prose Writings*, I, pp.5-61. '"Adelphi"' was Cowper's 'tormented, self-accusing autobiographical narrative' which 'had its foil in the gentle and sensitive rendition of his brother John's conversion to the truths [he himself] had learned...it is a direct and primitive account of the torments of the suicidal mind': see Introduction, p.xxiii.

Lies down secure, her heart and pocket light:
She for her humble sphere by nature fit,
Has little understanding, and no wit,
Receives no praise; but though her lot be such
(Toilsome and indigent) she renders much
Just knows, and knows no more, her Bible true -
A truth the brilliant Frenchman never knew; [123]
And in that charter reads, with sparkling eyes,
Her title to a treasure in the skies.[124]   (317-330)

Third, Cowper had produced some of the *Olney Hymns* which
Eliza probably sang, and both Cowper and Newton had died
comparatively recently - in 1800 and 1807 respectively. Finally, in
his poems such as 'Yardley Oak' and 'The Task', Cowper had
imaged the day-to-day human, animal and plant life of her familiar
rural landscape.[125]

Eliza's long poem expressed her intensely personalized
reflections in the simplest of terms. Her plain, simple style may
have been the only way in which she could write, but it might be
judged that simplicity was her strength. She was following the
mode set by the great Evangelical versifiers, such as the Wesleys,
Cowper and Newton, whose aim was to appeal to all in familiar
and easily understood language. Her use of 'I' and 'me' throughout
was an expression of the individualistic religious outlook of
Evangelicals. Conversion was a deeply personal experience and it
carried individual responsibilities. The only mediator between God
and man was Christ,[126] and direct communication with the
Almighty was possible through prayer. Hannah More's comment

123 Referring to Voltaire.
124 Cowper, *Poetical Works*, pp.37-8.
125 *Ibid.*, 'Yardley Oak' (1791), pp.410-14. (MS in Newton & Cowper Museum, Olney). See
   also *The Poetry of William Cowper*, pp.180-6, on 'Yardley Oak' in which Cowper made a
   winter tree a 'self-reflexive' image 'of his own old age'. The tree stood in Yardley Chase,
   a hunting area just beyond Salcey Forest and only about four miles from Hackleton. See
   also Cowper, *Poetical Works*, 'The Task', Book I (1785), pp. 132-3, picturing the local
   scene: 'The distant plough slow moving, and beside\His lab'ring team...The sturdy swain
   diminish'd to a boy!\Here Ouse, slow winding through a level plain...The sloping land
   recedes into the clouds...square tow'r,\Tall spire...Groves, heaths, and smoking villages,
   remote.' (160-76). (Its high elevation and spire mounted on a tower make Piddington
   Church visible from miles around.) According to Hutchings, *The Poetry of William
   Cowper*, p.234, 'The Task' is really about the randomness of life and God's hand in its
   resolution.
126 1 Timothy, 2:5.

expressed the general Evangelical view thus: 'Prayer is the
application of want to Him who alone can relieve it; the voice of
sin to Him who alone can pardon it. It is the urgency of poverty,
the prostration of humility, the fervency of penitence, the
confidence of trust'.[127] Eliza's prayerfulness at times of distress and
joy is evident in her 'Verses'.

She opened with reference to her childhood:

> I at an early age was taught
> That God should be in every thought,
> My Mother brought me up with care,
> And led me to the house of prayer. (1-4)

Her introduction to a spiritual life at 'an early age' was undoubtedly
within her own home. 'That God should be in [her] every thought'
is an all-encompassing doctrine difficult to analyze in a few words.
It can be taken that Eliza had been taught to develop a code of
living governed by awareness of God's perpetual presence, keeping
his laws constantly in mind and nurturing a desire to do his will.
Furthermore, Mrs Westbury's loving 'care' had extended to leading
her infant daughter to a place of organized religion. Here is
evidence that it was not only middle-class Evangelical parents who
felt responsibility for the spiritual nurture of their children.[128] In
the second and third stanzas of this poem we can learn something
of Eliza's early education:

> Unto a Sabbath School I went,
> To gain instruction I was sent;
> And there it was my constant aim
> To strive to gain the greatest name.
> 'Twas my desire (the truth I'll tell)
> That I in reading might excel;
> My chief concern and labour then,
> Was how to gain the praise of men. (5-12)

The 'Sabbath School' Eliza attended was obviously one where
both reading and writing were taught. Eliza has given the
impression that she was sent there as much to learn these skills as

127 More, *Practical Piety*, p.49. See also, Gordon, *Evangelical Spirituality*, p.113.
128 See Rosman, *Evangelicals and Culture*, p.97.

for religious 'instruction'. Laqueur has confirmed that part of the reason why working-class children attended Sunday Schools was because of the education facilities provided.[129] But reading could be harnessed to further knowledge of the faith and, as Laqueur put it, 'literacy was the *sine qua non* of religious life'.[130] Evangelicals encouraged individual study of the Bible in the domestic situation. We know from the 'short Account' that Eliza 'made pleasing progress in learning' but here she confessed an ulterior motive. A working-class girl with good reading ability would be particularly admired in a community where literacy was still by no means general, especially among females in a male-dominated society, and Eliza was no doubt fully aware of this.

There is no firm evidence of which Sabbath School Eliza attended. However, in the Government's 1818 *Digest of Education Returns, County of Northampton,* a 'national' Sunday school containing 100' pupils was shown to exist at 'Piddington containing Hackleton'.[131] Eliza was ten years old at the time. No Baptist Sunday School at Hackleton was mentioned. Yet there is indication that such a one existed continuously until the 1880s, 'with varied success', from the time it was founded by Eliza's father and the two other men.[132] Perhaps Hackleton's 'Sabbath School' was thought not worth mentioning in the Return, but it cannot be said with certainty that this was a separate organization and the one providing Eliza's education. Most likely Hackleton Baptists had joined forces with the local Anglicans and others to become part of the 'national' school, which was a member of either the Sunday School Society or the Sunday School Union. Both organizations were interdenominational and expressions of Evangelical activism.[133] In any case, it can be seen that Eliza certainly gained 'instruction' on Sundays. Interestingly, the 1818 Return also

129 Laqueur, *Religion and Respectability*, p.158.

130 *Ibid.*, p.9.

131 *Parliamentary Papers, IX/(2): Digest of Education Returns, County of Northampton, 1818* (1819), Piddington (pop. 413) and Hackleton (pop. 343), p.658. Percentage of population enrolled, 7.56, almost exactly agrees Laqueur's figure of 7.6 for Northamptonshire, in *Religion and Respectability*, Table 7, p.49.

132 Anon., *History of Hackleton Sabbath School*, p.1.

133 Laqueur, *Religion and Respectability*, pp.33-40: The Sunday School Society was founded in 1785, 'primarily through the efforts of a Baptist merchant, William Fox';...'twelve lay Churchmen and twelve Dissenters' made up the governing body. The Sunday School Union 'went public in 1812'; though 'theoretically ecumenical, most [local] Unions contained only Dissenters'.

included 'a national school supported by voluntary contributions open to all the children' of Piddington and Hackleton 'and the adjoining parishes of Horton and Preston Deanery' but this would have been a day school.[134] A note in the Return, under 'Observations', highlighted the situation of the less fortunate when it came to daytime instruction: 'The poor have not the means of educating their children'. Therefore, it can be said that without her 'Sabbath School' Eliza would have received no other organized religious or secular education.

However, the *Government Digest of Education Returns, 1833* shows that at Piddington (population 558) there were by then 'Two Day and Sunday Schools', one for males that was 'wholly supported by subscription', the other for females '(commenced 1828)' in which 'a certain number' paid 'only 1d. per week, the deficiency being made up by subscription, but a few [were] wholly paid for by their parents.'[135] Significantly, the Return also shows that at Hackleton (population 425) there was a well-established 'Sunday School' consisting of 37 males and 42 females...supported by Dissenters of the Baptist Denomination' and it had 'a lending Library attached'.[136] Its numbers probably included adults as well as children. The Return was completed only five years after Eliza Westbury's death and it is likely that William Knowles had re-established the Baptist Sunday School some time after the date of the previous Return in 1818.[137] There can be little doubt that Eliza attended the Baptist School in her later childhood for it appears that another local facility for female instruction was not provided until 1828.

Eliza's 'Verses' continued with a simple confession of her former waywardness and spiritual confusion. It must be remembered that all this was written retrospectively, in the remorse of guilt after her conversion, and that she was probably referring to

---

134 It contained 35 children and, as the returns for Horton and Preston Deanery indicated, it was run according to 'Dr Bell's plan'. This gave it an Anglican bias.

135 *Parliamentary Papers XLII: Digest of Education Returns, County of Northampton, 1833* (1835), p.654. 64 males attended daily...70 on Sundays; 22 females daily, 50 on Sundays. The School for females did not open until the year of Eliza's death.

136 Enrolment in this one Sunday School was 8.0% of the parish population. Lacqueur's figure of 9.3% for Northamptonshire included all denominations, see Table 7, *Religion and Respectability*, p.49.

137 By this time, the interdenominational Sunday schools were beginning to break up; for reasons, see Laqueur, *Religion and Respectability*, pp.73-4.

her early teenage years:

> I many strong convictions had,
> But I to stifle them was glad:
> I knew my ways did God offend,
> But I to this would not attend.
> I for my chief companions chose,
> Those who religion did oppose,
> Who disobey'd each warning voice
> They were the objects of my choice.
>
> Thus with the thoughtless, gay, and vain,
> God's holy day I did profane;
> For oft we in the fields did walk,
> To join in vain and trifling talk.
> But conscience told me all along
> That I was surely acting wrong:
> This fill'd my soul with sore dismay
> And oft I did attempt to pray.   (13-28)

'Sunday sets a thousand tongues agoing that have nothing to say' was but one of the seven 'evils that follow a profanation of the Lord's-day', according to an article in the Baptist Magazine, which Eliza may have read.[138] Yet the simple amusements Eliza thought had profaned the Sabbath were very different from the activities the Evangelical middle-class girls sacrificed on Sundays through their religious commitment. Despite good intentions, Eliza's 'solemn vows were broke at length' (30) for she found 'Religion...Too gloomy and too dull' (31-32). By 'religion' it can safely be taken that she meant Evangelicalism and, understandably, the constant hammering home of human depravity and mortality, along with severe demands for asceticism, were difficult for a lively, intelligent adolescent to accept. It can be understood that Eliza had learned at Sunday School the awful consequences of disobedience and following one's own desires, especially on the Sabbath.

Catechizing was accepted as a correct method of instructing children in the articles of their faith.[139] Learning the Anglican catechism was probited for 'Chapel children',[140] and the Rev.

---

138 Rev. R. Robinson, 'On Sabbath-breaking', *Baptist Magazine*, XVI (1824), pp.8-9.
139 See Bebbington, *Evangelicalism*, p.123.
140 M. Farningham, *A Working Woman's Life: An Autobiography* (1907), p.17.

Knowles devized his own system of indoctrination in his *Scripture Principles: A Catechism for the Young.*[141] This printed booklet contained fifty-four questions with the answers expected. It can be viewed as a statement of Evangelical biblicism, spelling out the principal truths of the Bible and God's warnings of retribution for the young sinner who refused to see the way of salvation. There is every reason to consider it a rival to the catechism contained in the Anglican Prayer Book.[142] Today Knowles's method might be judged an ordeal to which the younger Baptists at Hackleton were subjected, either by himself or the Sunday School teachers, though degrees of severity and paternalism were matters of individual personality. The booklet was undated, therefore it cannot be said with certainty that Eliza underwent questioning directly from it. However, it can be expected that Knowles had developed a procedure on similar lines before going into print and we can depend upon it that he had always expounded on Biblical laws, the horrors of hell and the delights of heaven.

The following questions and answers have been selected to illustrate what Knowles endeavoured to instil in the minds of local young sinners:

8. Q. What is declared in the Bible concerning those
        who have not perfectly obeyed the divine Law?
    A. Cursed is every one that continueth not in all
        things written in the book of the law to do them.
9. Q. Then are you not as a transgressor condemned by
        the law, exposed to great danger?
    A. Yes; I am righteously condemned by the law
        which I have broken, I am unworthy of any
        favour, and justly deserve death and hell.

141 Rev. W. Knowles, *Scripture Principles: A Catechism for the Young* (Leicester, undated),
    N.C.R.O., attached inside HBC8.
142 The catechism appears in the Book of Common Prayer between 'The Order of Baptism
    of those of Riper Years' and 'The Order of Confirmation'. See Knight, *The Nineteenth-
    century Church*, pp.96-8, for catechizing in the Anglican Church and published teaching
    materials that broke down the lengthy catechism into small component parts to assist
    learning by rote.

52. Q. What will be the state of the wicked?
    A. They will be wicked and miserable forever, and
       will have their portion with the devil and his
       angels.
53. Q. As you have the word of God, which makes
       known these important truths, what will be the
       consequence if you disbelieve them?
    A. I shall be left without excuse and my eternal
       condemnation will be just.

The notion of duty faith can be detected in that last question. The
good sense philosophy of obeying divine command was made
obvious in the final answer:

54. Q. Is it not, then, your wisdom to attend to the great
       concerns of religion in your youth?
    A. God has commanded me to 'remember my
       Creator in the days of my youth', and it will be to
       my unspeakable advantage, for then I shall obtain
       mercy, I shall escape many dangers, I shall find
       wisdom's ways, ways of pleasantness and when I
       die I shall be received into the kingdom of
       heaven.

According to her 'Verses', Evangelicalism appears to have been
a divisive element between Eliza and her village contemporaries.
She was 'mocked and ridicul'd' (34) when she returned to the
company of those among whom her 'conscience could be fast
asleep' (40). In hindsight of final conversion she judged them
'ungodly' and 'wicked' in taking 'the scoffer's seat' (42-44). They
revelled in her wickedness, made the more extreme by having
believed and then forsaken her beliefs:

> All sacred things I did deride,
> But my companions would me chide,
> And oft they unto me would say,
> That I indeed was worse than they. (45-48)

She became 'of true wisdom void, the existence of a God
deny'd', and chose 'the paths of infidelity' (57-59). Her faith was
lost and she wanted answers to some fundamental questions:

Who hath ascended up, thought I,
And seen a God above the sky?
Who of the dead came back to tell,
That there was either heaven or hell? (61–64)

Eliza was asking for empirical evidence of God's existence. Could true knowledge of Him be substantiated? Great Evangelical minds had sought the same proofs but we cannot tell how much Eliza was aware of the writings that issued from them.[143] However, she probably knew Watts's hymn that began: 'Lord, we are blind, we Mortals blind,\We can't behold thy bright Abode;', but went on to present a recognizable vision of God 'in human form, sitting on a throne, walking on feet, looking with eyes'.[144]

Eliza remained sceptical. Having daily 'waxed worse and worse/Regardless of the Saviour's curse'(55 & 56), she rejected the Bible and 'determin'd ne'er to read it more' (68). She ignored warnings of the dangers she was piling up for herself. Thus began the long struggle between unbelief and conviction characteristic of other gradual conversions.[145] The heightened introspection demanded by Evangelicalism affected most those prone to melancholia or, in its extreme form, manic depression. They were particularly vulnerable to its doctrine of man's depravity. Deep feelings of inadequacy in the struggle against evil and constant desire for reassurance of God's grace could lead to inner conflict of almost unbearable magnitude. Moments of spiritual exaltation could alternate with long periods of darkest despair.

Eliza's descriptions of her fluctuating emotions followed this pattern and are strikingly similar to William Cowper's account of his mental distress. It can be argued that she identified herself with

---

143 See Bebbington, *Evangelicalism*, pp.48-50, for eighteenth-century empiricist difficulties in applying rationalism to religious faith. According to Enlightenment thinking, only knowledge gained through the senses, i.e. experience, was considered certain so for some Evangelicals the 'range of senses available to a human being' was extended. John Wesley described faith as 'a supernatural inward sense or sight'. See also, M. J. McClymond, 'Spiritual perception in Jonathan Edwards', *The Journal of Religion*, Vol. 77, No. 2 (Chicago) 1997. Newton's hymn, 'Faith a new and comprehensive Sense' deals with the subject in J. Newton & W. Cowper, *Olney Hymns in Three Parts* (1779, 1859 edn), III, 43.

144 Marshall & Todd, *English Congregational Hymns*, p.37.

145 See *Baptist Magazine*, XIX (1827), pp.618-19: for 'Obituary of Mrs Keene' whose feelings 'fluctuated considerably between sorrow and joy, hope and fear, darkness and light... Her 'faith and patience...were rendered ultimately more firm' by overcoming the 'series of painful temptations' that had 'assailed her'.

Cowper in the agony of mind he suffered from his obsessive Evangelical self-scrutiny, his heightened sense of guilt and terrifying premonitions of eternal misery in hell.[146] David Cecil gave this summary of Cowper's experience:

> Once or twice God had let fall a ray of His grace upon him, but, seduced by the pleasures of the world, he had shut his eyes. On the threshold therefore of his manhood God had plunged him into a melancholia, had overwhelmed him with spiritual fears; and then, as suddenly had removed them and filled him with spiritual happiness. But again he had neglected His message...But just when Cowper, maddened by misfortune, was about to decide his damnation by committing the frightful sin of self-murder, God miraculously rescued him, showed him to himself as the vile creature he really was, and revealed the hell that was in store for him if he proceeded in his evil doings.
>
> Finally, when he was still trembling under this newly-found consciousness of sin, He turned the full light of His grace upon Him. He saw it and was converted.[147]

Continuing with Eliza's account, a similar pattern of events can be recognized. She was 'determined to go on\in the sad course [she] had begun' (71-72) and felt she must enjoy her 'youthful days' (75). 'Thus [she] went on from year to year\Till stopped in [her] mad career' (77 & 78).[148] Then she was urged to change:

> A minister of God above,
> Bid me from Christ no longer rove,
> But now to seek in days of youth,
> The God of mercy, love, and truth.
> He bid me also not to be
> A servant of God's enemy.[149]   (81-86)

---

146 See Gordon, *Evangelical Spirituality*, p.80.

147 Cecil, *The Stricken Deer*, p.86.

148 Newton used the phrase '"stopp'd my wild career"' in 'one of his many hymns exploring conviction of sin': see Gordon, *Evangelical Spirituality*, p.72.

149 These were probably the 'few words spoken to her after... hearing a Sermon to young people', no doubt by Knowles: see the 'short Account'.

The inner suffering Eliza experienced in subsequent efforts to repent was to be expected as it was part of the process according to these words from an article in *The Baptist Magazine*, which she may have been given to read. 'Repentance is sorrow for sin; having the heart broken and contrite on account of it...Guilt and confusion will fill the heart of the once rebellious, but now contrite, humbled, abased sinner', along with 'shame and remorse'.[150]   Like Cowper, Eliza fell into melancholy and anxiety. Her 'sins as mountains did appear\Which fill'd [her] soul with grief and fear' (91-92). She continued in describing her desperation:

> No hope of mercy could I see,
> For bold transgressors such as me.
> I thought I oft heard something say,
> That t'was in vain for me to pray;
> I at religion used to scoff,
> And now the Lord would cast me off.
> At length God's holy word I took,
> But fear'd to open that blest Book,
> Lest in its pages I should see
> A curse denounc'd on such as me. (99-108)

She 'tryed to pray' but still 'thought t'was all in vain\For mercy [she] should ne'er obtain' (109-112). Depression took over. Her 'mind' was 'devoid of peace'\And fast [her] misery did increase' (113-114).

James Gordon might have been describing Eliza's state of mind when he wrote of Cowper's unrelenting feelings of guilt that 'triggered recurring bouts of self-despair', and an inescapable 'subterranean dread...of a God who was unalterably indifferent to him and his fate. In such a bleak atmosphere assurance was impossible and breakdown all but inevitable'.[151]   Again like Cowper, Eliza became suicidal: 'At length, [she] fully did intend\To [her] own life to put an end' (115-116) and prepared to carry it out, possibly by hanging.[152]   Cowper had intended to hang himself but

---

150 W.B., 'On Evangelical Repentance', *Baptist Magazine*, XVI (1824), pp.233, 235.

151 Gordon, *Evangelical Spirituality*, p.90.

152 Some thought 'melancholy madness' was due to a medical condition rather than to 'any peculiar religious tenets newly embraced': see, A. P. F. Sell, *Dissenting Thought and the Life of the Churches: Studies in an English Tradition* (Mellen, U.S.A., 1990), quoting G. Burder, *A Vindication of the Dissenters in Lichfield from the Charges brought against them* (1808), with 'An appendix on Religious Melancholy' by Dr. Clarke (1762-1832).

this, like his other suicide attempts, had not been accomplished.[153] However, just before committing her final, irreversible act Eliza prayed that she 'might find a place in heaven', but then recalled 'these awful words' (119-120) of warning clearly stated in the Bible:

> No murderer shall enter heaven,
> His crimes shall never be forgiven;[154]
> And should I be my murderer now,
> To endless torment I must go.   (121-124)

Yet remembering God's alternative promise that he would hear all those who cried for pardon, she realized that if she abondoned her plan, he might still forgive her (125-128). 'Thus God in mercy did appear'; he stopped her in her madness, and thus she escaped the terrors of 'hell\Where wicked men and devils dwell' (129-132). She had been saved by divine intervention at the crucial moment. Here again Eliza's experience was similar to Cowper's, except that in his case God's intervention had been in the failure of the mechanics of his attempt and might be seen clearly as a particular providence.[155] The 'atrocious nature' of the sin he had committed was suddenly apparent to Cowper also, 'that there wanted nothing but murder to fill up the measure of [his] iniquity', that he was as guilty as if his 'crime' had been successful; living would be better than facing God's wrath in eternity.[156]

After this incident Eliza resorted to immediate prayer for mercy. God fulfilled his promise of 'pardon' and 'aid', thus freeing her from all her 'grief and misery' (133-136). In her new state of relief, she re-joined the Hackleton congregation and 'with the saints [she] lov'd to meet\To worship at the Saviour's feet' (141-148).[157] However, joy was only temporary. The personified Satan

---

153 Cowper, *Letters and Prose*, I, pp.23-24.

154 There are warnings in 1 John, 3:15: 'ye know that no murderer hath eternal life abiding in him', and Revelations, 21:8: 'But...murderers...shall have their part in the lake which burneth with fire and brimstone: which is the second death'.

155 Evangelicals believed in particular providences that displayed God's judgement or mercy and these could be 'individual or national': see Bebbington, *Evangelicalism*, p.61. In this context Bebbington has mentioned Newton and Thomas Scott. The latter was curate of Ravenstone and Weston Underwood near Olney.

156 Cowper, *Letters and Prose*, I, p.25.

157 'Saints' was a term for the converted and used in similar context by Cowper: see *Olney Hymns*, I, 64, v.5, 'Thy saints are comforted, I know,\And love thy house of prayer'. Here Cowper was himself 'rewriting Watts (with the allusion to "thy saints", and to "loving thy house of prayer" (from Watts's *Divine Songs*)': see Watson, *The English Hymn*, p.290.

came to sow seeds of doubt in her mind yet again:

> But soon my mind was fill'd with care,
> For Satan tempted to despair;
> He told me 'I did not believe,
> 'But only did my self deceive,
> 'That mercy I need not expect,
> 'For I was not of God's elect;'
> Could I forgiveness hope to find,
> A sinner of the vilest kind?   (149-156)

Eliza's use of the word 'elect' in this context is a clear expression of her moderate Calvinism.   For Newton, Satan was 'that raven unclean\Who croaks in the ears of the saints'.[158]   Possibly these other lines of his suggested Eliza's own: 'When sin revives and shows its power,\When Satan threatens to devour...\We tremble lest we were deceiv'd\In thinking that we once believ'd.[159]

Eliza went on:

> This state of mind continued long,
> Through these temptations sharp and strong;
> But then my real case was known
> Unto Almighty God alone.   (157-160)

Although her personal relationship with God was undoubted, she was still uncertain that her conversion was real and questioned whether it would be wise to join the 'saints' of Hackleton Baptist Church 'Lest [she] should stray from God again' (161-172). 'But [she] at length his name confess'd\Love to [her] Saviour [she] profess'd' (173, 174) and was received 'into the church\As one who in the Lord believ'd' (177, 178).   Here it can be understood that Eliza was referring to the occasions on which she 'spoke her experience', was baptized and became a full member of her Church.   However she was not complacent, as Evangelicals were urged never to be, and the next three verses evidence her continuing feelings of spiritual weakness.   Like other Evangelicals, she feared backsliding and realized 'How often [her] wandering heart' departed 'from God' (181-192).

---

158 *Olney Hymns*, I, 35.
159 *Ibid.*, 141, v.5 & 6.

Though her words may not have been read until after her death, Eliza hoped others might share her experience: 'Now those who read these lines may see\The goodness of my God to me' (193-194). She referred again to the divine intervention that stopped her suicide:

> He could have stop'd my feeble breath,
> And sent me to eternal death:
> But he has spar'd me still to tell
> How he has sav'd my soul from hell.   (197-200)

She began to take the sacrament 'at the glorious gospel feast' to which she had 'long refused to be a guest' (205-206). She knew the matter had been in her own hands. This seems to confirm that Hackleton Baptists withheld communion from those who had not been baptized as believers.[160] At last, with true Evangelical optimism, Eliza proclaimed that God's offer of redemption was unrestricted to all who repented:

> God's grace to sinners doth abound,
> I sought the Lord and mercy found;
> The vilest sinner need not fear,
> For God will his petitions hear.   (209-212)

And there was one final, simply-worded plea:

> Lord, may thy spirit guide me now,
> While I am in this world below:
> And then when I am call'd to die,
> Receive my soul above the sky.   (213-216)

Eliza was soon to know if her prayer was answered. It seems that her Evangelical confidence did not diminish before she died. For Cowper the 'conviction of sin and despair of mercy' he suffered following his attempt to hang himself in 1763 were sufficiently overpowering to cause insanity and a stay in a lunatic asylum.[161] His conversion came after an interval of eight months' residence there.

---

160 For Calvinistic Baptist divisions on this, see Payne, *The Baptist Union*, p.40. According to the Hackleton Meeting minutes the newly-baptized took Communion on the Sunday following their baptism.

161 For Cowper's account of this period, see: *Letters and Prose*, I, pp.34-46.

However, he did not maintain his belief that 'God is love and changes not',[162] for after another period of mental illness in 1783, he never again found complete spiritual peace.[163]

5.5 Eliza Westbury's hymns

Alan Everitt has referred briefly to 'the vast development of Dissenting hymnology' during the eighteenth century, that began 'with Isaac Watts and Philip Doddridge' and continued 'through Charles Wesley and his many imitators well into the nineteenth century'.[164] Hutchings has shown how the hymn writing of William Cowper and John Newton (1725-1807) was influenced by Watts's innovative ideas in the development of Evangelical hymnography.[165] Watts, a Nonconformist, had recognized a necessity to move away from traditional metrical psalms to a new style of English hymn suited to the times, that would better express the everyday experiences of a congregation and speak in linguistic terms they would find familiar.[166] Newton, an Anglican Evangelical and moderate Calvinist,[167] took up the curacy of Olney in 1764 and in 1771 Cowper agreed to join him in producing their famous *Olney Hymns*, which were eventually published in 1779.[168] They were probably two of the imitators Everitt had in mind. Cowper and Newton were near to Eliza Westbury in time and place and I would argue that they were the greatest influences on the style and content of her hymns. Evidence of her borrowing from both writers in her poems has already been mentioned, but it will be shown that this can be detected to a larger extent in her hymns. Limits of space permit none other than *Olney Hymns* to be used for comparison here.[169]

---

162 Cowper, 'Peace after a Storm', *Olney Hymns*, III, 23, v.3.

163 Gordon, *Evangelical Spirituality*, p.83.

164 Everitt, *Pattern of Rural Dissent*, p.66.

165 Cowper, *The Poetry of William Cowper*, pp.22-36.

166 *Ibid.*, p.24.

167 Bebbington, *Evangelicalism*, p.63; Walsh & Taylor, 'The Church and Anglicanism', p.49.

168 *Olney Hymns* totalled 348; only 67 were by Cowper. Newton gave Cowper's 'long and affecting indisposition' as the reason for the discrepancy in numbers; p.iii.

169 Eliza Westbury's hymns might also be compared with those of Anne Steele (1717-1778) who has been called 'the first major woman hymn-writer', Watson, *The English Hymn*, p.191. Steele was the daughter of a Particular Baptist timber merchant *cum* minister: See *Hymns by Anne Steele* (1760), J.R.B. (ed. 1967), p.xvii. She wrote before 'Fullerism' had split the denomination. 'Olney Hymns' more accurately portray Eliza's moderate Calvinism.

Subject matter was governed by the doctrine acceptable to the congregations for whom hymnodists were writing. Members of Evangelical churches expected what they were singing to fully reflect their beliefs. Most hymnodists suffered limitations for, to fulfil these expectations, they must try to bring in as much Scriptural imagery and wording as possible.[170]   Hutchings has suggested that the following should be borne in mind when considering Cowper's hymn-writing task, but the same can be applied to Eliza's works. We should

> acknowledge a whole series of defining and related factors: the scriptural basis which affect[ed] both theme and language, the circumscribed form of communal song, the lack of metaphorical possibilities beyond a point fixed by biblical precept and Nonconformist tradition, the specific dogmas of a Calvinistic creed, the need to communicate directly to all the members of a congregation, and the strict limitation of the expressed personality of the poet to that which the whole church can recognise and identify with.[171]

It might be thought unwise to examine a young lace-maker's hymns alongside those of the educated Cowper and the ordained Newton, both mature Anglican Evangelicals, though the latter had risen from humbler beginnings than his friend.[172] However, there is sense in such alignment because Bebbington's four defining characteristics of Evangelicalism (conversionism, activism, biblicism and crucicentrism) are reflected in the hymns of all three writers. Another significant tie is that, in some instances, they drew from the same Biblical passages. My purpose here is not to produce a critical, qualitative assessement of Eliza's works or to compare their merits with those of others. It is to place them in context and to illustrate how they expressed her responses to Evangelicalism.

Cowper and Newton aimed to communicate with their singers plainly and simply,[173] in a style that would appeal to a whole congregation, regardless of social differences. Bebbington has seen

170 Elliott-Binns, *Early Evangelicals*, pp.415-6.
171 Cowper, *The Poetry of William Cowper*, pp.42-3.
172 See Balleine, *A History of the Evangelical Party*, pp.103-4; Marshall & Todd, *English Congregational Hymns*, p.90; Watson, *The English Hymn*, p.284.
173 Gordon, *Evangelical Spirituality*, p.71.

Enlightenment features in the simple and didactic nature of the earliest Evangelical hymns.[174] In his introduction to *Olney Hymns*, Newton offered the publication 'to all who love[d] the Lord Jesus Christ in sincerity' and he 'more particularly' dedicated it to his 'dear friends in the parish and neighbourhood of Olney, for whose use the hymns were originally composed'.[175] The Olney community of the time was characterized by its lace-makers and families engaged in agriculture. The 1811 Population Returns for the town have pointed to a continuing attraction for female employment in lace-making.[176] Eliza's hymn writing was her form of activism and probably she hoped that one day her verses would be sung or read by members of Hackleton Baptist Church and other people. However, there is no evidence that the hymns were ever used in local congregational worship.

It has already been shown that in the early nineteenth century Hackleton congregation were singing from Watts and Rippon.[177] The 1802 edition of Rippon's *Selection* occasionally extracted from *Olney Hymns* but it is feasible that, by the time Eliza was converted in 1826, a complete volume of the latter was in regular use at Hackleton. A spirit of ecumenism at Olney was well-established and John Sutcliff, William Knowles's mentor, had been there in Cowper and Newton's time.[178] Evangelicalism had broken down barriers between Anglicans and Dissenters in the town.[179] Newton regularly joined the Baptists in their meetings. Knowles's diary shows that he went to preach at Olney on at least one Sunday each year, so Hackleton's relationship with the Baptists there was maintained after Sutcliff's death. It is likely that Knowles held a special regard and favour for the 'Olney Hymns' and encouraged his own congregation to sing them.

174 Bebbington, *Evangelicalism*, pp.67-8.

175 *Olney Hymns*, p.v.

176 Of the 497 families in Olney, 96 were employed in Agriculture, 377 in Trade, Manufacture and Handicraft. Population was 1,277 females, 991 males: see *Abstract of Answers and Returns, 1811*, p.78.

177 Undoubtedly, one of the many editions of Rippon's, *A Selection of Hymns from the Best Authors* would have been used. The 13th Edition (1802) contained 9 of Cowper's and 9 of Newton's 'Olney Hymns'.

178 See Cowper, *Letters and Prose*, I, p.197, for his letter, 18 June 1768, mentioning a recent 'Holiday Week at Olney' when 'the [Northamptonshire] Association of Baptist Ministers' and Anglican clergy (including Newton) together held meetings for preaching and prayer.

179 E. Routley, *English Religious Dissent* (Cambridge, 1960), p.151.

All 141 hymns in Book I of *Olney Hymns* were based, as the heading indicated, 'On select passages of Scripture' and the text for each was given. Eliza Westbury readily drew from Biblical texts for her stanzas, and mention will be made of where her words echoed those of Cowper and Newton. No specific Biblical sources were noted in Eliza's hymn book, but it can be detected where she used them. It was customary for writers to name their hymns and several might be classified under the same title. Occasionally, up to seven of Eliza's hymns were grouped under a single heading, yet it cannot be claimed that any of the titles had been suggested by herself. Only around fifty per cent of her works were included in *Hymns by a Northamptonshire Village Female*. Even so, not all of these can be discussed here. A selection has been made from those most clearly representative of Evangelical doctrine and a few have been chosen for their other particular interest. The hymns will be placed under the titles given and looked at in their original numerical sequence.

HYMNS:

BY

A Northamptonshire

VILLAGE FEMALE.

Hymn 1, 'The omnipresence of God'.

This hymn will be quoted in full because it was given pride of place as first in the book. Its message was wholly biblical: 'Can any hide himself in secret places that I shall not see him? saith the Lord. Do not I fill heaven and earth?',[180] and his eyes 'are in every place, beholding the evil and the good.'[181] The unseen presence meant that no-one anywhere, at any time, escaped the divine eye of judgement, a consideration to be borne constantly in mind by Evangelicals; they should be ever mindful of their innate sinfulness and tendency to lapse.[182] But here Eliza saw God as protective more than retributive:

180 Jeremiah, 23:24.
181 Proverbs, 15:3.
182 For how this message was conveyed to children in hymns and stories, see Thompson, *Making of the English Working Class*, pp.413-4.

1.   The Lord Jehovah reigns on high,
          But he is present every where;
     Though he is cloth'd in majesty
          Yet he is with us ever near.

2.   'Tis he supports us every hour,
          And guards us midst the shades of night;
     'Tis he upholds us by his power,
          And keeps us safe till morning light.

3.   If with the morning wings we fly
          Beyond the great and mighty sea,
     Still our Creator's watchful eye
          Will ever with his creatures be.

4.   If in the caverns of the earth
          We from our maker strive to hide,
     'Tis he supports our feeble breath,
          Nor can his presence be deny'd.

5.   If up to heaven we take our flight,
          Or if we make our bed in hell,
     Yet we are constant in his sight,
          And ever in his presence dwell.

'Jehovah' was the most solemn name given to God, signifying the self-existent, and in the English Bible distinguished by capital letters. Eliza's first line was taken from the last verse of Psalm 83, 'That men may know that thou whose name alone is JEHOVAH, art the Most High over all the earth'. For Cowper, 'Jehovah Jesus' was 'The great supreme, the mighty God'.[183] The imagery of the Psalms was especially appealing to such artistic imaginations and it can be said with certainty that Eliza based the real substance of her hymn on these words from Psalm 139: 7-11.

7.   Whither shall I go from thy Spirit? or whither shall I
       flee from thy presence?
8.   If I ascend up into heaven, thou art there: if I make
       my bed in hell, behold thou art there;

183 Cowper, *Olney Hymns*, II, 38.

9. If I take the wings of the morning, and dwell in the uppermost part of the sea;
10. Even there shall thy hand lead me, and thy right hand shall hold me.
11. If I say, Surely the darkness shall cover me; even the night shall be light about me.

Hymn 2, 'Value of the Scriptures'.

> 1. How precious is the Book divine,
> By inspiration given;
> In sacred truths do all combine,
> To teach the road to heaven.

Clearly, Eliza held a simple Evangelical belief that the Bible was inspired by God and felt a hymn should be dedicated to its spiritual values. In subsequent verses biblicism is fully expressed. Eliza spelt out her conviction that the Bible: 'guides the Christian on his way', tells of 'Christ's love' and 'makes known his will' (v.2); 'The drooping saint' can derive 'fresh courage' from its promises (v.3.); 'The wounded conscience' might find 'substantial peace' in its words and be healed by its 'sov'reign balm' (v.4). In *Olney Hymns* two titles were placed under the heading 'On the Scriptures' - Cowper's 'The Light and Glory of the Word' and Newton's 'The Word more precious than Gold'.[184] In his hymn, Newton also had written of the reviving and healing properties of the Bible's metaphorical 'Food and med'cine' when 'faith' was 'faint and sickly'.[185] In the second line of her last verse, Eliza may well have borrowed from Newton's title:

> 5. The statutes of our dearest Lord,
> More precious are than gold;
> The value of his holy word,
> Cannot on earth be told.

Hymns 4, 5, 6, 'Sufferings of Christ'.

Three of Eliza's hymns were included under this heading. In

---

184 *Olney Hymns*, Book II, 62 (Cowper's), 63 (Newton's).
185 See L. Adey, *Class and Idol in the English Hymn* (Vancouver, 1988), pp.27-8.

these she has given good illustration of what Bebbington called 'crucicentrism'. In verse 2 of Hymn 4, she dealt with the doctrine of Christ's substitutionary atonement, 'a belief' that 'originally distinguished Evangelicals from even the strictest divines of other schools' and at the beginning of the nineteenth century was strongly defended by Robert Hall.[186] First she invited her readers to witness the Crucifixion in a re-enactment of the scene:

> 1.   Come and behold the bleeding Lamb
>   Nail'd and expiring on the tree:
>   He from his throne in glory came
>   And bore the shameful cross for thee.
>
> 2.   What sufferings did our Lord endure,
>   When the vast debt for us he paid;
>   God's weighty vengeance then he bore,
>   Our numerous sins on him were laid.

The sacrificial 'bleeding Lamb' gave potential for imagery of the most gory nature and for harrowing descriptions of Christ's suffering, which Watts and Cowper had exploited to the full.[187] A sense of reality and authenticity was often added by quoting Christ's own words, as Eliza did here:

> 4.   Hear how he prays – 'Father, forgive
>   'These cruel enemies of mine,
>   'And now, O father, me receive,
>   'To Thee, my spirit I resign.' [188]

The Crucifixion was accompanied by darkness during normal daylight hours and an earth tremor. In verse 5 Eliza drew upon the Gospels for her comment on these terrifying phenomena that reflected the evil human behaviour and cruelty of Calvary: 'Well might the sun forbear to shine,\And well the temple veil might rend'.[189]

186 Bebbington, *Evangelicalism*, pp.15–16.

187 See Marshall & Todd, *English Congregational Hymns*, pp.125–6.

188 Luke, 23: 34 & 46. Newton also quoted v.34 for *Olney Hymns*, I, 109, entitled 'Father, forgive them'.

189 See Luke, 23:45, 'And the sun was darkened'; Matthew, 27:51, 'And, behold the veil of the temple was rent in twain, from the top to the bottom; and the earth did quake, and the rocks rent.'

Her second and third Crucifixion hymns also firmly supported the doctrine of substitutionary atonement. These lines from Eliza's Hymn 5 will suffice as further illustration:

> 2.   No one for sinners could atone,
>   But Christ, the Son of God.

Hymns 11, 12, 13, 'Repentance'.

The lengthy article in *The Baptist Magazine* dated June 1824 was a clear and easily understood explanation of 'Evangelical Repentance'. It began:

> The Bible, it should never be forgotten, is the religion of sinners, and it follows, as a necessary consequence, that repentance is an essential part of vital godliness. Without repentance, we must perish, in body and soul eternally.

> Repentance is founded in conviction of the evil nature, and awful consequences of sin. In some, it is more pungent than in others, yet it is essentially the same in all who believe in Christ, and turn to God. Till we are the subjects of [E]vangelical repentance, we shall never seek pardon through the blood of Christ, nor live to the glory of God...Repentance constitutes a leading feature, in a truly [E]vangelical ministry. John, the harbinger of our Lord, preached the baptism of repentance.[190]

It has already been noted from the 'Short account' that Eliza was deeply conscious of the evil of sin. Proof of this can be seen again in many of her hymns; Hymn 11 is a good example. Here, with repentant heaviness of heart, she pleaded for God's mercy:

> 1.   In wrath, O Lord, rebuke me not,
>   Spare me when thy displeasure's hot;
>   Sin like a burden weighs me down,
>   Beneath its pressure, Lord I groan.

---

190 W.B., 'On Evangelical Repentance', p.233.

And in Hymn 12 she recognized a continuing propensity for sinning, not only in herself, but also among her singers:

> 2.   We, too long, O Lord have been
>   Slaves to Satan, slaves to sin;
>   We have gone too far astray,
>   Rushing on the downward way.

Then in these verses from Hymn 13 she returned to an individual seeking for pardon 'through the blood of Christ':

> 1.   Saviour, unto thee I pray,
>   And on thee for mercy call,
>   Grant that I, a sinner, may
>   Find in thee my all in all.

> 3.   I approach thy holy throne,
>   Pleading what the Lord has done,
>   I've no merit of my own;
>   But accept me through thy Son.

Hymn 18, 'Resignation'.

'Resignation', 'submission', 'patience', imply acceptance of something unpleasant and inevitable. Eliza used each of the words in her hymn: 'Saviour, grant me resignation\To whatever be thy will' (v.1); 'Dearest Saviour, grant submission\To what ills may me betide' (v.2);

> 3.   Should thou please to send affliction
>   Calm the murmuring of my breast,
>   May I cherish this conviction,
>   That thou knowest what is best,
>   And with patience,
>   May I wait for promis'd rest.

That physical and emotional sufferings were to be anticipated and endured because they were God's will had probably been instilled in Eliza's young mind from childhood. The Bible dealt with the theme in several places, for example in James, 5:10, 'Take my brethren, the prophets, who have spoken in the name of the

Lord, for an example of suffering affliction and of patience'; v.11, 'Behold, we count them happy which endure'; and Romans, 5: 3-4 '...but we glory in tribulations also: knowing that tribulation worketh patience; And patience, experience; and experience, hope.' Cowper's hymn, 'Prayer for Patience',[191] presented the sufferings of Christ as a far heavier burden than our 'lighter cross' and put human pain and distress in perspective:[192]

> 1. Lord, who hast suffer'd all for me
>   My peace and pardon to procure,
>   The lighter cross I bear for Thee,
>   Help me with patience to endure.
>
> 6. Let me not angrily declare
>   No pain was ever sharp like mine;
>   Nor murmur at the cross I bear,
>   But rather weep, remembering thine.

However, in his hymn entitled 'Submission' Cowper more nearly expressed what Eliza was saying:

> 1. O Lord, my best desire fulfil,
>   And help me to resign
>   Life, health, and comfort to thy will,
>   And make thy pleasure mine.[193]

Yet endurance of life's hardships must surely have been easier for Cowper than for the poor. It can be seen from 'Adelphi' that he was able to procure creature comforts and medical care that were far beyond the resources of someone like our young lace-maker from Hackleton.

Hymn 27, 'Discontent'.

Another of Eliza's hymns was written in a similar spirit of 'resignation' but it appeared later in the hymn book under this different heading. Here she may have had in mind the 'discontent' generated by the social position of the local poor as well as their

191 *Olney Hymns*, III, 28.
192 Marshall & Todd, *English Congregational Hymns*, p.128.
193 *Olney Hymns*, III, 29.

day-to-day afflictions, or perhaps it was a reflection of the
'calamities' occasioned by the 1826 enclosure of Salcey Forest:

> 1.   Christians, beware of discontent,
>   'Tis a besetting sin;
>   It will all happiness prevent
>   When once it is let in.

> 2.   We murmur at our Maker's will
>   Complain of our hard lot;
>   Calamities remember still,
>   But mercies are forgot.

> 4.   Pardon, O Lord, our discontent;
>   Forgiveness now display;
>   And may thy spirit now be sent
>   To guide us lest we stray.

With her use of 'we', 'our' and 'us', Eliza was identifying with
her singers and bringing a communal element into their worship.
Those in authority usually expected the poor to be industrious,
long-suffering and resigned to their lot.[194]   These lines from
Cowper's hymn 'For the Poor' can be judged a typical, consolatory
acceptance of such attitudes:

> To Jesus then your trouble bring;
>   Nor murmur at your lot;
> While you are poor, and He is King,
>   You shall not be forgot.[195]

Thompson has given his notion of how Evangelicalism turned
multifarious hardships of life into some kind of blessing:

> Since joy was associated with sin and guilt, and pain
> (Christ's wounds) with goodness and love, so every
> impulse became twisted into the reverse, and it became
> natural to suppose that man or child only found grace in
> God's eyes when performing painful, laborious or self-

194 Hammonds, *The Village Labourer*, p.208.
195 *Olney Hymns*, III, 57.

denying tasks. To labour and to sorrow was to find pleasure and masochism was 'Love'.[196]

Hymn 30, 'The Harvest is past'.

The title appears seasonal in a rural context and Eliza probably thought her hymn appropriate to autumn, when the various local harvests had been gathered in. Her sense of activism can be observed as she advised conversion – repentance and the turning to God in faith – before it was too late. Jeremiah, 8:20, 'The harvest is past, the summer is ended, and we are not saved' was clearly the inspiration for the heading of this hymn and content. However, Eliza reversed the first two parts of the biblical extract for the last line of each stanza. Only two of the four verses will be quoted as, throughout, she expanded on the concept of wasted time during a life spent without spiritual growth and yielding no crop of heavenly rewards.

1. What direful remorse those sinners will feel,
    Who for their transgressions, are sent down to hell;
    Their torments for ever and ever will last,
    For summer is ended and harvest is past.

2. When Jesus as judge on his throne shall appear
    Though trembling and fearful, they all will be there;
    They then will remember the time they did waste:
    But summer is ended, and harvest is past.

Her cautionary tone emphasized that 'human life is short, and yet it is the only period in which repentance is available'.[197] Evangelical moderate Calvinism is again very evident here. *Olney Hymns* included two by Newton on harvesting. These had special significance for his parishioners employed in agriculture. 'Haytime', in similar vein to Eliza's, was about using time wisely and being prepared before the 'scythe of death' mowed the singers down. Contrastingly, his 'Harvest' hymn imaged 'precious seeds of heavenly joy' producing 'grace's crop', which 'Death the reaper' finds 'fully' ripened.[198]

196 Thompson, *The Making of the English Working Class*, p.409.
197 See W.B., 'On Evangelical Repentance', p.234.
198 *Olney Hymns*, II, 35, 36.

Hymn 33, 'The Fiery Lake'.

This seeming oxymoron ended each of the four verses of Eliza's hymn, the theme of which again is conversion. The lake was that of fire and brimstone described in Revelations, 19:20; 20:10,14,15. Like other Evangelicals she used the image to effect:

> 1. How dangerous is the way
> Which careless sinners go,
> Repentance they delay,
> And thus their folly shew;
> They no advice nor warning take,
> While standing near the fiery lake.

> 3. They think they will repent
> Before they come to die,
> And thus with one consent,
> Their precious souls destroy:
> But they will see their great mistake
> When in that awful fiery lake.

Eliza's hymn and one by Newton in *Olney Hymns*, his second of three under the heading 'Solemn Addresses to Sinners', were distinctly similar. They were based on identical texts. Though the two hymnwriters were not in the same literary league, here their messages were equally simple. We can see this in Newton's first verse alone:

> 1. Stop, poor sinner! stop and think
> Before you farther go!
> Will you sport upon the brink
> Of everlasting woe?
> Once again I charge you, stop!
> For, unless you warning take,
> Ere you are aware, you drop
> Into the burning lake.[199]

The same stanza was quoted by Watson to make his point that, 'When Newton preaches in his hymns, the result can also be a

---

199 *Olney Hymns*, III, 2.

rather disagreeable authoritarianism, mixed with threats, although his skill with rhymes makes the verse very dramatic.'[200]   The comment might also be applied to Eliza's didactic works.

Hymn 36, 'Prepare to meet thy God'.

At least one hymn in any Evangelical collection was almost bound to bear this title and Eliza's version was merely a variation of the message hammered home with regularity in her other hymns:

> 1. Sinner, prepare thy God to meet,
>   This awful warning ne'er forget,
>   For God himself has said that they
>   Shall perish who do not obey.

The heading was used by Newton for one of his Olney Hymns.[201] A distinct class bias can be observed in these words from it, which would have appealed to the many poor in his congregation. It was 'the rich, the great, the wise,' he saw as 'Trembling, guilty, self-condemn'd' who 'Must behold the wrathful eyes\Of the judge they once blasphem'd'. Eliza's 'Prepare to meet thy God' was followed immediately by four others, all under 'Danger of the Wicked' and each repetitive of the same theme urging repentance and conversion.

Hymns 42-48, 'On death'.

Eliza's approach was unpretentious and matter-of-fact in her seven hymns 'On death'. She was able to accept the inevitable with Evangelical confidence in the 'perfect harmony and bliss' of 'where Jesus is' for 'all the favour'd throng' (Hymn 42). She recognized the inequalities of society, yet 'death the tyrant' was the great leveller (Hymn 43):

> 2.   He takes the aged and the young,
>   The weak, the healthy, and the strong:
>   He visits those of humble mien,
>   And in the palace he is seen.

200 Watson, *The English Hymn,* p.287.
201 *Olney Hymns,* III, 4.

3.   Now one of royal blood is dead,[202]
      His soul has from his body fled;
      Though he of late in splendour dwelt,
      Yet he the stroke of death has felt.

It has been suggested that lace-makers were particularly prone to
serious lung diseases through working long hours from childhood
sitting with others in cramped, airless cottage rooms. Were these
first lines of Eliza's other hymns 'On death' evidence of her own
personal, short life-expectancy or were they another reminder for
any singer that her or his end could come at any time?

'Soon I shall be call'd to enter\Into endless bliss or woe;
                                                    (No. 45)
'Soon I must leave this world below\And to eternity must
go;
                                                    (No.46)
'When a few more years are come\I must go into the
tomb;
                                                    (No. 47)
'Since I soon must leave for ever\Every thing below the
sky;
                                                    (No.48)

Hymns 62, 63 (No heading).

Evangelical congregations might be requested to remember their
ministers in their prayers and sometimes complete hymns were
devoted to encouragement of those with pastoral duties. A letter
headed 'On ardent concern for the conversion of sinners among
members of Churches' appeared in the *Baptist Magazine* of July
1828. It contained this message:

His people's prayers are among the supports of a minister,
and since the certain efficacy of prayer cannot be limited
by us, earnest supplications for success in his labours should
never be omitted. Besides, should those who are partially
impressed hear such supplications from a church, in aid of

202 Probably Frederick, Duke of York, brother of William IV, who died in January 1827,
aged 64.

the addresses which have arrested their attention from the
pulpit, the effect may be important. What may not be
expected from a church striving, both in preaching and in
prayers, for the conversion of sinners?[203]

Activism was at the heart of the letter. It was written soon after
Eliza Westbury's death but, in the following two hymns, she had
already requested the Hackleton congregation to remember their
preachers. This was the first of them:

1.   Who can describe the grief of mind
Of those who preach the word of God,
When those around them seem inclin'd
To persevere the downward road?

2.   They many tears in private shed,
O'er those who do their souls despise,
That are by Satan captive led;
They long to see poor sinners wise.

3.   They love to hear when sinners pray,
When they begin to seek the Lord;
When they to Zion ask the way,
And set their faces thitherward.

5.   They watch for souls while here they live,
God's counsel they to men declare,
For they account will have to give,
Of those committed to their care.

Here singers were reminded that endeavouring to convert
unbelievers was sometimes a burdensome, thankless task for
ministers, yet could have its rewards. Eliza's second hymn on this
theme was a prayer specifically for their own pastor, no doubt
written with feeling for William Knowles. It contained only a
couple of verses:

1.   Dearest Saviour, bless thy servant,
        Who to us thy word makes known;
        May our prayers for him be fervent,
        May they rise before thy throne;
        Saviour, bless him,
        And do thou his labours own.

2.   May our prayers be never ceasing,
        That thou wilt our Pastor bless,
        May thy church be here increasing,
        Crown his labours with success;
        Him encourage,
        And increase his happiness.

Two of Newton's Olney Hymns concerned the sorrows and joys of 'ministers' employ' and signalled their need for encouragement. In singing them, as with Eliza's hymns, the congregation were reminded of the 'pain' their own pastor could suffer in trying to convert parishioners and the 'pleasures felt' when sinners' hearts 'began to melt'.[204] Of course, Newton's 'Prayer for Ministers' was written subjectively.[205] In Evangelical phrases such as these, he prayed for help and support from 'The Chief Shepherd': 'With plenteous grace their hearts prepare\To execute thy will (v.2)'; 'And let them live, and let them feel\The sacred truths they preach' (v.3).

Hymn 64, 'For Revival'.

Membership of the Baptist Churches belonging to the Northampton Association as a whole had increased little from 1820 onwards and 29 June 1826 was fixed as a day of prayer for revival.[206] Eliza may have produced her hymn for this or some other occasion,

204 *Olney Hymns,* 'Travailing in birth for souls', II, 26. See Marshall & Todd, *English Congregational Hymns,* p.112.

205 *Olney Hymns,* II, 50.

206 *The Circular Letter from the Ministers and Messengers in The Northamptonshire Association assembled at Kettering, 16th & 17th May 1826,* p.15. The Association, formed in 1764, included Particular Baptist churches in Northamptonshire, Leicestershire, Buckinghamshire and Nottinghamshire. Its early leaders were Robert Hall, the elder, John Collett Ryland, followed by Sutcliff, Fuller, the younger Ryland, the younger Hall and Carey: see Payne, *The Baptist Union,* p.37. Hackleton Church joined the Association in 1817.

particularly as the variation in numbers at Hackleton from 1820 to 1828 was between only sixty and sixty-five.[207] It began:

> Saviour, hear our weak petition
> That thy cause may here revive.[208]

In the fourth stanza she pleaded for spiritual renewal amongst them:

> May poor sinners turn from folly,
> And to thee devote their days;
> May thy people be more holy,
> May they daily grow in grace:
> Lord, revive us,
> Thou alone shalt have the praise.

Her lines seem 'calculated to inspire the congregation to want to do better', as Marshall and Todd commented on the final stanza of Newton's 'Travailing in Birth for Souls'.[209] Eliza's last six words here were identical to those that ended Newton's hymn.[210]

Hymn 71 (No heading).

It is appropriate for Eliza's final hymn to end this discussion and here are three of its five verses:

> 1.   What is this world with all its joys?
>   Vain are its transitory toys:
>   It can afford no real place,
>   'Tis vanity of vanities.

207 *Hackleton Baptist Church Book*, N.C.R.O., HBC16. *Abstract of Answers and Returns, 1821*, for Piddington and Hackleton, p.228, reveals a much greater majority employed in agriculture: Piddington, 93 families out of 120, Hackleton, 63 out of 84; with only 25 families at Piddington and 19 at Hackleton still in trade, manufacturing, handicraft. This marked change may explain the low new membership figures locally.

208 Newton's 'Prayer for Revival' and 'Hoping for Revival' had their Anglican purpose, *Olney Hymns*, II, 51, 52.

209 Marshall & Todd, *English Congregational Hymns*, p.113.

210 *Olney Hymns*, II, 26.

3.   While you indulge in sinful mirth,
      You may be call'd away from earth;
      Death unexpected may you seize,
      'Midst vanity of vanities.

4.   O then no longer dare delay;
      Seek not those joys that fade away,
      Do not the God of heaven despise;
      But love him more than vanities.

These words were on Ecclesiastes 1:2, 'Vanity of vanities, saith the Preacher, vanity of vanities; all is vanity.' 'Vanities' here means material assets and 'Vanity' the conceit they might generate. Evangelicals accepted the biblical teaching that earthly wealth held no spiritual value or lasting security. There were two Olney Hymns built on the same text, 'Vanity of Life' by Newton, 'Vanity of the World' by Cowper.[211] For Newton, 'The gourds, from which we look for fruit\Produce us only pain'; for Cowper, 'The joy that vain amusements give,\Oh! sad confusion that it brings'...'God knows the thousands who go down\From pleasures into endless woe'. The local poor could take comfort in the idea that the rich were not to be envied. Eliza's last verse suggested an alternative way for those she addressed as 'you':

5.   Then quickly to the Saviour come,
      For he has said, 'there yet is room';[212]
      From sinful pleasure may you cease,
      And flee from earthly vanities.

In her own surroundings, Eliza probably had the reputation for being a young woman of unusual character and talents when she was alive but, in the publication of her hymns and verses after her death, she gained a wider, acceptable and lasting identity, unlike most of her class at that time. Through her Sabbath School she acquired the literacy and learning that gave her confidence to express her spirituality in writing. It has already been mentioned that generally women did not hold positions of authority within Dissenting churches and their decision-making role was still

211 *Olney Hymns*, I, 54 & 55.
212 Luke, 14:22.

limited, but Evangelicals welcomed female activity, 'provided that it remained within its proper sphere'.[213] Hymn writing was regarded 'as a respectable and ladylike thing to do'.[214] Women hymn writers were accepted in Nonconformist circles before they were recognized within Orthodox Anglicanism. However, those whose works were published, usually through private funding, were overwhelmingly from middle-class backgrounds. It can be safely assumed that William Knowles was behind the publication of Eliza's hymns and for this he might be considered progressive because of her working-class background. Yet it is noticeable that her name did not appear in the title 'Hymns by a Northamptonshire village female', making it sound impersonal as well as class divisive. Clearly, Eliza was not thought of as 'a Northamptonshire village lady', unlike Charlotte Elliott, sister of a clergyman, whose *Morning and Evening Hymns for a Week* (1839) were marked 'by a Lady'.[215] Though women were regarded as spiritually equal, such discriminating terminology accentuated their social inequalities. However, Knowles may have been proud to indicate that Hackleton Baptists could produce a female hymn writer from the lower classes. Eliza's conversion and subsequent dedication to hymn writing can be recognized as a success story for Evangelical religion in a small, close-knit, rural community set within a Midland area where Particular Baptists had become widely established.

213 Davidoff & Hall, *Family Fortunes*, p.141.
214 Watson, *The English Hymn*, p.422.
215 *Ibid.*, p.427-9.

Chapter 6

CONCLUSION

Female responses to Evangelical religion during the first half of the nineteenth century were widely diverse. For some women it was central to their existence, for others it was a source of irritation and fear of losing social and religious traditions. A powerful spiritual movement that energized countless women and claimed their complete dedication was bound to generate undiluted reactions. In this study of contemporary wives, mothers, daughters and sisters living in Kent and Northamptonshire, some interesting relationships between women and men in local matters of religion and society have been revealed. Furthermore, it can now be understood that, in the Northamptonshire parishes investigated, Evangelicalism was not an exciting, short-term phenomenon. Instead, through the influence of well-known historical figures, it left a lasting impression on local communities.

As David Bebbington confirmed only four years ago, the spirituality of nineteenth-century Protestants, especially Evangelicals, remains a neglected topic - 'the patterns that affected the people en masse have been very little traced. The soul of the ordinary churchgoer has its own history waiting to be recorded'.[1] Valuable evidence presented in my chapters has shown that primary sources of various kinds, concerning female Anglicans and Dissenters, do exist for tackling the deficiency. However, the limited nature of my investigation is acknowledged. Having worked within certain parameters, I must declare it a partial attempt to locate women whose concerns with Evangelical religion differed. Female Methodists have not come under scrutiny here, neither have I included English Presbyterians,[2] Quakers,[3] Congregationalists, or the New Connexion wing of the Arminian General Baptists. My research has dealt only with the city of Canterbury, a small number of other areas in Kent, and parts of Northamptonshire. Nevertheless, it is a pointer to avenues of detailed enquiry that can be useful in bringing something new to

1 Bebbington, *Holiness in Nineteenth-Century England*, p.3.
2 The Dissenters 'least influenced by Evangelicalism': see Bebbington, *Evangelicalism*, p.18.
3 Among the Quakers, there was a 'grouping' of Evangelicals who were 'most active in the period from 1830-85': see Davidoff & Hall, *Family Fortunes*, p.87.

the local history of women and Evangelicalism within the denominations not covered here for those two counties. Other English counties provide scope for investigation of all their 'serious' Anglican and Dissenting women. Parts of this present work add to existing knowledge of how Evangelical religion was established and sustained in parishes. Landscape and geographical position were, undoubtedly, key factors in governing hierarchical influences and employment patterns in the areas discussed. Demographic evidence has been important in my assessments of local Evangelical involvement. As Dennis Mills has pointed out, family history is fundamental to community history 'both in terms of practicality and of concepts, since a community can readily be treated as a collection of families'.[4] That women's responses to Evangelicalism were shaped predominantly by family influences and environmental factors has remained undisputed. Significantly, the women featuring most prominently in my investigation, even those whose lives were restricted by Evangelical religion, or whose attitudes and activities changed considerably after spiritual conversion, did not divert from their childhood religious associations. Social and economic circumstances presented individual opportunities for active female participation in local Evangelical church or chapel life. For many women these were chances for closer interaction with classes of society other than their own, which could be to mutual advantage.

Although my work has added little to what was already known about the social base of Nonconformist Evangelicalism, something has been contributed to an area of investigation much less well documented, especially with regard to women. That is, the people who made up Anglican Evangelical congregations during the first half of the nineteenth century. It can be concluded that, in the districts of Kent and Northamptonshire studied here, Anglican Evangelicalism attracted women and their families from the middle and working classes, as well as the landed gentry. There are surely many more primary sources relevant to this question of 'serious' Anglican congregations lying hidden in local archives. Then again, in English churches and churchyards there is always the possibility of discovering nineteenth-century memorials with epitaphs reflecting Evangelical beliefs of women. If the social class of the

4   D. Mills, 'Community and nation in the past: perception and reality', in M. Drake (ed.), *Time, Family and Community; Perspectives on Family and Community History* (Oxford, 1994), p.282.

deceased is not evident, nominal record linkage might provide answers. Census enumerators' books have been of little use in this present work because returns for censuses before 1841 did not contain individual names, ages and occupations. In 1988, it was claimed that there was still room for analysis to be made of the 'social origins, age-structure, numerical strength and geographic distribution' of Anglican Evangelicalism in Victorian Britain.[5] Searching even for parishes in which Evangelical clergymen were appointed between 1800 and 1836 could prove worthwhile in this respect for, as we have seen, from that period a curate or incumbent might remain in the same parish for some years after Victoria's accession.

Although the number of Anglican women studied here has been limited, my investigations have been sufficient to reveal extreme contrasts in their responses to Evangelical religion. Strong negative views of Evangelicalism were held by some of them, while others adhered positively and steadfastly to its doctrines. This has been well illustrated in personal letters, particularly valuable in their conversational quality. Much of the correspondence can be considered a double source, for it has indicated attitudes shared by both writer and recipient. Most women in the Church of England had little power to express antagonism towards Evangelicalism other than in conversation or writing, and probably there remain few unpublished, original sources conveying such feelings. As has been shown, some nineteenth-century female authors used their novels as vehicles of opposition. The Orthodox Anglican at the centre of my second chapter must have been representative of many women who were more than ready to criticize Evangelical religion in its various manifestations. Perhaps others also commented on the deficiencies within the Established Church. Though undistinguished in wider circles, within her own social network Mrs Lukyn appears to have been respected for her critical views. Search for further written evidence of antipathy towards Evangelical religion left by unknown Anglican women would prove an interesting exercise. Only through such historical legacies shall we know more of the reactions of ordinary women in the Church of England who felt traditional doctrines and social customs were being changed by the advance of Evangelicalism.

---

5   D. Englander, 'The word and the world: Evangelicalism in the Victorian city', in G. Parsons (ed.), *Religion in Victorian Britain, II Controversies* (Manchester, 1988), p.23.

We have seen that, for some pious women in the Established Church, personal monetary wealth, land ownership or status gained through male relatives with similar advantages, gave freedom to respond to Evangelicalism in ways usually closed to lower-class parishioners of both sexes. Literate women might express their faith in writing, whether for private or public reading, but females from all classes could respond to the call for practical piety and activism within their own households. Through expression of newly-acquired Evangelical beliefs, some wives and daughters of landed gentry were able to assert themselves in their Orthodox Anglican families and their parishes. Although they challenged established norms of society, they held sufficient power to remain within the folds of their parish churches. Open female opposition to close relatives inside these privileged circles appears to have been a new departure and was disruptive of domestic harmony. Yet the responses of women featuring here were not so extreme as George Eliot's 'refusal to go to church' at all when, in 1841 at the age of twenty-two, she discarded the Evangelical faith in which she had been nurtured.[6] Subsequent 'confrontations with her father and other members of the family' were 'long and painful'.[7]

The virtues of nineteenth-century clergy wives, daughters and sisters were extolled in obituaries and memoirs, and their supportive roles have been discussed in historiographies containing references to women members of the Anglican Church. Furthermore, they were of sufficient importance in clerical lives and local society to be characterized by more than one contemporary novelist. Thus, it might appear that an Anglican minister without female relatives in his household lacked domestic comfort, and was likely to be other than fully effective in his church concerns. The case of Thomas Jones of Creaton belies the supposition for, with the affectionate support of generations of women from a family other than his own, he gained national and local Evangelical success. Seemingly, he was able to achieve more from his home in a village hostelry, for several years owned and run by widows, than most clergymen of his time living a conventional married life in Church property. Jones had no need to consider a wife whose duty it was to settle in an area, make friends and become accepted in her husband's parish. That the Bosworth

6   G. Eliot, *Scenes of Clerical Life* (1973 edn), pp.13-14.
7   *Ibid.*

women were of a local family with established religious, social and business relationships in the community was probably advantageous for him. During the first half of the nineteenth century the role of clergy female relatives was limited and they were never to usurp his authority. Their customary involvement was with the Sunday School, other Church organizations and as parochial visitors, though some did write hymns, poems, or children's stories. Clergy wives 'were expected to have no independent existence of their own, but to be incorporated into the profession of their husbands'.[8] The Bosworth women had an 'independent existence' in running Highgate House and this was the focus of much of their interest and activity. Their need to devote some time to other than parish church affairs might in part have contributed to Thomas Jones's domestic harmony and ministerial success. Nevertheless, it is transparent that the love, moral and practical support given him by the Bosworth wives and daughters was considerable and should never be underestimated. We still know little of what it was like for nineteenth-century clergy families living on inadequate stipends, and the practical difficulties posed by loss of freehold if the breadwinner died. There is room for local research on this subject. The few Evangelical female patrons mentioned in my study were, typically, concerned with propagating their own form of piety through the clergymen they appointed. Clearly, knowing or being related to such women could be of significant advantage for Evangelical incumbents or curates when it came to finding a living.

Of the several early nineteenth-century missionary and philanthropic organizations involving women, only the Church Missionary Society and the British and Foreign Bible Society have been looked at here. Though I have dealt with collectors and visitors operating on behalf of both Societies within a limited area of Northamptonshire, they were working to the same ends as other such women throughout England. Female commitment at local level was real and vital to the success of these two national networks of Evangelical missionary endeavour. The report from the Ladies' Associations forming the Creaton Branch of the British and Foreign Bible Society has revealed the surprisingly large number of women in a country area who were willing to work together in their interdenominational unity of purpose, and to accept

---

8   S. Gill, *Women and the Church of England: From the Eighteenth Century to the Present* (1994), p.139.

continuing subordination to men. The Bible Ladies evangelizing voluntarily on behalf of the British and Foreign Bible Society were not pioneers of women's organized philanthropic visiting. Nevertheless, they helped to pave the way for those who later established new societies run by women and employing salaried female visitors. The British city and town missions, such as the London City Mission founded in 1835, also were male-administered. In their early years they favoured employment only of men as their paid visitor-evangelists.[9] However, in 1837 a former member of the London City Mission created the British and Foreign Mission (later known as the Town Missionary Society) and this 'was willing to countenance the hiring of women evangelists'.[10] Though recruitment of female paid agents was not wholehearted during the new Mission's first twenty years or so, gradually more women were employed. They visited female workers 'congregated together' in 'large workrooms' and women at their homes in town and country areas.[11]

When Mrs Ellen Ranyard (1810-79) founded her London Female Bible and Domestic Mission (later known as the Ranyard Bible Mission) in 1858, she addressed the issue of which class of woman could be most effective in paid home missionary work.[12] Mrs Ranyard, married to a philanthropist, had experience of dealing with the poor through her earlier parochial work in Kent for the Bible Society.[13] She was a Low-Church Anglican and set in motion some of the most highly imaginative ideas on reaching the poor in their own communities.[14] Mrs Ranyard's organization was unsectarian. She appointed her bible-women from among those suffering greatest poverty as she argued that they were more likely than any others to communicate with families living in similar circumstances to their own, and to have sympathetic awareness of their distress.[15] The Mission was an imaginative scheme for paid

9   D. M. Lewis, '"Lights in dark places"; women evangelists in early Victorian Britain, 1838-1857', in W. J. Shiels & D. Wood (eds), *Studies in Church History, 27, Women in the Church* (1990), pp.416-18.
10   *Ibid.*, p.418.
11   *Ibid.*, pp.419-21.
12   *Ibid.*, p.421.
13   B. Heeney, *The Women's Movement in the Church of England, 1850-1930* (Oxford, 1988), p.46. The funds of the Ranyard Bible Mission were supplemented by grants from various donors, but largely from the British and Foreign Bible Society.
14   Prochaska, *Women and Philanthropy*, p.126.
15   Lewis, 'Lights in Dark Places', p.421.

and volunteer, working-class and middle-class workers respectively, the lower-class bible-women being under the administration of lady superintendents.[16] Middle-class women were restricted to the latter role and were not allowed to be visitors. Mrs Ranyard's salaried 'bible-women' (noticeably not 'Bible Ladies') received a degree of instruction on relevant subjects to help them fulfil their roles as purveyors of the Scriptures and as limited advisers on health and domestic affairs.[17]

The young Particular Baptist featured in my Chapter 5, though rebellious as a child, grew to respect her Evangelical roots and became a shining example of what spiritual conversion could achieve. Facts have been presented to bear out my suggestion that the Hackleton Particular Baptist community was unusual because so many well-known Evangelical personalities were connected with it. This hamlet was no backwater of irreligion in early nineteenth-century England, being one small, yet significant area contributing to the development of Northamptonshire as a stronghold of dissent by 1851. That a young lace-maker from a fatherless domestic background could come to the commitment shown in her hymns, has given testimony to the inclusive worth of working-class women in Evangelical Nonconformity. For Eliza Westbury, living throughout her short life in a rural parish near Northampton, the value of Sunday-school attendance has been highlighted. Evidence has indicated that Hackleton's Sunday provision of 'religious education' was probably not 'based on denominational assertiveness' or 'employer...sources of power'.[18]

Eliza Westbury's birth (1808) was twenty-six years earlier than that of the better known Particular Baptist, Marianne Farningham, in 1834. Both had spent their girlhoods in rural England, but Marianne's first home was in Kent. Her autobiography, *A Working Woman's Life*, tells of her parents' involvement as teachers in the chapel Sunday School. Though Marianne described her early 'church' as 'absolutely Calvinistic', the minister's wife 'wanted to tell the people that every one who would might be saved'.[19] There are

16 Prochaska, *Women and Philanthropy*, p.128.
17 *Ibid.*, p.127-8.
18 See argument in K. D. M. Snell & P. S. Ell, *Rival Jerusalems; the Geography of Victorian Religion* (Cambridge, 2000), p.319. However, at Creaton some Anglican Sunday School helpers were female relatives of the wealthy Evangelical landowner who financed it, and of others holding local agricultural land. Therefore, that Sunday School can be associated with a source of child labour.
19 Farningham, *A Working Woman's Life*, p.15.

implications of moderate Calvinism here. If Eliza had lived longer, doors might have opened for her to achieve more in the literary world. Even so in 1828, when acknowledgement of her talents was made in the printing of her verses, it could have been an innovation for a young working-class woman. Perhaps local recognition of this kind was the prelude to someone like Marianne Farningham being able to win much wider publication of her writings in religious magazines a few decades later. Marianne was baptized at Farningham in 1848 when she was only fourteen. Her early verses were published through her own initial contacts five years later. Subsequently, she was given the opportunity to reach a more extensive readership through a new 'religious newspaper', *The Christian World Magazine*, which 'would be decidedly [E]vangelical, but wholly unsectarian'.[20] In 1857 one of her poems was printed in the first number under a new pen-name, Marianne Farningham. This was suggested by her minister, who was involved with the magazine.[21] Hearn was her family name, but Farningham had been her place of birth. For Marianne the way to a long career in teaching and writing was opening up. It is interesting to note that she finally spent more than fifty years in Northampton, where she undertook to instruct a Bible class for young women attached to the Particular Baptist Church in College Street. As we have seen, this was the very same establishment that had such close connections with Hackleton in the late eighteenth century.

A more optimistic strand of theological liberalism had been developing among Nonconformist Evangelicals since 1830, 'but did not become sufficiently prominent to be seen as a general shift in thought until the 1860s'.[22] The new image presented was of a gentler God. 'The Fatherhood of God was a typical theme, eternal punishment a typical omission', and hell as the assured place for the unregenerate no longer held the majority view.[23] In the few of Marianne Farningham's verses included in her autobiography there is no mention of Satan, God's wrath, or hell's fiery lake which figure so dramatically in some of Eliza Westbury's compositions. Marianne indicated something of how and why concepts changing. 'The great controversy on eternal punishment was going on' in *The Christian World* and the movement was 'toward a broader

20   *Ibid.*, p.77.
21   *Ibid.*, pp.75-6.
22   Knight, *The Nineteenth-century Church*, p.57.
23   Bebbington, *Evangelicalism*, p.145.

outlook' over religious doctrine, and 'a more generous theology'.[24] In her autobiography, she quoted this extract from that magazine dated 3 May 1873, which helped to explain the new theological approach:

> Our age, impetuous, daring, headstrong, requires to be admonished as to the duties of reverent faith and patient obedience, but it has reached forward to truth which was not known to our fathers, and this truth it is bound to accept and make the most of. It has found that neither the Bible nor common sense sanctions the whole figment of universal, verbal, infallible inspiration. It has formed expanded conceptions of the Divine Love and the freedom of the Gospel Offer. It has divested itself of many hard, un-Christianlike tenets of the theology of blood, and brimstone, and fire.[25]

This was a diversion from Evangelical doctrine of the Bible's infallibility.[26] After a period of heart-break and anxiety, Marianne Farningham reconciled herself to the liberal theology thus: '"The larger hope" had already attracted me, and I decided to wait, hoping and praying that the light which it was necessary for me to have would come to me gradually. So I laid down the burden, and found there was nothing to be afraid of.'[27] Other Evangelical women perhaps reacted several years earlier than Marianne and more strongly, but is there evidence of this yet to be discovered?

Hymn singing, already so much a part of worship for Dissenters and Anglican Evangelicals, became generally acceptable within the Church of England after about 1820. The number of female hymn writers grew during the first half of the nineteenth century and many were from middle-class backgrounds.[28] Some funded their own earliest publications. Women assumed an increasingly

---

24 Farningham, *A Working Woman's Life*, pp.136-7.
25 *Ibid.*, p.137.
26 Bebbington has explained that the 'Down Grade Controversy of 1887-8' among Baptists was an expression of opposition to the liberal approach. C. H. Spurgeon, the great Baptist preacher, 'condemned the tendency to theological vapidity', and though he lacked support from most of his own denomination, he 'was widely applauded by Evangelical Anglicans': see Bebbington, *Evangelicalism*, pp.145-6.
27 Farningham, *A Working Woman's Life*, p.138.
28 For several of the best known, see Watson's chapter on 'Victorian women hymn-writers', *The English Hymn*, pp.422-60.

important role in hymn writing, which came to be seen as their particular contribution to ministry.[29] However, anonymity of early nineteenth-century women composers was perpetuated by themselves; they were often reluctant to reveal their identities. Charlotte Elliott in 1839 designated her hymns 'by a Lady',[30] but later female Victorian hymn writers were pleased to be acknowledged by name. As the century moved on, the less threatening Evangelical tone was adopted in most hymns. This was especially evident in those for the very young, who were now presented as possessors of innocence rather than innate wickedness. Though still 'didactic' the majority of the later Victorian hymns for children were no longer so openly terrifying.[31]

In most public and private spheres male supremacy remained distinctive during the early decades of the nineteenth century. Yet my research has signalled changing attitudes in a move towards feminine equality, or even dominance, within some elite Kentish families where women had been converted to Evangelicalism. Such change might be regarded as constituting one brave step supporting women's demand for female autonomy and equal rights in society, a movement that gained strength during the second half of the century. Bearing this in mind, Barbara Caine's argument that the Evangelical view of women's role as guardian of domestic moral standards 'was one of the formative influences of Victorian feminism' is worthy of particular note.[32]   Evangelicals were instrumental in establishing the domestic ideology of separate spheres for men and women,[33] and it has been claimed that this way of thinking idealised the increasing separation of home and workplace caused by advancing technological means of production.[34] Along with the new ideology came the middle-class notion of virtuous womanhood - that of 'angel in the house' maintaining 'the home as a haven' from external pressures. The old prescriptive view of women being tainted by Eve and the fall was denied so long as they kept to their proper domestic sphere.[35]   It

29   *Ibid.*, p.339.
30   *Ibid.*, p.427.
31   Tamke, *Make a Joyful Noise*, p.83.
32   B. Caine, *Victorian Feminists* (Oxford, 1992), p.43.
33   Hall, *White, Male and Middle Class*, p.75. See also Hall, 'The early formation of Victorian domestic ideology', p.24.
34   P. Levine, *Victorian Feminism, 1850-1900* (1987), p.12.
35   See E. J. Yeo, 'Introduction: Some Paradoxes of Empowerment', in E. J. Yeo (ed.), *Radical Femininity: Women's Self-representation in the Public Sphere* (Manchester, 1998), p.7.

was in their domesticity that women could be glorified for their nurturing qualities, compassion, moral sense and chastity.[36] These 'natural characteristics' associated with potential or actual motherhood made them significantly different from men.[37] Part of the Victorian feminist argument was founded on this view. Seen as morally purer than men, women were expected to supervise correct behaviour in male members of the family and to ensure their application to religious and social duties.[38] The contradictory nature of this ideology was obvious, for woman's role in most spheres of influence was one of subordination.[39] As Philippa Levine has claimed, for many women fighting for female rights their argument lay not in rejecting Victorian domestic ideology but in manipulation of its fundamental values; 'if women's purity made them the natural custodians of religious teachings and values, then their effect in public life could only be uplifting'.[40]

David Bebbington has recognized the persuasive arguments presented by Olive Anderson and Prochaska[41] that 'Evangelical religion, despite its emphasis on the domestic role of women, was more important than feminism in enlarging their sphere during the nineteenth century.'[42] It has been shown here how females in Kent and Northamptonshire engaged in activities to further Evangelical interests within their communities during the first half of the century, and many must have gained confidence from being able to play their individual public roles. It is not within the scope of this present work to go further into later countrywide Evangelical organizations run by women, such as the Young Women's Christian Association,[43] and the Girls' Friendly Society,[44] both set up for

36 Caine, *Victorian Feminists*, pp.52-3. As Caine has said here, the ideology always implied that women could retain their moral purity only so long as they remained innocent of the carnal world beyond the home, for once outside their 'domestic confines', they 'would lose their innocence and subside into sensuality and evil'. The 'separate spheres' ideology made little impact on the existence of working-class women who needed to find employment outside the home: see P. Levine, *Victorian Feminism, 1850-1900* (1987), p.106.

37 Caine, *Victorian Feminists*, pp.52-3.

38 Hall, *White, Male and Middle Class*, p.86, and Caine, *Victorian Feminists*, p.44.

39 Hall, *Ibid.*; Caine, *Ibid.*

40 Levine, *Victorian Feminism*, p.13. See also Caine, *Victorian Feminism*, p.53.

41 In O. Anderson, 'Women preachers in mid-Victorian Britain: some reflexions on feminism, popular religion and social change', *Historical Journal*, vol. 12, no.3 (1969), and Prochaska, *Women and Philanthropy*, pp.227-30.

42 Bebbington, *Evangelicalism*, p.129.

female spiritual nurture, self-help and physical protection. Furthermore, women's nineteenth-century involvement with temperance societies, which reflected Evangelical concern for moral reform of the individual as well as female protection, has not entered into my discussion but has received attention elsewhere.[45] Evangelical women's views on the Oxford Movement within the Anglican Church have received only brief mention here, yet clearly they point to displeasure at early signs of local Anglo-Catholic revival. As Bebbington has said, 'Ritualism touched a raw nerve in Evangelicalism'.[46] It would be interesting to search for more on women's reactions in the parishes of Northamptonshire and Leicestershire where Tractarian practices were being introduced during the 1840s. A similar exercise could be taken up for other counties.

It can be safely argued that the women at the centre of my research, who were 'cradle' Evangelicals or converted to Evangelicalism in later life, shared the same basic religious beliefs and sense of purpose. Interestingly, even a staunch Orthodox Anglican woman found a little space in her letters to admire others' commitment to a belief system she usually denigrated. Not only this anomaly, but much of my research has indicated the complexities for women in their responses to Evangelical religion. During the second half of the nineteenth century, Evangelical values and virtues of individual moral and social responsibility, which Bebbington has called 'high Victorian values',[47] could be seen in the lives of many women from all classes. In most families, maintaining respectability was a priority. By virtue of hard work, self-help, sexual morality, sobriety, integrity, paying their way, Sunday observance, neighbourliness, cleanliness and good social behaviour, family members could hold their heads high. These codes of living, as has been indicated in this study, had been advocated by serious Christians and Evangelical organizations

43   For a short history, see S. Tall, *The Y.W.C.A. of Great Britain and the Women's Movement, 1855-1900* (unpublished M.A. dissertation, Victorian Studies Centre, University of Leicester, 1998).

44   See B. Harrison, 'For Church, Queen and family: the Girls' Friendly Society, 1874-1920', *Past and Present*, No.61 (1973), pp.108-134.

45   For example, see Banks, *Faces of Feminism*, pp.17-20; also Shiman, *Women and Leadership*, pp.151-5.

46   Bebbington, *Evangelicalism*, p.146.

47   *Ibid.*, p.105.

during the early part of the century. Yet Victorian women in general were expected to set an example to their families and were considered responsible for directing members of their households in the recognized ways of good conduct. Even those women who seldom, or never, attended a place of worship might try to attain these virtuous standards. Evidence has shown that in the areas of Kent and Northamptonshire covered here some women living during the first half of the nineteenth century found it far easier than others to achieve such aims.

BIBLIOGRAPHY

Primary sources: originals, or authorized copies as described

Documents in Northamptonshire County Record Office: call numbers given where possible

The Bosworth Collection (uncatalogued)

Letters

T. Jones to C. Bosworth, 14 May 1813.

T. Jones to C. & S. Bosworth, c.1815.

Fanny to C. Bosworth, 12 March 1816.

T. Peck to C. Bosworth, Tuesday night, c.1816.

T. Peck to C. Bosworth, Monday evening, c.1816.

T. Jones to C. Bosworth, 6 June 1821.

T. Jones to C. Bosworth, 29 August 1821.

T. Jones to C. Bosworth, 10 May 1823.

T. Jones to C. Bosworth, 28 January 1825.

D. Owen to C. Bosworth, 12 December 1826.

H. Middleton to C. Bosworth, 20 April 1830.

J. Owen to C. Bosworth, 20 September 1831.

T. Bosworth to C. Bosworth, 12 March 1840.

T. Jones to C. Bosworth, c.1840.

E. Bosworth to M. and T. Bosworth, 19 June 1841.

C. Bosworth to T. Bosworth, Saturday, 1841.

C. Bosworth to M. Bosworth, August 1841.

A. White to M. Bosworth, 4 October 1841.

T. Jones to C. Bosworth, undated, c.1841.

C. Bosworth to T. Bosworth, Wednesday, 1842.

E. Bugg to M. Bosworth, 22 November 1842.

J. Owen to T. Bosworth, 29 March 1843.

M. Owen to M. Bosworth, March 1843.

M. Owen to C. Bosworth, Tuesday night, c.1843.

M. Owen to M. Bosworth, 20 February 1846.

C. Bosworth to T. Bosworth, 12 July 1847.

S. Owen to T. J. Bosworth, 29 September 1863.

S. Owen to T. J. Bosworth, c.1864.

S. Owen to T. J. Bosworth, 16 April 1878.

Other material in the Bosworth Collection

Leases, C. Davenport to E. Bosworth, 5 January 1785.

Bosworth, T., *The Particulars of an Experiment respecting Smut in Wheat* (Wellingborough, 1798).

Owen, J., *Lines to the Endearing Memory of a Departed Wife* (Leicester, 1822).

Knight & Clarke, The Valuation of the Personal Estate and Effects of the late Mrs A. Bosworth of Highgate House (1833).

Probate of the Will of Ann Bosworth, deceased, 20 July 1833.

Certificate of Marriage: T. W. Bosworth to M. B. Pearson, 10 June 1841.

Smith, H., *Early Associations and Recollections*, H. P. Owen Smith (ed.)(St Albans, 1886).

Resolutions: Creaton Sunday School (undated manuscript).

Creaton Branch of the Church Missionary Society documents:

Annual Reports, 1822-3, 1823-4, 1824-5, 1825-6, 1826-7, 1827-8, 1828-9, 1830-1 (Northampton).

Poster: The Church Missionary Society, 14 May 1834.

Creaton Branch of the British and Foreign Bible Society documents:

First Annual Report (Northampton, 1826).

First Annual Report of the Spratton Ladies' Association (manuscript, 1826).

Paper setting out the Districts and the rounds of the collectors, Spratton Association (manuscript, undated).

Collecting Book, no.42.

Hackleton Baptist Church documents: (HBC)

Hackleton Baptist Church Book, 1781-1869, HBC16.

Rev. W. Knowles, Diary, 1811-1833, HBC8.

Hymns by a Northamptonshire Village Female. To which is added, A short Account of her Life (Northampton, 1828), HBC71/1.

Rev. W. Knowles, Diary of texts preached, 1833-1856, HBC10.

Rev. W. Knowles, *Scripture Principles: A Catechism for the Young* (Leicester, undated), inside HBC8.

Choirmaster's Notebook (undated), HBC64.

Anon., History of Hackleton Sabbath School (c.1881), HBC43.

Album of illustrations and photographs, etc., c.mid-1900s, HBC11.

The Strong Collection: S(T)

Letters

Mrs A. M. Lukyn to Mrs M. Strong: S(T)230-315 (dated 1809-35).

Quoted:

S(T)230, S(T)235, S(T)238, S(T)240, S(T)241, S(T)242, S(T)243, S(T)245, S(T)246, S(T)253, S(T)256, S(T)257, S(T)258, S(T)261, S(T)264, S(T)266, S(T)268, S(T)269, S(T)270, S(T)271, S(T)272, S(T)273, S(T)274, S(T)279, S(T)280, S(T)281, S(T)282, S(T)283, S(T)284, S(T)285, S(T)286, S(T)287, S(T)289, S(T)293, S(T)295, S(T)297, S(T)298, S(T)300, S(T)303, S(T)306, S(T)307, S(T)309, S(T)314, S(T)315.

Mrs M. Strong to Mrs Strong (junior): S(T)113 (undated).

Census and Parish records, Northamptonshire

Census Enumerators' Returns (1841), microfilm M345 (containing Creaton, Thornby).

Census Enumerators' Returns (1841), microfilm M348 (containing Spratton).

Constable's (Militia) List, Hackleton, Wymersley Hundred (1786), 984/9.

Constable's (Militia) List, Parish of Creaton in the Division of Daventry in the County of Northampton (1819), D2837.

Reconstruction of map from Award Document, Great and Little Creaton Parishes Inclosure Award, 1782-3 (1978), Map 5498.

Parish Inclosure Award, Piddington and Hackleton (1782), ref. 0710.

Parish Inclosure Award and map, Salcey Forest (1826), Stack 71,c3.

Parish registers (microfiche nos. given in text):

Creaton, microfiche 90p/5.

Holdenby, microfiche 171p/4.

Piddington, microfiche 266p/3/4/11.

Spratton, microfiche 295p/3/4/6.

Thornby, microfiche 318p/1.

Spratton Vestry Minute Book, 295p/11.

Payment of Tithes, Creaton, 1800-50, 90p/38.

Valuation of the Lands, Buildings and Property within the parish of Spratton in the County of Northampton, 30 November 1837, 295p/71.

Creaton Church Book, Creaton Congregational 5.

Miscellaneous documents in Northamptonshire County Record Office

Peterborough Diocese, *Institutions Book* (1764-1839), ML733.

Peterborough Diocese, *Institutions Book* (1839-1862), ML734.

Peterborough Diocese, *Bishop's Triennial Visitations* (1792-1798), ML582.

Letter, Sir Rbt. Gunning to the Bishop of Peterborough, 21 February 1780, G(H)734.

Letter, T. Jones to Rev. Mr Griffin, 6 November 1799, ZB1052/2.

Letters, Spencer Perceval to Sir G. Gunning, 1804: 21 August, 1 October, 4 December G(H)756, 758, 759.

Letter, Tenants to Sir James Langham, 6th December 1830, L(C)1181.

Sale catalogue (1858), Highgate House, D1562.

Indenture (Conveyance), 18 June 1864, ZB1158/51.

Indenture (Lease), 3 January 1867, B/G79.

Documents, etc. in other Archives, Record Offices and Local Collections

Canterbury Archaeological Trust

St Margaret's Church, Canterbury, stone no. 218 (photocopy 1997).

Canterbury Cathedral Archives

Parish Register, Nonington, microfilm U3/118/1/5.

Parish Register, St Margaret's Church, Canterbury, microfilm U3/6/1/1.

Registration certificates, places of religious worship (Dissent). Canterbury, H/A/185-600 (1813-24); in particular Certificates H/A/525, H/A/535, H/A/542.

Canterbury City Library

National Portrait Gallery to Canterbury City Librarian, *Letter*, 5 June 1959.

Price, R., *Diary* (1769-1773) (transcript, 1975).

Wollaston, J., *Portrait, 'Anthony Lukyn, a celebrity of Canterbury'* (1742) (photograph, 1959; copy also in possession of S. M. Phillips).

Centre for Kentish Studies, Maidstone

Probate of Will, Anthony Lukyn, PRC17/100/f114, proved 23 November 1778.

Leicester County Record Office

Presentation deed 7D55/1008/1, 7 August 1845.

Public Record Office

Probate of Will, John Lukyn, PROB11/811 F191RH+F192LH, proved 30th October 1754.

Northamptonshire County Library, Local Studies Room

Northampton Mercury, 7 June 1822.

The Circular Letter from the Ministers and Messengers in The Northamptonshire Association assembled at Kettering, 16th & 17th May 1826.

Sutcliff Chapel Archives, Olney, Bucks.

Olney Baptist Church Book, c.1752-1854.

Pre-1900 publications: Place of publication is London unless otherwise stated.

Austen, J., *Jane Austen's Letters (1796-1817)*, D. Le Faye (ed.) (Oxford, 1995, 1997 edn).

Austen, J., *Pride and Prejudice* (1813, 1994 edn).

Baker, G., *The History and Antiquities of the County of Northampton*, pt. 1 (1822).

Bridges, J., *The Histories and Antiquities of Northamptonshire* (Oxford, 1791).

Bronte, A., *The Tenant of Wildfell Hall* (1847, 1980 edn).

Burke, B., *History of the Landed Gentry of Great Britain and Ireland*, I, II, A. P. Burke & brothers (ed.), (1894 edn).

Burke, E., *Reflections on the Revolution in France* (1790, 4th edn).

Butler, J. E., *Social Purity: an Address* (1879).

Byron, G., *Childe Harold's Pilgrimage and other Romantic Poems* (1807-23), in J. D. Dump (ed.) (1975).

Clare, J., 'My Mary', in E. Robinson & D. Powell (eds), *The Oxford Authors*, John Clare (Oxford, 1984).

Cowper, J. M., *Memorial Inscriptions of the Cathedral Church of Canterbury* (Canterbury, 1897).

Cowper, W., *The Letters and Prose Writings of William Cowper*, J. King & C. Ryskamp (eds), I (Oxford, 1979), IV (1983).

Cowper, W., *The Poetry of William Cowper*, B. Hutchings, (ed.) (Beckenham, 1983).

Cowper, W., *Poetical Works*, I, (1782-99), H. S. Milford (ed.) (1934, 1967 edn).

Cozens, Z., *Ecclesiastical Topographical History of Kent*, I (1795).

Crabbe, G., 'The Village' (1783), in *George Crabbe: Selected Poems*, G. Edwards (ed.), (1991).

Cunningham, J. W., *The Velvet Cushion* (1814, 3rd end).

Dudley, C. S., *An Analysis of the System of the Bible Society* (1821).

Dudley, C. S., *Hints Relative to The Duties that Devolve on the Officers and Collectors of the Bible Associations Extracted from the Analysis of the System of the Bible Society* (1823).

Eliot, G., *Adam Bede* (1859), B. Gray (ed.), (1994).

Eliot, G., *Middlemarch* (1872, 1982 edn).

Eliot, G., *Scenes of Clerical Life* (1858), D. Lodge (ed.), (1993).

Eliot, G., 'Silly novels by lady novelists' (Westminster Review, October 1859), in *Selected Essays, Poems and Other Writings*, A. S. Byatt & N. Warren (eds) (1990).

Fuller, A. G., *Andrew Fuller* (1882).

Gordon, Rev. A., 'James Janeway (1636?-1674)', in S. Lee (ed.), *Dictionary of National Biography*, XXIX (1892).

Greenwood, C., *An Epitome of County History: County of Kent* I (1839).

Hasted, E., *A History and Topographical Survey of Kent*, IX (Canterbury, 1800, 1972 edn).

Jones, T., *Baskets of Fragments or Notes from Sermons*, 2 vols (1832-3).

Kelly, *Northamptonshire Directory, 1847*.

Lee, S. (ed.) *Dictionary of National Biography*, XXIX (1892).

Marsh, H., 'A speech delivered to the House of Lords on Tuesday, June 14, 1821, by Herbert Marsh, Lord Bishop of Peterborough respecting his examination questions', in Anon., *Tracts on the Bishop of   Peterborough's Questions* (1821).

May, G., *Circular Letter to the Inhabitants of Herne*, (Canterbury), 22 February 1823.

More, H., *Coelebs in Search of a Wife: Comprehending Domestic Habits and Manners, Religion and Morals* (1809).

More, H., *Practical Piety; or, the Influence of the Religion of the Heart on the Conduct of the Life* (1811, 1812 edn, New York).

Newton, J. & Cowper, W., *Olney Hymns: in Three Parts* (1779, 1859 edn).

Overton, J. H., *The English Church in the Nineteenth Century, 1800-1833* (1894).

Owen, J., *The History of the Origin and First Ten Years of the British and Foreign Bible Society*, V (1820).

Owen, J., *Memoir of The Rev. Thomas Jones* (1851).

Rippon, J., *A Selection of Hymns from the Best Authors, intended to be an Appendix to Dr. Watts's Psalms and Hymns* (1787, 1802 edn).

Seeley, M. *The Later Evangelical Fathers* (1879).

Sherwood, M. M., *The History of the Fairchild Family, or the Child's Manual, being a Collection of Stories calculated to show the Importance and Effects of a Religious Education*, Part I (1818, 1879 edn).

Skeats, H. S., *A History of the Free Churches of England from A.D.1688- A.D.1851* (1869, 2nd edn).

Steele, A., *Hymns by Anne Steele* (1760), J. R. B. (ed. 1967).

Trollope, F., *The Vicar of Wrexhill* (1837).

Watts, I., *The Psalms of David Imitated in the Language of the New Testament And apply'd to the Christian State and Worship* (1719, 1734 edn).

Wilberforce, W., *A Practical View of the Prevailing Religious Systems of Professed Christians in the Higher and Middle Classes in this Country contrasted with Real Christianty* (1797, 1834 edn.).

Wollstonecraft, M., *A Vindication of the Rights of Woman* (1795), in R. Todd & M. Butler, *The Works of Mary Wollstonecraft*, V (1989)

Wright, T., *The Town of Cowper* (1893).

Periodicals: Items by Editors unless otherwise stated.

Baptist Magazine (2nd Series)

'Report of speech of William Wilberforce to Bath Missionary Society', XIII (1821).

W.B., 'On Evangelical repentance', XVI (1824).

Robinson, Rev. R., 'On Sabbath-breaking', XVI (1824)

'Memoir of the late John Ryland, D.D.', XVIII (1826).

'Obituary of Mrs Keene', XIX (1827).

'On ardent concern for the conversion of sinners among members of Churches', XX (1828).

Christian Observer

Anon., 'The state of the Established Church', X (1811).

Members of the Established Church, 'Review of "A Defence of the Bible Society"', XVII (1818).

Evangelical Magazine and Missionary Chronicle

M[ends, H.], 'Thoughts on the importance of catechising youth', VIII (1800).

Anon., 'Review, T. Jones, "Scripture Directory: or an Attempt to assist the unlearned Reader to understand the General History and Leading Subjects of the Old and New Testaments"', XXI (1813).

The Edinburgh Review (or Critical Journal) (Edinburgh)

Smith, S., 'Critique, "Coelebs in Search of a Wife"', XIV (1809).

'Lord Byron's "Childe Harold"', XIX (1811-1812).

'Publications on the education of the poor' and 'Papers on Toleration', XIX (1811-12).

'Crabbe's Tales', XX (1812).

'Papers on Toleration', XX (1812).

The Gentleman's Magazine: and Historical Chronicle

'Clerical appointments: Anthony Lukyn', XXV, 1755.

'Obituary, Anthony Lukyn', XLVIII (1778).

'Evening Lectures not suited to Country Parishes', LXXXII (1812).

Scrutator Oxoniensis, 'Letter on the Bible Society', LXXXII, (1812).

'Cowper's Mental Sufferings', XCIV, pt.1 (1824).

Government Publications

Abstract of the Answers and Returns pursuant to an Act, passed in the Fifty-first Year of His Majesty King George III intituled "An Act for taking Account of the Population of Great Britain, and of the Increase or Diminution thereof", 1811 (1812).

Abstract of the Answers and Returns pursuant to an Act, passed in the First Year of the Reign of His Majesty King George IV intituled "An Act for taking Account of the Population of Great Britain, and of the Increase or Diminution thereof" 1821 (1822).

Abstract of the Answers and Returns pursuant to an Act, passed in the Eleventh Year of the Reign of His Majesty King George IV intituled "An Act for taking Account of the

Population of Great Britain, and of the Increase or Diminution thereof", *1831*, Vol. I (1833).

Parliamentary Papers IX/(2): Digest of Education Returns, County of Northampton, 1818 (1819).

Parliamentary Papers XLII: Digest of Education Returns, County of Northampton, 1833 (1835).

....

Post-1900 publications: Place of publication is London unless otherwise stated.

Anderson, O., 'Women preachers in mid-Victorian Britain: some reflexions on feminism, popular religion and social change', *Historical Journal*, vol. 12, no. 3 (1969).

Anderson, W. E. K. (ed.), *The Journal of Sir Walter Scott, 1771-1832* (Oxford, 1972).

Balleine, G. R., *A History of the Evangelical Party in the Church of England* (1908).

Barrie-Curien, V., 'The clergy in the diocese of London in the eighteenth century' in J. Walsh, C. Haydon, S. Taylor, *The Church of England c.1689-c.1833: From Toleration to Tractarianism* (Cambridge, 1993).

Bebbington, D. W., *Evangelicalism in Modern Britain: A History from the 1730s to the 1980s* (1989, 1993 edn).

Bebbington, D. W., *Holiness in Nineteenth-Century England: The 1998 Didsbury Lectures* (Cambridge, 2000).

Best, G. F. A., 'The Evangelicals and the Established Church in the early nineteenth century', *Journal of Theological Studies*, N.S., X, Pt.1, (1959).

Best, G. F. A., *Temporal Pillars: Queen Anne's Bounty, the Ecclesiastical Commissioners, and the Church of England* (Cambridge, 1964).

Bradley, I., *The Call to Seriousness: The Evangelical Impact on the Victorians* (1976).

Braine, R. K., *The Life and Writings of Herbert Marsh, 1757-1839* (unpublished PhD. thesis, Cambridge, 1989).

Bready, J. W., England: *Before and After Wesley; The Evangelical Revival and Social Reform* (New York, 1938, 1971 edn).

Burns, R. A., 'A Hanoverian legacy? Diocesan reform in the Church of England c.1800-1833', in J. Walsh, C. Haydon, S. Taylor (eds), *The Church of England, c.1689-c.1833: from Toleration to Tractarianism* (Cambridge, 1993).

Bushell, T. A., *Barracuda Guide to County History, I: Kent* (Chesham, 1976).

Caine, B., *Victorian Feminists* (Oxford, 1992).

Cecil, D., *The Stricken Deer: the Life of William Cowper* (1929, 1943 edn, Constable & Robinson Pub. Ltd).

Chadwick, O., *The Victorian Church, pt 1* (1966, 1971 edn).

Chambers Biographical Dictionary, M. Magnusson (ed.) (Edinburgh, 1990 edn).

Conrad, B., *Coach Tour of Joseph Conrad's Homes* (1974).

Daiches, D., *Sir Walter Scott and his World* (1971).

Davidoff, L., & Hall, C., *Family Fortunes: Men and Women of the English Middle Class, 1780-1850* (1987).

Denny, J., 'The Epistles to the Thessalonians', in W. Robertson Nicoll (ed.), *The Expositor's Bible* (1909).

Ditchfield, G. M., *The Evangelical Revival* (1998).

Dods, M., 'The Gospel of St.John', I, in W. Robertson Nicoll (ed.), *The Expositor's Bible* (1910).

Dunhill, R., 'The Rev. George Bugg: the fortunes of a 19th century curate', *Northamptonshire Past and Present*, VII, 1 (1983-4).

Dymond, D., 'God's disputed acre', *Journal of Ecclesiastical History*, vol. 50, no. 3 (Cambridge, 1999).

Elbourne, E., 'The foundation of the Church Missionary Society: the Anglican missionary impulse', in J.Walsh, C. Haydon, S.Taylor (eds), *The Church of England, c.1689-c.1833: From Toleration to Tractarianism* (Cambridge, 1993).

Elliott-Binns, L. E., *The Early Evangelicals: A Religious and Social Study* (1953).

Elwyn, T. S. H., *The Northamptonshire Baptist Association: a Short History of the Association, 1764-1964* (1964).

Englander, D., 'The word and the world: Evangelicalism in the Victorian city', in G. Parsons (ed.), *Religion in Victorian Britain, II Controversies* (Manchester, 1988).

Evans, E., *Daniel Rowland and the Great Awakening in Wales* (Edinburgh, 1985).

Evans, E. J., 'Some reasons for the growth of English rural anticlericalism c.1750-c.1830', *Past and Present*, No. 66 (Oxford, 1975).

Everitt, A., *The Pattern of Rural Dissent: The Nineteenth Century* (Leicester, 1972).

Farningham, M., *A Working Woman's Life: An Autobiography* (1907).

Gash, N., *Aristocracy and People: Britain 1815-1865* (1979).

Gilbert, A. D., *Religion and Society in Industrial England: Church, Chapel and Social Change, 1740-1914* (1976).

Gill, S., *Women and the Church of England: From the Eighteenth Century to the Present* (1994).

Gordon, J. M., *Evangelical Spirituality: From the Wesleys to John Stott* (1991).

Gotch, J. A., *Squires' Homes and other Old Buildings of Northamptonshire* (1939).

Grant, J. (ed.), *Northamptonshire: Historical, Biographical, Pictorial* (c.1915).

Hall, C., 'The early formation of Victorian domestic idealogy', in S. Burman (ed.), *Fit Work for Women* (1979).

Hall, C., *White, Male and Middle Class: Explorations in Feminism and History* (Cambridge, 1992).

Hammond, J. L. & B., *The Village Labourer, 1760-1832: a Study of the Government of England before the Reform Bill* (1911, 1987 edn).

Harrison, B., 'For Church, Queen and family: the Girls' Friendly Society, 1874-1920', *Past and Present*, No.61 (1973).

Heeney, B., *The Women's Movement in the Church of England, 1850-1930* (Oxford, 1988).

Hennell, M. M., *John Venn and the Clapham Sect* (1958).

Houghton, W. E. (ed.), *The Wellesley Index to Victorian Periodicals*, Vol. I (1966, Toronto).

Igglesden, C. *A Saunter through Kent with Pen and Pencil*, XXVI (1932).

Jackson, S. M. (ed.), *The New Schaff-Herzog Encyclopedia of Religious Knowledge*, Vol IV (Michigan, 1967 edn).

Jay, E., *The Religion of the Heart: Anglican Evangelicalism and the Nineteenth-Century Novel* (Oxford, 1979).

Jay, E., 'Introductory essay', in E. Jay (ed.), *The Evangelical and Oxford Movements* (Cambridge, 1983).

Johnson, E., *Sir Walter Scott, The Great Unknown*, Vol. I (1970).

Kiernan, V. G., 'Evangelicalism and the French Revolution', *Past and Present*, No. 1 (Oxford, 1952).

Knatchbull-Hugessen, H., *Kentish Family* (1960).

Knight, F., *The Nineteenth-century Church and English Society* (Cambridge, 1995).

Lane, S., *Forgotten Labours: Women's Bible Work from 1804-1895, with particular reference to the British and Foreign Bible Society* (unpublished M.A. dissertation, Bristol University, 1994).

Laqueur, T. W., *Religion and Respectability: Sunday Schools and Working Class Culture, 1780-1850* (1976).

Levine, P., *Victorian Feminism 1850-1900* (1987).

Lewis, D. M., '"Lights in dark places"; women evangelists in early Victorian Britain, 1838-1857', in W. J. Shiels & D. Wood, *Studies in Church History, 27, Women in the Church* (1990).

Longden, H., *Northants and Rutland Clergy from 1500-1900*, VIII (1940), XIII (1942) (Northampton).

Marshall, M. F., & Todd, J., *English Congregational Hymns in the Eighteenth Century* (Kentucky, 1982).

Martin, B., *John Newton: a Biography* (1950).

Martin, R. H., 'Anglicans and Baptists in conflict: the Bible Society, Bengal and the Baptizo controversy', *Journal of Ecclesiastical Studies*, XLIX (1998).

Martin, R. H., *Evangelicals United: Ecumenical Stirrings in Pre-Victorian Britain, 1795-1830* (Matuchen, N.J., 1983).

McClymond, M. J., 'Spiritual perception in Jonathan Edwards', *The Journal of Religion*, vol. 77, no. 2 (Chicago) 1997.

Mills, D., 'Community and nation in the past: perception and reality', in M. Drake (ed.), *Time, Family and Community: Perspectives on Family and Community History* (Blackwell, Oxford, 1994).

Mingay, G. E., *A Social History of the English Countryside* (1990).

Moorman, J. R. H., *A History of the Church in England* (1953, 1973 edn).

Nockles, P. B., 'Church parties in the pre-Tractarian Church of England 1750-1833' in J. Walsh, C. Haydon, S. Taylor (eds), *The Church of England, c. 1689-c. 1833: From Toleration to Tractarianism* (Cambridge, 1993).

Norman, E. R., *Church and Society in England, 1770-1970: a Historical Study* (Oxford, 1976).

O'Dea, T. F., *The Sociology of Religion* (Englewood Cliffs, N.J., 1966).

Page, W. (ed.), *Victoria History of the Counties of England: Kent*, III (1974).

Parsons, G., 'Reform, revival and realignment: the experience of Victorian Anglicanism', in G. Parsons (ed.), *Religion in Victorian Britain: I, Traditions* (Manchester, 1988).

Payne, E. A., *The Baptist Union: a Short History* (1958).

Pevsner, N. & Newman, J., *North East and East Kent* (1969, 1998 edn) in series B. Cherry & J. Nairn (eds), *The Buildings of England*.

Plummer, A., 'The General Epistles of St Jude and St James', in W. Robertson Nicoll (ed), *The Expositor's Bible* (1907).

Prochaska, F. K., *Women and Philanthropy in Nineteenth-Century England* (Oxford, 1980).

Rack, H. D., 'Domestic visitation: a chapter in early nineteenth-century evangelism', *Journal of Ecclesiastical History*, vol. 24, no. 4 (Cambridge, 1973).

Reardon, B. M. G., *From Coleridge to Gore: a Century of Religious Thought in Britain* (1971).

Reardon, B. M. G., *Religion in the Age of Romanticism: Studies in Early Nineteenth Century Thought* (Cambridge, 1985).

Reay, B., 'The context of meaning of popular literacy: some evidence from nineteenth-century rural England', *Past and Present*, No. 131 (1991).

Reid, D. A., 'The decline of Saint Monday, 1766-1876', *Past and Present* No. 71 (1976).

Roberts, M. J. D., 'Private patronage and the Church of England, 1800-1900', *Journal of Ecclesiastical History*, vol. 32, no.2 (1981).

Robinson, E. & Powell, D. (eds), *The Oxford Authors, John Clare* (1984), (with permission of Curtis Brown Group, Ltd)

Rosman, D. M., *Evangelicals and Culture* (1984).

Routley, E., *English Religious Dissent* (Cambridge, 1960).

Royal Commission on Historical Monuments, England, *An Inventory of the Historical Monuments in the County of Northampton*, III (H.M.S.O., 1981).

Saltzman, L. F. (ed.), *The Victoria History of the County of Northampton*, IV (Oxford, 1937).

Sargeantson, R. M. & Adkins, W. R. D. (eds), *The Victoria History of the County of Northampton*, II (1906).

Sell, A. P. F., *Dissenting Thought and the Life of the Churches: Studies in an English Tradition* (Mellen, U.S.A., 1990).

Shelton Reed, J., *Glorious Battle: the Cultural Politics of Victorian Anglo-Catholicism* (Nashville, Tennessee, 1996).

Smith, G., *The Life of William Carey, Shoemaker and Missionary* (1909, 1922 edn).

Snell, K. D. M., *Annals of the Labouring Poor: Social Change and Agrarian England, 1660-1900* (Cambridge, 1985, 1995 edn).

Snell, K. D. M., & Ell, P. S., *Rival Jerusalems, the Geography of Victorian Religion* (Cambridge, 2000).

Solloway, R. A., *Prelates and People: Ecclesiastical Social Thought in England, 1783-1852* (1969).

Stanley, B., *The History of the Baptist Missionary Society, 1792-1992* (Edinburgh, 1992).

Summers, A., 'A home from home - women's philanthropic work in the nineteenth century', in S. Burman (ed.), *Fit Work for Women* (1979),

Tall, S., *The Y.W.C.A. of Great Britain and the Women's Movement, 1855-1900*, unpublished M.A. dissertation, Victorian Studies Centre, University of Leicester (1998).

Tamke, S. S., *Make a Joyful Noise unto the Lord: Hymns as a Reflection of Victorian Social Attitudes* (Athens, Ohio, 1978).

Tatton-Brown, T., *St. Margaret's Church, Canterbury* (Canterbury, 1986).

Thompson, E. P., *The Making of the English Working Class* (1963, 1980 edn).

Tolley, C., *Domestic Biography: the Legacy of Evangelicalism in Four Nineteenth-Century Families* (Oxford, 1997).

Underwood, A. C., *A History of the English Baptists* (1947).

Venn, J. & Venn, J. A., *Alumni Cantabrigienses: A Biographical List of All Known Students, Graduates and Holders of Offices at the University of Cambridge, from the Earliest Times to 1900; Part I, from the Earliest Times to 1751* (Cambridge, 4 vols, 1922-7), IV (1927). *Part II, from 1752-1900* (Cambridge, 6 vols, 1940-54), II (1944), IV (1951), VI (1954).

Vickers, J. A., *The Story of Canterbury Methodism* (Canterbury, 1961).

Walsh, J. & Taylor, S., 'Introduction: The Church and Anglicanism in the "long" eighteenth century', in J. Walsh, C. Haydon & S. Taylor (eds), *The Church of England, c.1689-c.1833: From Toleration to Tractarianism* (Cambridge, 1993).

Ward, W. R., *Religion and Society in England, 1790-1850* (1972).

Watson, J. R., *The English Hymn: a Critical and Historical Study* (Oxford, 1997).

Watts, M. R., *The Dissenters, from the Reformation to the French Revolution*, II (Oxford, 1995).

Whyman, J., *Kentish Sources, VIII: the Early Kentish Seaside* (Gloucester, 1985).

Wilson, L., '"She succeeds with cloudless brow..." How active was the spirituality of Nonconformist women in the home during the period 1825-75?', in R. N. Swanson, (ed.), *Studies in Church History, 34: Gender and Christian Religion* (1998).

Wolffe, J., *The Protestant Crusade in Great Britain, 1829-1860* (Oxford, 1991).

Yates, N., Hume, R., Hastings, P., *Religion and Society in Kent, 1640-1914* (Canterbury, 1994).

Yeo, E. J., 'Introduction: Some paradoxes of empowerment', in E. J. Yeo (ed.), *Radical Femininity: Women's Self-representation in the Public Sphere* (Manchester, 1998).

INDEX